CREATING THE CAPACITY FOR ATTACHMENT

CREATING THE CAPACITY FOR ATTACHMENT

Treating Addictions and the Alienated Self

by Karen B. Walant, Ph.D.

JASON ARONSON INC.
Northvale, New Jersey
London

Credits

"somewhere i have never travelled, gladly beyond" is reprinted from *Complete Poems 1904-1962*, by E. E. Cummings, edited by George J. Firmage, by permission of W. W. Norton & Company, copyright © 1931, 1979, 1991 by the Trustees for the E. E. Cummings Trust and George J. Firmage and by permission of the Liveright Publishing Corporation, copyright © 1931, 1952, 1959, 1980, 1991, by the Trustees for the E. E. Cummings Trust, and copyright © 1979 by George James Firmage.

Selections from *Look Homeward, Angel*, by Thomas Wolfe, are reprinted with the permission of Scribner, an imprint of Simon & Schuster, Inc. Copyright © 1929 Charles Scribner's Sons; copyright renewed © 1957 Edward C. Aswell, as administrator, C.T.A. of the Estate of Thomas Wolfe and /or Fred W. Wolfe. World rights: renewal copyright by Paul Gitlin, Administrator, C.T.A., of the Estate of Thomas Wolfe.

Production Editor: Judith D. Cohen

This book was set in 10 point Palacio by TechType of Upper Saddle River, New Jersey.

Library of Congress Cataloging-in-Publication Data

Walant, Karen B.
    Creating the capacity for attachment : treating addictions and the alienated self / by Karen B. Walant.
        p. cm.
    Includes bibliographical references and index.
    ISBN 1-56821-509-6
    1. Intimacy (Psychology) 2. Personality disorders—Treatment.
3. Substance abuse—Treatment. 4. Empathy. 5. Alienation (Social psychology). 6. Child rearing. I. Title.
    RC554.W35   1995
    616.89—dc20
                                                                    95-3405

Manufactured in the United States of America. Jason Aronson Inc. offers books and cassettes. For information and catalog write to Jason Aronson Inc., 230 Livingston Street, Northvale, New Jersey 07647.

To David
for our children Anna, William, and Benjamin
and to the indissoluble bond
that awaits every moment of oneness

CONTENTS

Acknowledgments   ix

1. The Indissoluble Bond   1

2. Symbiosis Revisited   37

3. The Oneness/Separateness Paradox   73

4. The Immersive Moment   103

5. Unlocking a Deaf Heart   139

6. Alcoholics Anonymous and Transcendence   165

7. The Power of Immersion   187

8. Point-Counterpoint and Other Treatment Issues   223

9. Working in the Immersive Transference   247

10. Gaslighting   275

References   293

Index   301

ACKNOWLEDGMENTS

My psychoanalytic thinking has been influenced by numerous teachers and supervisors, most notably Jane Spivack Brown, C.S.W., whose analytic wisdom has always been most helpful. I thank Jeffrey Seinfeld, Ph.D., for his supervision and sharing of theoretical ideas, as well as his encouragement regarding expansion of my dissertation into book form. I am grateful to New York University School of Social Work for the excellent education and intellectual stimulation that I received throughout my masters and Ph.D. coursework. I wish to thank Steve Rosman, Ph.D., M.S.C., for his ongoing interest and support. My thanks to Four Winds Hospital in Katonah, New York, and to its chief executive officer and executive medical director, Samuel Klagsbrun, M.D., for providing me with a rich forum to apply and develop my theoretical ideas. In addition, I am grateful to the late Kent Cunow, Ph.D., for his supervision and lively clinical discussions. I also thank Marlene Bartolo for sharing her knowledge and expertise.

I wish to express gratitude to Jason Aronson, M.D., for his interest and encouragement of this work, and to Michael Moskowitz, Ph.D., acquisitions editor, Judy Cohen, production editor, and Gail Chalew, copy editor, for their invaluable guidance, knowledge, and expertise. They have made the process of publishing this book a truly pleasurable experience.

This book has incorporated the efforts of several family members. I am most grateful to my mother, Beverly Gural, who was a thorough researcher, proofreader, and editorial assistant, and to my father, I. Jack Gural, who provided research back-up and ongoing support. I am honored to provide one of my grandmother's poems, "Mirror," which appears in Chapter 4. I thank my brother, Ken Gural, for his translation of the Baudelaire poem entitled "Enivrez-vous" at the beginning of Chapter 9. And I thank my husband David for his ongoing support and encouragement.

I wish to thank my patients, who have allowed me into their private worlds of pain and detachment. Many of the immersive moments we have shared together are reflected in this book and will remain embedded in my heart. To those who have allowed me access to their personal writing, I am especially indebted.

1

THE INDISSOLUBLE BOND

"'We cannot fall out of this world.'[1] That is to say, [the 'oceanic feeling'] is a feeling of an indissoluble bond, of being one with the external world as a whole."

Freud, summarizing Rolland's "oceanic feeling"
in *Civilization and Its Discontents*

THE TWENTIETH-CENTURY emphasis on self-reliance and individuality has greatly affected the psychological conditions most frequently requiring psychotherapeutic treatment in later life, including personality disorders and addiction. Autonomy and separateness have been emphasized in early childhood, in part because of the psychoanalytic view that the infant begins life in a state of non-differentiation with mother and gradually, through the first two to three years of life, becomes an individuated, separated, and cohesive being. Merger has been seen as a fusion state normal only to the early mother–infant dyad. The neonate cannot separate himself from his mother and therefore remains in a state of symbiotic bliss, comforted by her self-state, which protects his own. From this viewpoint, merger is seen as a dangerous threat to the burgeoning self of the infant; it encourages the child to remain fused and to seek only more moments of oneness. The child has no wish for self-actualization or self-mobilization because the symbiotic state is seen as heavenly.

I have another view of this infant, albeit an infant seen from my

---

1. Freud paraphrased this passage from a Christian Dietrich Grabbe (1801–1836) play entitled *Hannibal*. Before the hero dies from a self-inflicted wound, he says, "Indeed, we shall not fall out of this world. We are in it once and for all."

particular bias: an infant struggling to maintain both connectedness and separateness. This infant senses, even in utero, his separateness from others while feeling connected to a larger and, it is hoped, protective mother. Our society's long-standing denial and devaluation of merger phenomenon throughout the life cycle have actually increased the likelihood of personality disorders and addiction, precisely because autonomy and independence have been encouraged *at the expense of* attachment needs. These disorders, which are so pervasive in our current world, illustrate that beneath the veneer of self-reliance lies the core of powerlessness, alienation, and detachment. The push for individuation and self-determination in young children has greatly affected the acting out and repressed behavior of adults we later see in our psychotherapy practices, patients who suffer from what has been termed the *basic fault* (Balint), the *false self* (Winnicott), or the *empty core* (Seinfeld).

He somersaults, he moves with the sounds that surround him, he sucks his thumb and plays with his fingers. He moves back and forth with the pulsating movement around him. He pushes at the wall, the cavern in which he lives. He recognizes familiar sounds, relaxes to soothing ones, jolts with the jolting of the walls around him. And he cannot fall out of this world.

That is my perception of what the womb experience feels like. The neonate has some perception of his own being while he is surrounded by what I term a more *powerful, protective other*. Indeed, to extend the poetic description of the "oceanic feeling," the baby moves around in a sea of amniotic fluid[2] while still being held in, safely and securely. He is connected to the world by an *"indissoluble bond"* — the *umbilical cord* — and he *"cannot fall out of that world."*

My view is no doubt influenced by my own experiences as a mother, having had the experience of *separate* beings inside my body. It was not, as the poets have described, a continual state of bliss and oneness between my fetuses and me. Rather, it often felt like a tug of war, they wanting to somersault this way and that, moving their arms, legs, and body into alternating positions, looking for a comfortable space in a container that continually shrank as they continually grew. One incident comes to mind that furthers my point. I was comfortably reading one night, six months along in my first pregnancy, when suddenly I felt an intense, insistent

---

2. Of interest, the amniotic fluid is a saline solution, composed of salt water.

banging from my baby. I moved around, thinking that somehow she must have gotten into a difficult position. Still the banging, banging, banging. I stood up—still the banging, banging, banging. Then I realized that perhaps it was the elastic waistband of my pants that, admittedly, had felt a little tight when I had moments ago put them on. So I moved the elastic away. No banging. I sat down again, with the waistband removed—still no banging. Indeed, if I needed convincing that this being had some sense of her own body, this was it. She was telling me to get this pressure *off* her— and she was communicating this to the outside of her world, the outside of her container.

Freud and other psychoanalysts have postulated that birth is in itself a trauma that produces tremendous anxiety. Rank (1929) took the idea further than Freud, postulating that birth trauma is the root of neurosis. These ideas presuppose that the fetus is so pleased and content in the womb that he would have no desire to be interrupted from this blissfully serene world. But babies are designed to leave the womb—that is inherent in the human condition. By the end of the ninth month, the baby has filled to capacity the cavernous space that used to allow him room for somersaults and backflips. Now, he is a little like Alice in Wonderland— grown too big for the small space he is living in. In the last few days or weeks before birth, his head has been locked in position, upside down, so that he is readied for release. He is no longer free to move his head and body around, although his arms and legs can still flail about. How joyous can this be? Perhaps the birth experience actually brings a sense of relief to the baby because he is no longer confined, no longer claustrophobic inside the shrinking womb.

It need not be assumed, therefore, that babies would never leave the womb unless pushed. This way of looking at the infant demonstrates the bias that exists in the psychoanalytic literature. The fusion state is viewed as regressive and serving as a powerful force in opposition to separation and individuation. On the contrary, the womb can be seen metaphorically as a symbol for human growth and development, not a regressive haven that leads away from life. The womb is, at first, the perfect place for the fetus and meets all of his demands. But when it is no longer sufficient for his increased level of maturation, it is time for him to leave and to embark on a new course. There is balance between separation and oneness, and there is an innate human need to grow, thrive, and mature. Birth, therefore, need not be viewed as trauma. Birth occurs, most usually, when both baby and mother are ready to embark on the next stage of life, together.

A child is born, eager to socialize, to be part of and held by the mother, who is seen as a giant comforter, to nuzzle at her breast, to snuggle on her shoulder, to feel part of the vast world around him. The child is held, comforted by mother, sucking on her being that provides the substance of life—sweet, delicious breast milk. The child sleeps, knowing he is safe in the protective embrace of his mother's arms.

The child is put down, feels his own size, touches hand to hand, feet to feet. He cries and hears his own voice. He turns his head and sees different views of the world. He feels the warmth of his body against his blanket, feels that he is no longer touching the giant comforter who held him against her body.

The child knows the difference.

From the beginning of life, the baby experiences himself as small and powerless. He has a sense that he can manage certain actions by himself, and yet he is so dependent on the responsiveness of the external, giant breast-mother. Stern (1985) observes that the infant knows the beginning and ending of his own being, that even conjoined infant twins know when they are sucking their own fingers or the fingers of their joined-at-the-stomach sister.

Feeling separate, little, and yet having what Stern (1985) calls an emergent self-state, the infant wants to remain close to mother not because he feels he *is* she, but because he knows his littleness needs protection from the larger other. Why does a baby cry when put down, when separated for sleep, if not because he feels his separateness and littleness? He is crying as if to say, "Where is the other whom I can fall into, whom I can feel protecting the little me?" Certainly, there are blankets, pacifiers, and teddy bears, but these are not animate objects. They are only secondary substitutes for mother, and although the baby may need to settle for them, he knows they are not mother. Liedloff (1975) argues that an "in-arms" period for infants is crucial to their emotional development. In this period, which ideally lasts through the first six to eight months of life, mothers should carry their children whenever possible, and, as in tribal cultures, emphasize attachment needs, physical touching, and emotional comfort. My perspective is not that the baby requires twenty-four hours a day of merger and not that separation is inhumane, but rather that we must examine the results of the amount of separation, the amount of aloneness, that we insist upon in our twentieth century child-rearing practices and our current psychotherapy orientations. How we understand the needs of childhood affects how we understand the treatment issues and the therapeutic interventions we provide for our patients.

I hope to offer the reader an affective, evocative experience, as well as to convey technical knowledge. In so doing, I have found it useful to draw upon literature, both poetry and prose, to help convey the many-textured feelings of merger and detachment. The following is a descriptive narrative written by Thomas Wolfe (1929), which I offer to demonstrate the painfulness of an alienated, detached childhood. In this passage, he is describing a young child (autobiographically himself) about 1 year old.

Lying darkly in his crib, washed, powdered, and fed, he thought quietly of many things before he dropped off to sleep—the interminable sleep that obliterated time for him, and that gave him a sense of having missed forever a day of sparkling life. At these moments, he was heartsick with wary horror as he thought of the discomfort, weakness, dumbness, the infinite misunderstanding he would have to endure before he gained even physical freedom. He grew sick as he thought of the weary distance before him, the lack of co-ordination of the centers of control, the undisciplined and rowdy bladder, the helpless exhibition he was forced to give in the company of his sniggering, pawing brothers and sisters, dried, cleaned, revolved before them. . . .

And left alone to sleep within a shuttered room, with the thick sunlight printed in bars upon the floor, unfathomable loneliness and sadness crept through him: he saw his life down the solemn vista of a forest aisle, and he knew he would always be the sad one: caged in that little round of skull, imprisoned in that beating and most secret heart, his life must always walk down lonely passages. Lost . . .

His brain went black with terror. He saw himself an inarticulate stranger, an amusing little clown, to be dandled and nursed by these enormous and remote figures. He had been sent from one mystery into another: somewhere within or without his consciousness he heard a great bell ringing faintly, as if it sounded undersea, and as he listened, the ghost of memory walked through his mind, and for a moment he felt that he had almost recovered what he had lost. [pp. 30–31]

I have given an alternative, experiential sketch of the fetus's womb-life and his very early days. A young child does not have a continuous sense of omnipotence, nor does he have a phase-specific experience of being the conqueror, with "the world [as] his oyster" as Mahler (1975) suggests in a phrase borrowed from Greenacre (1957). Rather, the child has an ongoing dialectical experience between feeling powerless and powerful. Nor does he look in the mirror, as Lacan believes, and feel himself to be whole, in form similar to his mother. Rather, he looks in the mirror and, although he feels delight at seeing the varied body parts that he knows so well—his arms, stomach, legs, and toes—all put together, he also realizes *his smallness*. He sees the truth, which is that he does not even resemble the mammoth body or mature face of his mother. He already knows his body parts are connected, but it is the image of his *smallness* that is so shocking. If nothing else, a child's childhood is about being little, uncoordinated, wordless, and powerless.

The 5-month-old sees a rattle just out of reach of his little hands. He grunts for mother to get him this shiny red thing. He remembers its ringing sound, its smooth, cold feel, and he wants it. He tries to reach again. He cannot. Mother! Mother! Come and help me! She comes, she sees he wants something . . . she brings him . . . the . . . pacifier. No! Not that, I want the other thing. She tries again. She brings him the stuffed pig. No! No! No! I want that rattle thing—right over there! Please, Mommy, understand what I want. She tries once more. The rattle is his. SUCCESS!! Until it drops from his grasp and rolls away. And he has to start all over again.

The 9-month-old has discovered pointing. What a delicious discovery. Now he can surely show Mommy what he wants. What is that thing on the wall, so high up? Hey, that made the light go on. I want to try it—me too, Mommy—me too; I want to make the lights go bright. She picks him up, he tries and tries, but his strength is not like his Mommy's. She helps him **again** *and the light goes on. Hey! I did that—let me turn it off now. He tries and tries and tries. This time he does it all by himself. Hooray! A new game to do for the rest of the day. What's this? Mommy doesn't want to do this anymore. Oh please come back—*I can't do this without you. I can't reach this without you. *He points to the light, and Mommy comes back again to the light. He tries again, and does it* **all by himself!** HOORAY! I am a big guy, I am just like Mommy!

The 15-month-old is not hungry. No, not now, he thinks. **NO!** He tells his Mommy that he doesn't feel like drinking a glass of milk now, and he doesn't want an apple, and he doesn't want any Cheerios. She says, as always, that she knows he's hungry, just be a good boy, eat this all up. She says it's important to eat so he'll grow big and tall. She says that he wouldn't know if he's hungry, that's **her** job. But he knows he's not hungry. And certainly not for this. Where is that ice cream stuff, if he has to eat? Or the pizza? No, he says again. No, no, no, no. But Mommy will not stop. She pushes the food into his mouth, insists that he has to eat now. **What else can he do, but eat?** When he finishes, she says that, see, she had been right—he was hungry.

The 20-month-old walks proudly with his toy pull-dog. He can do it, all by himself! He can make the dog walk a straight line, right behind him. Now Mommy comes with another pull-toy, and she walks behind him as if in a parade. What fun! I love her, he thinks. How big I am—I'm the leader of the parade.

The 2-year-old is sleepy, but doesn't want Mommy to leave. Not just yet, he thinks. Please not now, just one more story. I don't want to be alone. It's dark, it's lonely. The stuffed toys aren't you, they don't really talk to me. I want you! But Mommy wants him in bed, she's had a long day, and this is (quite frankly) her time for rejuvenation. Besides, she thinks, he's supposed to sleep through the night by now; he's old enough to have a regular bedtime. She places him gently back in his crib and firmly tells him, "Good night, my sweet child. You have your toys, you have the light on, and Mommy knows you can go to sleep **all by yourself.** Nighty-night!" She leaves the room, and he screams out for her. She doesn't return. He's stuck in this prison-crib, and he needs to get out! Where is she? He panics. He screams again. She's not coming for me, she won't help me. He cries, he cries again, and he sobs heavily while shaking furiously at the crib. I can't get out of here! I need to get her! I can't get out and find her. I'm stuck here. Help me Mommy! When he can cry no more, he closes his eyes, exhausted with fear and sadness at the tinyness of his being. (And his mother thinks, Well, it didn't take him too long tonight to settle down. He's getting used to this.)

The 2½-year-old says, "Me want sberryyut." "Sberryyut?" says Mommy, "Sberryyut? I don't know what you are saying. Sberryyut? Let's see. You want the stereo? No? You want to see Sherry?" "No, no, no, no." He points to the refrigerator. She opens it, and he sees the strawberry yogurt. That is what he wants. He proudly says again, "Sberryyut." She laughs. "Oh, you mean strawberry yogurt!" And laughs again. He feels shamed, ridiculed, his pride in his language shifting to embarrassment in his awkwardness.

These are momentary snippets from a child's life, any child's life. There is a mixture of achieving goals, communicating effectively, and failing. These examples serve to counter the psychoanalytic perspective that the baby inherently feels omnipotent and that only over time, as frustrations mount, does this grandiosity lessen. The Freudian idea of "His Majesty the Baby"[3] refers more to how parents may feel, in catering to the infant's many demands, than to the baby's actual subjective experience. The infant primarily feels helpless and little, and it is only in moments when his mother will do his bidding that he can feel powerful or omnipotent. When he has been able to communicate exactly what he needs to an external other, and when she responds to his request, then all is right within his world. Of course, moments when he has been able to accomplish a task without assistance are powerful too—but these are, certainly in early childhood, few and far between.

I agree with Miller and Bowlby that there are much greater and deeper wounds in childhood than have been readily acknowledged by psychoanalysts, child-rearing experts, and parents. Miller (1990) has spent most of her career building a case for increased attention to the dangers of "normal" parenting. She has detailed in her many books incidents which, like some of the moments described above, are traumatic to the child's development. "Some people accuse me of exaggeration when I speak of child abuse in cases of a strict but nevertheless 'normal' upbringing that has 'nothing unusual' about it. Yet it is precisely the widespread nature of this type of child-rearing that makes a warning imperative" (Miller 1990, p. 20). Not only do I agree with Miller, but I am suggesting we examine the damage to children whose childhoods might not even be called strict.

Our culture allows for a certain threshold of parenting practices that I term *normative abuse*. Normative, because these are included in some of the basic tenets of child-raising that are endorsed by the culture in which we live. Normative, because, like the generations before that believed "a child should be seen and not heard," these are parts of current parenting philosophy. Normative, because these are often tiny moments in a child's life, moments that may be followed by a loving interaction or a sweet caress. Normative abuse occurs when the attachment needs of the child

---

3. Freud (1914a) used this phrase to describe the infant's position in his family. According to Strachey, Freud's editor and translator, it was probably a reference to a Royal Academy picture with this same title, in which two London policemen stopped traffic so that a nanny and baby carriage could cross the street.

are sacrificed for the cultural norms of separation and individuation. Normative abuse occurs when parental instinct and empathy are replaced by cultural norms. Although these incidents are not as severely trauma-tizing as incidents of verbal, physical, or sexual abuse, they nevertheless affect the overall development of the child's personality. In many cases, normative abuse occurs alongside of alcoholism or in conjunction with other forms of abuse.

Bowlby (1979), whose work is presented in greater detail in later chapters, was convinced that much of our child-rearing practices, in-cluding the daily minutiae, creates more frustration than necessary. In a lecture in the late 1950s on child care, Bowlby stated:

> An immense amount of friction and anger in small children and loss of temper on the part of their parents can be avoided by such simple procedures as presenting a legitimate plaything before we intervene to remove his mother's best china, or coaxing him to bed by tactful humoring instead of demanding prompt obedience, or permitting him to select his own diet and to eat it in his own way, including, if he likes it, having a bottle until he is two years of age or over. The amount of fuss and irritation which comes from expecting small children to conform to our own ideas of what, how, and when they should eat is ridiculous and tragic—the more so now that we have careful studies demonstrating the efficiency with which babies and young children can regulate their own diets and the convenience to ourselves when we adopt these methods. [p. 13]

I agree with Bowlby's parenting philosophy, but would add that it is more than "friction and anger" that are at stake: it is the child's overall sense of powerlessness, worthlessness, and alienation.

Mitchell (1988) has noted the tendency of psychoanalytic theory to overemphasize early infant experiences in the development of the person-ality. He states, "Developmental-arrest theory, drawing heavily on the metaphor of the modern baby, has swung the pendulum back too far, viewing neurosis as frozen, aborted development, with infantile experi-ences of deprivation and parental failure underlying and predisposing adult experience and psychopathology" (p. 172). Certainly, each life event affects a personality throughout the life cycle. A death in the family when the child is 5, a move when the child is 8, a struggle with schoolwork when the child enters seventh grade, all will have a significant impact on overall personality development. As I often say to patients, "We are a work in progress." And that is as true at 6 months as it is at 60. The difference is that the impact, the impressionability for a 2-year-old is that much greater than for a 20-year-old. When mother and father are the child's whole world, when there are no other models, no other friends, no other homes to feel secure in, then the world of the child is that much more important. And, when the self is just beginning to crystallize and to form a way of relating to others, these early moments of normative abuse matter greatly. These unempathic ruptures between mother and child bring a separation in their interrelationship, a detachment that edges them slightly further apart. When mother does not respect her child's refusal to eat, when she does not cuddle him to help him sleep, when she laughs, even lovingly, at his language struggles, there is a momentary split, a break, in the empathic attunement or fusion that had existed before. The more often these moments occur—even in normative abuse—the larger the split and the deeper the sense of detachment. This slow process leads to the overall personality development of what has been called, variously, the *basic fault*, the *false self*, and *the empty core*. The detachment of, and in, the self forms in response to the rupture of empathic, intersubjective relating. And the extent of this detachment is directly related to the quality and quantity of normative, verbal, physical, and sexual abuse that the child has received throughout his life.

Many examples from patients come to mind.[4] One woman, a talented musician, responded to my request to share an early memory, with the following:

> I was little, no more than 2 or 2½. My crib was under the window. I can still see it now. Outside, it was thundering and lightning, and I was frightened. I was scared that the lightning would come in through the window and, like an arrow, pierce my heart. I can still remember seeing shadowed lines on the floor, from the bars of the crib being illuminated as the lightning erupted. "Did you call for help?" Oh yes, I did. But no one came. And the thing is, I knew my parents could hear me in their room next door, but they were purposely ignoring me, leaving me to be frightened

---

4. Certain of the behaviors, symptoms, and descriptive features of the individuals and patients referenced in the case histories included in this book have been altered for purposes of publication in the interest of protecting the true identity of those upon whom the case histories have been based.

and helpless, all alone and trapped in that crib. [The patient began to cry. When she spoke again, she said] *I think this has a lot to do with why I never ask for help. This is part of it. I cried out, I asked for it, and no one came. It was awful.*

Another memory from this patient furthered an understanding of her long-standing belief that she should never ask for anything, lest she be seen as a bother.

I had this pretty little dress, and I just loved wearing it. I wore it in the morning, afternoon, and I wanted to wear it at night too but I wasn't allowed. I must've been about 4 years old. One day, I went to put on my beautiful dress, but it was gone. I looked everywhere. I searched every closet in the house, every dresser drawer. I pleaded with my mother to find it with me. But she told me it was gone, that it had just "disappeared." And then she took out another dress for me and said that I would have to "get used to" wearing other things, like all the other good girls do.

A second patient was relating to me the trouble she was having with her 2-year-old daughter.

Patient: I just can't get her to listen to me. She's started this temper tantrum thing now, and I am so frustrated, you have no idea.

K.B.W.:   Give me an idea about what kinds of things set your daughter off.

Patient: Well, today is a good example. I carried her down for breakfast and told her we were going to have eggs, that I had hers already made and ready to eat. But she saw the lollipop on the counter from yesterday and wanted to eat this instead. Of course I told her no, that lollipops are not for breakfast, and have these yummy eggs. But she just couldn't get off it. No matter what I said or how I tried to distract her, she would have no part of it. She started to scream, to have a real temper tantrum. That's when I sent her to her room for a little time out.

K.B.W.:   So the problem was the lollipop. Did you consider giving her the lollipop?

Patient: Of course not. That's not something you should have for breakfast!

K.B.W.:   I know that, and you know that. First of all, in the future, don't leave lollipops out if you don't want her to have them. Second, what's wrong with her having a little taste of her lollipop, which had been left there from the day before, so I assume she doesn't usually finish them, and then giving her her eggs?

Patient: Well, I didn't think of that. Anyway, she needs to know that she can't have everything she wants to in this life.

K.B.W.: Really? At 2 years old? Wouldn't it be better if, for the most part, she experienced herself as being able to get the things in life that she wants to have, that she can ask for something, and receive it? Wouldn't it be great for her to know that she can use her determination to get what she wants?

Patient: But I want her to know that *I'm the boss.*

K.B.W.: Why is that? Isn't that what your own mother did? Don't you see how that is related to how indecisive you often are, how you are always so worried what others will say, as if to indicate that *they* are the boss? And how related this is to your continual seeking of a relationship in which you will be dominated, punished, and put down?

A third patient described two moments of her day with her 2½-year-old daughter. She was at her mother-in-law's home with Megan and a neighbor's child, who was 3½. They were playing nicely when, all of a sudden, the older child snatched away one of the toys. Her daughter slapped this other child's face, and then both started hitting and pushing each other. My patient ran to intercede, separated the two, and pulled Megan away to speak with her. Megan then slapped her mother's face. This patient has spent a good deal of time in sessions discussing the physical and verbal abuse she had experienced in her own childhood home, and how she had been somewhat rageful and abusive with her older child. She was learning through the therapy that there is another way, and now she was being tested to try it out. She kneeled down to her daughter and held her arms so that she could no longer swing them. "Sweetie, I know this made you angry. I know you are tired; it's been a long day. Hitting me or Amy when you are angry isn't appropriate. Let's go home now." She picked up her daughter to leave, only to hear her mother-in-law behind her shouting at her angrily, "You should've hit her back. HIT HER! Boy, have you gone soft with this child. No child of mine would've gotten away with that!"

Later that day my patient had a chance to sit with her daughter while she was playing at home in their sandbox. She thought about what I had once said about choosing a later moment to review, or process, any earlier difficulties. She thought about what I had said about little children lacking the vocabulary skills to say, "I'm angry, I'm sad," and using physical actions instead. She said to her daughter, "I know how angry you were with Amy. She was being a bully, bossing you around so much. Instead of hitting her, you could say, 'Megan mad,' or 'Megan sad,' or 'Megan tired.' " Her daughter immediately responded: she picked up sand and threw it in the sandbox, saying, "Megan mad." Over and over again she did this, practicing saying sad and mad. As they continued, her Daddy came home. Megan ran to hug her Daddy, telling him "Megan happy." In describing this to me in session, the patient said, tearfully, "But I had never told her the word 'happy.' She just put this together on her own. It was a wonderful moment, to see Megan express herself, and she was so proud of herself for having made us understand just what she felt."

Other patients have mentioned some of the childhood names their parents had used to describe them, names that do not constitute verbal abuse, but fall instead under normative abuse. These names include: "devil," "troublemaker," "rebel," "boob," "silly," "a bother," "a challenge," "a klutz." One patient, Rebecca, had been continuously told by her mother that her clinginess, hysteria, and tempestuousness caused her mother frequently to be "Rebecca-ed out." Throughout her treatment with me, she would anxiously ask if I, too, had been "Rebecca-ed out" yet. She was constantly preoccupied with the idea that her whole self could overwhelm others. In some cases, these kinds of stock phrases were used even in playful moments, but the labels still became fused in some way into their beings. What is important here is that these words were used not just once, but over and over, many times a day: they are striking in their frequency and forcefulness. The label is offered at any moment of exasperation, irritation, or frustration. One mother continuously labeled her beautiful daughter's behavior "ugly." If the child wanted someone else's toy, she was told to "stop being so ugly." If the child would not cooperate, she was "being ugly." If she was too insistent, she was "ugly."

Certainly these normative moments of abuse, such as the ones mentioned above, lead to an internalization of these labels. They also create a separation, a space between the interconnectedness of mother and child. In the case of Rebecca, for example, she continuously felt that she was unlovable in her total being, for after all, she knew that she would always be "too much" for anyone to love. In another case, the patient who was called a "devil" knew she could not rely on her mother for friendship or interaction, because every one of her favorite activities was frowned upon. She loved to go to the creek near her home and watch the bugs, frogs, and turtles. But her mother called that "rebellious" and "obstinate" behavior, angry that she would dirty her pretty dresses. Her burgeoning interest in nature was squashed and was replaced with an internal feeling of badness and a sense that she liked to do things that were rebellious and upsetting to others. The separation, the retreat into the self, leads to the activation of the *false self*. The development of an alienated sense of self can start in a childhood filled with normative abuse, just as it so often begins in a childhood filled with sexual or physical traumas. The culmination of so many moments leads to a feeling-state of detachment, separateness, aloneness. It leads to lack of merger experiences that are so important to living fully in this world. Another passage from Thomas Wolfe (1929), himself an alienated being, adds more descriptive evocation of a childhood filled with normative abuse and alcoholism.

> He saw that the great figures that came and went about him, the huge leering heads that bent hideously into his crib, the great voices that rolled incoherently above him, had for one another not much greater understanding than they had for him: that even their speech, their entire fluidity and ease of movement were but meagre communicants of their thought or feeling, and served often not to promote understanding, but to deepen and widen strife, bitterness, and prejudice. . . .
>
> He understood that men were forever strangers to one another, that no one ever comes really to know anyone, that imprisoned in the dark womb of our mother, we come to life without having seen her face, that we are given to her arms a stranger, and that, caught in that insoluble prison of being, we escape it never, no matter what arms may clasp us, what mouth may kiss us, what heart may warm us. Never, never, never, never. [pp. 31–32]

INCIDENTS FROM A CHILDHOOD FILLED WITH ALCOHOLISM AND NORMATIVE ABUSE

I first met James when he was 46. His wife had quite vehemently "dragged" him to therapy because she had *had* it. Their son was well into his teenage years, soon off on his own, and the future for the marriage looked bleak. The final incident involved yet another time in which James had usurped his wife's limit-setting position and had undermined a rule she had instituted with their son. As the marital sessions continued, it became apparent that James continually minimized everything around him. Whatever incident his wife related, be it from the present week or from the beginning of their marriage twenty years ago, he would always answer with, "Well, I really don't think it was as bad as she says it was." For almost the entire first year, James would sit in the corner of the room, trying to stay out of the limelight. In fact he even used to sit behind a large plant in my office and often gave me pointers on how I could care for it better. (I had always felt that his focus on the plant—was it cared for well enough?—was a self-statement about himself and me, that is, how well would I be able to care for him?) After the room was redecorated and the plant moved to another side of the room, James had no recourse but to become more visible.

Over the three years of marital therapy, the main theme of James's passive-aggressivity and his rather detached, uninvolved manner were continuously examined. His wife's strongly expressed emotions served in stark contrast to his mild, almost wordless demeanor. The sessions seemed productive in that the two were able to accept the many differences between them, yet there seemed to be little room to draw them closer together. Their separateness, which was a hallmark of their marriage, included how they spent evenings after work—she read or watched television while he was working on various projects in the basement, researching his next hiking trip, or perusing some poetry.

On occasion, he and I would have an individual session. In these, he seemed quite unlike the man in the marital sessions. He could articulate his feelings, was careful in presenting his completed thoughts, and seemed genuinely intrigued by the analytic frame. As a result of these few sessions, James began to feel courageous enough in himself to voice his opinions more openly to his wife. He told her some of the past incidents in their relationship that had bothered him and shared his own internal thoughts regarding any new conflict that they might encounter. Still, throughout the entire marital work, it became clear that these two individuals were never going to agree to spend much time together and were probably happier "doing their own thing." As would be expected, even vacations had started years ago to be separate, and the marital therapy did nothing to change this except to help the two of them feel more comfortable about this arrangement. They simply could not agree on activities to do together while vacationing—he loved camping, hiking, and bird watching, whereas she liked shopping, sightseeing, and relaxing on beaches. There was no compromising their individual pursuits; there was little accommodation of their separate emotional states.

As the fourth year approached, the two felt they had become more adjusted to their marital relationship. But James had some issues he felt he wanted to address individually, and so we moved into an individual frame of treatment. Every now and then his wife would come to a session to address the ongoing conflicts she was having with him—they actually became more numerous because, as the treatment progressed, James was better able to express his internal feelings and thoughts. In the individual sessions, we began to examine more of his childhood experiences, although it must be noted that, as usual, James would say, "This doesn't seem important to me" or "You're making too much out of this."

Despite his protestations, we began to uncover the history of his past. He was the younger of two boys who have never been close. He did have a circle of a few friends, particularly in high school, but in the earlier grades he was pretty much of a loner and he did not play much with other children. His parents were exclusively involved with one another, so much so that, as a result, they had minimal involvement with James. Furthermore, they were both alcoholics and, as the years progressed, drank away most of every evening together. According to James, the progression of their alcoholism became greater as he grew older, to the extent that, sometimes as a teenager, he had to help his father to bed or was held prisoner to his father's "soppy" spews of alcoholic romanticism. Usually the alcohol helped his father shed his repressed, cold, and extraordinarily tense demeanor. Under the glow of intoxication, he would wax philosophic on matters of the heart. Yes, there were a few times when he became violent or abusive, but James remembered him on the whole as being "harmless." The day after these alcoholic nights, his father would get up early and get ready for work, with nothing said about the previous night's events. He would spend the weekends working on numerous projects, continually repairing the house, landscaping the property, or building furniture. It was the same with his mother, who would retire earlier after her drink and would, like her husband, get up the next day to continue pushing for the completion of her many tasks. They were endless doers who enjoyed working on many projects together—refinishing antiques, renovating homes for resale, and creating stained-glass windows.

Throughout his adolescence, James remembers most weekends spent working with his father on continuous projects around the house— silently, separately, but yet together. This of course had great significance for his relationship with his wife: he repeated the need for solitude and detachment while having the other still nearby.

As the sessions continued, James began to awaken to other feelings, particularly those of love and the painfulness of abandonment. He realized that he had had few immersive moments, moments when he felt that an other was in tune with his own being. And he found that psychotherapy was one of the few places that afforded him this experience. Previously, he had found these moments only in the poetry he read or in the experience of being part of the larger natural universe. One of the reasons he loved being outdoors, traveling nature's expanse, was because he had found a kind of oneness in being surrounded by such beauty, stillness, and life. It was painful for him to have actually found attunement inside the thera- peutic relationship, because he could only focus on the inevitability of our separation. The relationship with me was going to end at some point, he would tell me, as surely as every session always ended. It became apparent that the sessions themselves were difficult, because each renewed contact with me meant renewed leaving. He often spoke of wanting to end his therapy because of this difficulty. In analyzing these feelings, we came to see that he had never really felt connected to others, especially not to his mother or father. He, like his parents, had become exclusively a doer, leaving little room for emotional connectedness. He carried this pain, this sense of detachment, into the rest of his life—he had not expected to find oneness in his marriage and indeed had not, and he had not expected to find attunement with his son, and indeed he did not. It seemed as though he felt the pain of separation from a loved one would be too great to allow himself entry into the attachment. Where had the painfulness of attach- ment begun? When did his minimization start? From what had his schizoid defense germinated?

After almost six months of individual treatment, James asked for "release." He spoke of the painfulness of attunement, which reminded me of Seinfeld's (1991) warning that "for the schizoid patient, empathy can be ensnaring and objectifying as any other intervention, even more so because, like pure honey, it tempts the patient into its sticky, thick warmth" (p. 38). For many sessions, James spoke of his wish to leave therapy because he continued to feel overwhelmed by the sadness of the separation and preferred to "get it over with." When, in the therapy, he abruptly announced that he was *definitely* leaving and that this was to be his last session, he asked, "What's the point? Why should I stay in something that is painful, makes me uncomfortable, and that I'll have to leave anyway?" When he added that he was not sure that psychotherapy could help him any more, I pointed out that he was now minimizing this experience as he has done with everything else—now he was lessening its importance, downplaying its value, and therefore reducing the intensity of his feelings. "Psychotherapy is a place to feel everything," I recall saying, "and if you don't want to do that, then yes, you really should stop the therapy. Since this seems like such a waste of time and money to you, then let's discontinue the analysis. Is today our last appointment?" James wrestled with his determined wish to leave and chose, as the session ended, to stop. He called me early the next day and apologized for his devaluation of the therapy. James had realized after the session that it was because the therapeutic work, and the nature of our relationship, were "too powerful" that he had requested distance. He asked to continue, although in a less concentrated and frequent way, because, although he had needed a "release," he felt that he also wanted the continued contact. To this I agreed, because I understood that James could not alter his internal state of feeling insignificant at too quick a pace, that he had been so used to minimizing his own self and to being minimized that the empathic attunements, and the moments of oneness, had to come under his control.

James also told me, during this conversation, that he was sending me some letters written by his father when James was a baby. He commented that, although he was "sure the letters were nothing of value," he thought I might be interested in glancing through the correspondence. And indeed I was. In fact, they provided some of the clues to answer the questions about James considered earlier, answers that he could not provide because he had so minimized his childhood drama. I have found that, very often, what constitutes normative abuse is not only forgotten by the patient but is also excused away, in part because the abuse occurs within the normal range of societal expectations. Bowlby (1973) notes this tendency as well, saying:

> In the first place, no child cares to admit that his parent is gravely at fault. To recognize frankly that a mother is exploiting you for her own ends, or that a father is unjust and tyrannical, or that neither parent ever wanted you, is intensely painful . . . [and] very frighten-

ing. Given any loophole, therefore, most children will seek to see their parent's behaviour in some more favourable light. This natural bias of children is easy to exploit. [p. 316]

James gave me his father's letters at a serendipitous moment for me, as I was in the process of organizing the material for this book. I am exceedingly grateful to him for giving me permission to include his father's letters, because they demonstrate, better than any explanation, the minutiae that make up the gestalt of normative abuse. These moments of everyday life reveal the beginnings of James's detachment from his own self and from others. One fascinating aspect of these letters is that, of course, they were not written by the father for the purpose of explaining his children's character development; on the contrary, the purpose of this correspondence was to give news to the relatives of his young, relocated family. The time period was 1944–1945, when letter writing still superseded telephone calls as a form of communication. James's family comes from a long chain of letter writers, with letters still intact from six generations past. So it was natural that Robert, James's father, would want to continue in this family tradition. One copy of the week's letter was sent to his father, mother, brother, and sister and another to his wife's mother and her several sisters and brother. Robert and Nancy had moved far from their families to New York City—all the more reason to attempt contact through letters.

The next few pages offer edited versions of Robert's letters that, unfortunately, extend for only one and a half years and were either stopped or have since been lost. The letters were written weekly, and each had a segment about each of the four family members. I have organized the material in a different way, by presenting Robert's observations of each family member in chronological order. James has told me that he found these letters to be more "cutesy" than he remembers his father ever being. And indeed, there is a somewhat sardonic, humorous tone to some of them; however, the underlying flavor of his sentiments still pervades.

It could be argued that a family in which alcohol played so prominent a role precludes any discussion of normative abuse. However, in these early years of Robert and Nancy's drinking, which is also quite early in their marriage, their use of alcohol was less than it became over the next thirty-five years. We have here only the first year and a half of James's life, and in that time, although alcohol is mentioned quite frequently by Robert there are also many entries (not included) that do not mention it.

Editing may actually have the effect of overemphasizing how much alcohol was used by his parents during these early years, as only the more disturbing entries are presented here. Another important factor is that the societal norm for drinking in the 1940s was not as it is today. Fifty years ago, having cocktails before dinner did not, in the public's eye, an alcoholic make nor did bingeing a few times a month. And that is precisely the point. Normative issues shift with the cultural tides. Today, awareness of alcohol abuse is much greater than in previous generations, just as consciousness regarding child abuse has been heightened. Given the societal context in which this family lived, then, we can examine the minutiae of their lives and discover the impact of numerous child-raising moments that created distance, fear, and separateness in their two very young boys. These children are now in their fifties—and have raised their own families as well. The effect of these normative moments has influenced more than their own childhoods, then, and has infiltrated their adult lives, their marriages, and their own child-rearing practices.

James has commented that it was a "puzzle" to him and to his brother just why his father became an alcoholic.

> He had had a normal childhood, with no traumas to speak of. With my mother, it was more understandable. She had had a great deal more suffering in her life, including the loss of her father at a young age and surviving a severe fire which left her body partially disfigured and burned. But my father—it has always been a mystery to me and to my brother just what had caused his need to drink. There was no history of alcoholism in the family—no one else in his family was like him. He was always so tense, he could never relax except when he was drinking. I think that's the only time he was ever at peace.

Historical Background

At the time of these letters, Robert was 35 and his wife Nancy was 32. They lived in a small apartment in the middle of Manhattan with their two small sons and were frequently visited by two of Nancy's five sisters. During 1945 Nancy also took care of the 4-month-old child of one of her sisters, who worked as a nurse and whose husband had deserted his family.

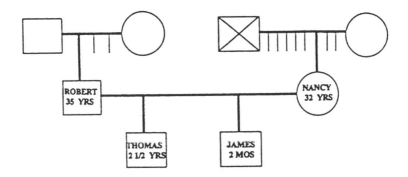

The first entry, on March 4, 1944, includes a somewhat apologetic opening:

> "We won't go so far as to say that the New York Smiths don't have any time to write letters, but it is sometimes a struggle. Rather than to dignify this by calling it a letter, we will just make it a report so that all of you will know that we are holding up under the strain."

James

March 4, 1944 (at 2 months old): The last couple of nights he forgot he was hungry (at least he did not yell too loud) so that his fond mother and father were able to enjoy a good night's sleep. Most of the time we do not know that he is around for he sleeps most of the time, and the rest of his energy is used to wave his arms and kick his covers off. It is thought he is beginning to see, at least he has a good idea of where the bottle ought to be when it is time to feed him.

March 10, 1944: The littlest one has been on his best behavior this last week and if there was a robot to do the feeding we would not know he is around the house . . . He is sure a credit to the system!

April 1, 1944: Last Sunday James and I kept house while the others went to Tuckahoe—the Little One cooperated beautifully for he did not peep all day. Based on a father's experience there is nothing to this business of raising a baby.

April 9, 1944: It is fun to watch the little one grow and especially since he does not cause us any trouble.

April 15, 1944: As long as he is awake he likes to play with the gadget that John sent him, and we are more than thankful for it keeps him quiet.

May 20, 1944: He is just as nice as can be so much so that there is only good to be spoken of him. He sleeps all night and does not cry so what else would you want.

May 27, 1944: Having a lot of fun with him now as he does not miss anything, and if there is a considerable rumpus he joins in.

June 10, 1944: We think he has caught on to this going-to-bed business for of late he starts to howl when we get him ready for the night. The present schedule has both of them going to bed at the same time, and it is not bad at all as far as we are concerned.

June 17, 1944: James is behaving like a little angel in that he is happy about everything and is not nearly as insistent as is his brother.

October 28, 1944: Being the only one in the family over whom we have no control, he is the boss: but our day is coming for he is starting to understand—no no.

December 16, 1944: That boy is right on his toes and does not miss a thing. He is almost as bad as his brother. Gone are the days when he could be left in bed and ignored. Does not sleep much in the morning any more and after lunch has to be strapped down if we want him to sleep; then he goes off in about ten minutes.

March 17, 1945 (at 14 months old): He is as stubborn as his *mother* and like her neither hell or high water can make him back down. Having a struggle with him over his milk—it is almost like a game with him, but sometimes it sort of tries our patience.

March 24, 1945: He has found that he can tease Sally [*the cousin who was three months older and was taken care of by his mother*] by biting her and is smart enough to know that it is best that N is not around. It used to be that we blamed Thomas for everything but that day is passing.

March 31, 1945: He is trying to talk. Of course we may be taking poetic liberty with what he has to say but we think that he can say bird and *beer* [*my emphasis*] so that it is understandable.

April 21, 1945: James is becoming as stubborn as his father so that it will not be long before someone will have to take a hand to the situation.

April 28, 1945: This little boy has usurped the prerogatives of his older brother and has been a terror. He seems to know that he is it and is taking advantage of the situation—he is as stubborn as all get-out and raises a devil of a fuss when he does not get his own way.

July 7, 1945: He is just fine but getting more and more stubborn as the days go on. He is starting on words, and once in a while he will parrot a phrase. He still has the tendency to bite if he is crossed.

July 30, 1945: James and his cousin have had the bit between their teeth lately and have been rather hard to feed. We are letting them do most of the spoon work now, but when they have decided that they have had enough then it takes the strong arm to get them to eat any more. That would be all right if they did not get hungry so soon—by the time that the regular time comes they are all a bunch of Indians.

September 6, 1945: During the course of the last week he has learned the trick of getting out of his crib. Of course we thought that it was fun when he did it first, but now we are not so sure. His hour of rising is between 6 and 6:30, which does not coincide with ours, so for a while in the morning there is a little temper in the air. . . . It has been a different picture at night too—now he is the one who is out of the bed a couple of dozen times before he settles down for the night. I can scare Thomas but not James—he is as independent as the devil.

Thomas

March 10, 1944 (at 2½ years old): In some ways it is too bad that we did not get the book which tells how to control the "little boys."

April 22, 1944: Aside from being too busy to eat, which can be right annoying at times, his only complaint is that the grown-ups do not play with him enough. From morning to night he is on the go, and he finds so many interesting things to do that it is hard to get him to take his nap.

April 29, 1944: If the little boy would only eat when he is supposed to eat, then he would have a quieter time of it and his parents would have better dispositions. But he has to be threatened and cajoled and cajoled and threatened before and during every meal. That might be natural but oh my . . . and the boy is busy, busy, busy all the time being a cross between a cyclone and a parrot.

May 20, 1944: By the time five o'clock comes around, he is rather mean, and then it is a job to put up with him. . . . Then too of late he has been rather stubborn.

June 3, 1944: After supper off he goes—in fact both of them go so that by 7:30 all is quiet.

June 10, 1944: This one has it in his mind that he is the one to run the park and so we have our troubles with him. He takes anything that he wants from the others and exhibits sort of a proprietary interest in the varied assortment of toys that are in the park. When the burden becomes too heavy then he has to be taken home—unwillingly is the word for it.

June 17, 1944: We are still having trouble in getting him to eat, but at times there are signs of improvement so that we have not given up all hope.

July 8, 1944: We had a little trouble in that he was right possessive and if the others tried to take anything away from him he would bite them, but I think that he is behaving better now. One thing is certain—that it will not do him any harm to learn that others have their rights too.

July 29, 1944: This week we have tried the starvation treatment. If he does not want to eat we do not force him with the result that he is hungry at mealtimes, but even then does not put much away. He sure is on the go enough so that he ought to be hungry. Otherwise he is the same.

August 26, 1944: He celebrated his birthday by biting a couple of the little boys in the park and by otherwise being right ornery.

February 3, 1945: He has developed one little habit that can be rather annoying at times, and that is his getting out of bed about six in the morning. He can be quiet but other times he is not with the result that James is up too, then there is no rest for the weary. N and I struggle and struggle, but it is no use and we might just as well get up.

March 17, 1945: Sometimes he is a help, and then there are times when he is as bad as his brother.

March 31, 1945: He can scare Sally by opening his mouth to bite (and sometimes does), but with James it is a different matter for J will bite right back.

Nancy

March 4, 1944: After feeding James at 6 AM there is the formula to make and the washing to do; then breakfast for Thomas and Robert; Thomas must be dressed and by that time James is ready for his bath and another feeding. Then she goes to the store and a walk with Thomas getting home in time for lunch. By the time Thomas is in for his nap James is ready again and so if all goes well she might have an hour for herself before Thomas is up and the supper started. After supper it is clean up, and the rest of the eve from 8 PM on her own. Of course James is ready to eat at ten and so by that time we are all ready to shove off for bed. And so it goes.

March 25, 1945: The chief cook and bottle washer of this household has been on her toes all this week. If she doesn't have sewing to do she wanders about like a cat, and it is not long before she will be out in the kitchen stirring up a cake. Me, I do not complain although most of the time I do mention that she ought to take it easy—that leaves me in the clear if they happen to burn a little on the bottom or do not come up to her expectations. Like Grandmother Smith, she hasn't made anything perfect yet, and I am beginning to think that she never will—to judge by her standards.

April 8, 1944: The days she can scarcely call her own and there is some doubt about the evenings. . . . The other nights she managed to find some sewing to do—fixing up blouses and dresses—so that she kept out of trouble.

May 6, 1944: If you asked the Lady what she did this week all that she would say was that she worked all the time—not too much of an exaggeration at that. But she found the energy to start on some sewing, so that it is not as bad as it sounds.

May 13, 1944: Although she mentions frequently that she should be in the house more doing the cleaning, she seems to be taking the outdoor periods with a certain amount of anticipation. . . . She finished her blouse and now has the skirt done—I would say all but the finishing touches.

June 17, 1944: Every morning N rushes around so that she will be able to take the little ones out—bringing them home for lunch, then it is out again until time to fix dinner. She has finished some sewing for Thomas, and I think is going out today to get some more material for herself.

July 29, 1944: By the time that the day is ended, with the weather and all, she has not had ambition to do a thing in the evening. Last night though she did get out her material for a skirt and at least looked it over.

August 26, 1944: As usual the Lady has had her hands so full of children that by the time that the evening comes around she is ready to just sit and take it easy.

October 21, 1944: A week or so ago she cut out Thomas' coat and most of the evening has been spent trying to interpret the pattern. As it is rather bulky material it is hard to sew, and since everything has to be just right she is having a time for herself. But it is coming along and looks right well.

October 28, 1944: She has started on the lining of the coat, which incidentally has been pronounced to be one fine job.

January 20, 1945: She says that all she does is work, but that can be no surprise. We always seem to have something going on, and there is always cleaning to be done.

February 10, 1945: Has just about finished her dress and is not at all happy about it. She thinks that she ought to have made it of a more expensive material. I think that it looks fine—come to think of it, if she were enthused about it at this stage then something would be wrong as it is not her nature to be too optimistic at this stage.

March 31, 1945: Is still trying to find enough energy to work after the kids are to bed. She like myself has lots of little things to do, but when comes night we are both more inclined to sit.

Robert

March 4, 1944: The only worry that he has is how to stretch the days into a 48-hour working day. There is so much to do, and the time is so short that one is on the go most of the time.

March 10, 1944: The work just keeps on building up though there are times when I can see through the fog. Taking work home helps a little, but for the most part I do not want to look at it in our "free hour."

March 15, 1944: There are so many things on hand that I do not dare stay out lest I get too far behind. The only irksome part is that I have to take some of the editing home at night for the printer is right after us all the time.

April 8, 1944: He has not been in too good graces with the mistress of the house for about every night he has brought home work and proceeds to drop out of circulation.

April 15, 1944: The weeks come and the weeks go, and there are times when he wonders if he will ever be caught up enough so that he can sit down without having a briefcase full of work behind his chair.

April 29, 1944: Last night, the girls feeling that it was a good night for a party, took up the ball and some. The Joneses came over carrying a liquid package so that all in all we had a nice quiet visit.

May 20, 1944: Last night the three of us after the little ones were sound asleep ran around the corner to visit the Joneses. Had a nice time visiting with a few on the side.

May 27, 1944: Last night we tried out the buttered rum—with the chill in the air it did hit the spot. . . . Almost every evening there has been something turn up that kept me working and that was not good for now I have it to do this weekend.

June 3, 1944: This has not been too bad a week though I did not do as much as I had hoped to, but that seems to be the way it goes.

July 8, 1944: We had a nice weekend [*visiting his parents*], although Dad and I were busy fixing up the other side of the house.

August 5, 1944: I am catching up on some of the work slowly but surely, and at times I can at least hope that I will have it easy for a while. But there is always so much to do that I will probably end in despair.

August 19, 1944: I have been trying to finish with my darn book and hope that I will see the last of it this coming week. Then I can do the other thousand things that have to be finished up. Last night Charlotte came over, and we had a quiet session at home with a little rum. Gave both the Smith and Stone families a good going over . . . [*we went out, later that week and*] when we came home we asked Miss T., the switchboard operator, and Mrs. M. who were looking after the children while we were out, in for a while. Had a few drinks and visited till the small hours.

August 26, 1944: The office always seems to be right busy and I think every day that I am going to take it easy and get home early, but somehow it is always the regular time or even later.

October 21, 1944: While the office has not been too busy, it seems that I can never get caught up.

January 27, 1945: With work piling up there has not been much that I could do. The other night I came back and did some work and there is still so much that I ought to do it. More often though when night comes I am tired enough to call it a day.

February 10, 1945: When I come home at noon more often than not I help put them in for their nap—my job is to go in and scare them so that they will stay quiet. Under the circumstances it is no wonder that I am watched by the small fry with a watchful eye. Last night for instance Thomas heard me go out and so was up in a flash. According to reports the lady had a time getting him back to bed.

March 17, 1945: Last Sunday I did take the day off to work a little around the house—washing windows and the like, but there is still a lot to do.

March 24, 1945: I made a gate to go in front of the boys' room. We can only say at the present time that the idea is good—how it will work out is a different matter for we can stand the holloring and wailing for only so long and then we let them out.

May 26, 1945: The other night Nancy, her sister, and I went out for a while. Knowing that the children would not go to sleep right away we had supper first. . . . By the time we went out N was hungry again so we went looking for a steak. T'was a bad night for that and we had no luck but did cover a couple of bars including the Commodore. We had a good time.

March 31, 1945: All I can say is that I go to work in the morning, come home to lunch, go back to work, come home for supper, and rest in the evening.

June 2, 1945: Tuesday night when I came home from work I found that the girls were in the mood for a party, but somehow it did not get started till late.

June 23, 1945: And this is a swell day, just right for a little beer. . . . A week ago was our wedding anniversary—five years of trouble for the lady. We were going out, but one thing and then another came up so we never did make it. Guess that was my fault; anyway N was not happy.

Have not done much this week, although we did go out one night for a while—nothing exciting—listened to an organ in a bar and visited with some of the characters. . . .

June 30, 1945: Last night N, her sister, and I were just sitting around being very careful not to do any unnecessary exertion other than to lift a cold glass . . . [*some neighbors came by*] and we sat around till nearly two.

Psychoanalytic Commentary

There are several issues raised by these vignettes from James's family life. Certainly, since he was so young when these were written, he has no personal recollection of these moments. One of the most striking observations is how quickly Robert's view of James changes from the "little angel" of 5 months old to the independent "devil" of almost 2 years. Robert makes it clear that he prefers James when he seems not even to exist—when he doesn't make a "peep" all day and when he "doesn't cause us any trouble." He misses the days when James "could be left in bed and ignored." As soon as James begins to establish a sense of self, to have likes and dislikes, he is labeled "stubborn" and "independent as the devil." Indeed, both Robert and his wife struggle with the powerful wills of their boys, wanting them to be quiet, compliant, and needing little attention. Surely, this has affected James's lifelong repression of his own self, his own thoughts, and especially his angry feelings. Of course, now when his wife wants agreement, he may tacitly give her an "okay" but move in a passive-aggressive way to defeat her wishes.

Throughout the letters, Robert is clearly more annoyed with his older son. He complains to the family that he needs a book to "control little boys." He tells them that his son bites, is a bully, and has trouble being "possessive." And by the end of the entries it is quite obvious that James is heading for the same kind of parental disapproval. The more individuated, the more emotionally expressive the child, the more angry Robert becomes. As he says, "someone will have to take a hand to this situation soon." My guess is that he is referring to spanking or hitting, if that was not already part of the parental repertoire.

The overall feeling tone of these letters is also quite striking. There are few, if any, entries in which Robert shares with the family any joy or happiness he has experienced with either child. Rarely are they seen as

wonders for the knowledge they continually accrue, or joyous for the fun
they have playing together. They are continually viewed as *burdens*, as
objects that get in the way of all the work he and his wife must do. Robert
takes his day off on Sunday so that he can wash windows, not play with his
children. Thomas complains that the grown-ups don't play enough with
him. Could it be that Thomas is referring primarily to his father, who is
frequently out of town on overnight business trips and works on Satur-
days too? Yes, Robert came home for lunch each day (his office was around
the corner), but his job was to put the children in for their nap, not to play
with them.

The impact of his father's feelings on James's personality is clear. He
is uncomfortable when any attention is focused on him. Until
psychotherapy he rarely socialized with his co-workers, but through the
process of being attended to, he is beginning to feel that he has something
worthwhile to say. He has begun to make friends with several others on
his staff, a noticeable shift from his previous, withdrawn manner. In the
therapy too, it has been difficult for him to focus on himself without
wanting to discuss me instead. When I point out how hard it is for him to
be the central focus, he characteristically responds with, "You think
there's something more special in here than I do. I don't think I have
much to offer, quite honestly." He has internalized the mirror that
reflected a burdensome, uninteresting child instead of the inquisitive,
thoughtful self he really is. The importance of psychotherapy for this
patient, to argue somewhat Seinfeld's (1991) point about empathic
attunement, is to help him gain a sense of importance about himself, to
help him stop minimizing both himself and others. And empathic
attunements provide him with the experience that what he says is
interesting, important, and valuable.

Food is an arena for power struggles with children, one in which
Robert and Nancy fully engaged with both boys. We are told that James
needed a "strong arm" to get him to eat more. There appear to be strict
meal times, and the parents hope to train the boys to eat only at the
appointed hour. As for Thomas, who was 2½ when these letters began
(and therefore we have an idea of what probably was in store for James in
the future), he was once given the "starvation treatment." Similarly, the
parents are more than annoyed that the children get up between 6:00 and
6:30 A.M., which is about an hour earlier than each parent would like. Yet
the children are sent to bed by 7:30 P.M. To hope that they would stay in
bed for twelve hours is certainly unrealistic! It probably did not escape the

children's notice that the minute dinner was over, they were sent to bed. Their parents clearly wanted the evenings to themselves and wanted the children out of the way. As well, this 6:00 A.M. awakening is consistent throughout the entire year and a half of writings—neither child ever changes *his* schedule, despite their parents' resentful wishes. (Furthermore, had the parents not been up until 2:00 A.M. drinking, then 6:00 A.M. might not have seemed so early!) Again, the needs of the children are minimized; they are seen as burdens and are angrily responded to. Robert later reports that it is his job to "scare" the children into going to sleep. How were the children scared? By threatening them? Spanking? Storming about angrily? Although we do not know what he did, we can assume he was comfortable with bullying his children into feeling frightened, powerless, and tiny.

I have asked James about his mother's need to "strap him down" after lunch for his nap. Characteristically, his answer was a deflected, "That does seem a bit curious, doesn't it?" Not only was he strapped down, but then it would take him "about ten minutes" to go to sleep. What, do we imagine, was he doing for those ten minutes? Cooing quietly in his crib? Not likely. He was probably screaming until he had exhausted himself. We can speculate that, in moments like these, he learned that no one was listening to his wishes. We can guess that, in moments like these, he felt powerless, little, and even foolish in his screaming. Where was anybody to help him? He was left alone, frantic in his fear. Robert writes about this incident in a detached, semi-humorous manner, not fully disclosing (or perhaps even realizing) what his baby son is suffering in those ten long minutes. Could it be that this style of being, in which Robert minimized the painful struggle of his son, has infiltrated James's being? That the patient's need to minimize any painful moment, any incidence of struggle, has come from a lifetime of being minimized, ignored, forgotten?

It is clear that these children experienced themselves as little; it is clear that they in no way felt omnipotent. Their wishes are seen as demands, their desires for autonomy, such as when to eat, are experienced as usurping control. Robert's decision to make a gate to lock the children in their room is especially disturbing to me, in view of the dangers of enforced separation.[5] Like strapping James into his crib, the boys are

---

5. Forced separation continues to be a fairly common parental practice. One mother recently described to me, in great detail, the lengths she and her husband had gone to find an "indestructible" gate to place between the family

"hollering and wailing" for quite some time until the parents can't "stand it" any more. The children know they are being heard, and yet they see that they are being ignored. Again, they experience their powerlessness; again, they feel like burdens for wanting to get out. They may even have felt foolish for wanting a relationship they cannot have. I do not know the source of James's conviction that love always dies, that nothing lasts forever, although I would suppose it comes from early childhood moments. Perhaps it came from some of these recorded events, when he might have wanted to remain in close contact with his parents, but was abruptly removed from them. Perhaps, in between his mother's busy schedule of cooking, cleaning, shopping, and sewing, he might have had just enough of her attention to long for more. Or perhaps he had felt particularly close to the babysitter, mentioned a few times in his father's letters, or to his two aunts who stopped by so frequently in these early years, or to the cousin he played with continually for over a year.

James's wife has frequently complained that he never believed her when she said she was sick. For example, she had complications during her pregnancy and was rushed to the hospital for emergency care. After the baby was born, she still was not well, and the doctor advised her to "take it easy, have someone else watch the baby" until she was on the mend. But two days after being home, James announced that he was going back to work, that she was fine enough to handle their son. In listening to the two of them tell this story, I was struck by the discrepancy between each one's view of it. To his wife, the return of James to work was an unforgivable action, one that furthered her resolve never to have any more children with him. She was left to attend to her newborn, and no amount of pleading could get her husband to stay home. To James, his wife was just being "histrionic." She seemed fine, and he believed she had, as usual, "made more out of this than what had really happened." Exploring with him the reasons behind his minimization was pointless, because he could not see that he was ignoring her state of being. And yet I never felt that it was a narcissistic inability to empathize, because he would be genuine in his feeling that, had it been "that bad," he would have certainly been home longer. Rather, it seemed that he had never known the attention that comes with illness, suffering, and pain. James claimed that his family was never sick and that he had never been sick either. With

---

room and the living room, so that their two young children would be unable to leave this area of play while their mother was busy with household chores.

the help of these letters, it is clear that he actually had been ill several times in his infancy, one time quite severely with pneumonia and tonsillitis. The difference between his self-perception and his early childhood memory is clear: while he had been sick, his own illnesses were hardly attended to with adequate devotion or care. Thus, his inability to comfort and care for his wife during her illnesses is a direct result of how his own illnesses were treated.

These letters were sent to grandparents, aunts, and uncles; the labeling of the children, therefore, was crystallized not only to them but also to the family at large. Furthermore, all these moments were being offered to the family for scrutiny and comment. There are no extant family archives to indicate how other family members reacted to the content of Robert's letters, but we can make the observation that Robert never altered in any way the descriptions of his child-rearing practices. If he had been scolded or cautioned by any family member, such as his parents or his wife's mother, it would seem likely that he would have left out, in subsequent letters, such moments as the need to "strap [James] down" in order for him to take a nap. Since he did not, we can conclude that Robert was comfortable showing his family that he had carried on their "family traditions" and that he had retained the same kind of overriding beliefs and behaviors that had been used with him. The impact of specific child-raising philosophies is just this: one often parents as one has been parented. Perhaps this inheritance of parenting beliefs provides answers to James's question about his father's drinking. Robert was as detached and isolated as his children because his own upbringing was, we can speculate, filled with similar moments of normative abuse. And so goes the chain of inherited child-raising practices—from parent to child, from son to son.

Although alcoholism was not part of the family inheritance, it is clear that, even in these early years of marriage, alcohol was a definite part of Robert and Nancy's lives. Many of the entries note drinking until the "wee" morning hours or saving a bottle of Scotch for a special party. As in later years, these parties were often held at home with the children "fast asleep." But the gestalt of these experiences is that James grew up with the flavor of alcohol in his being, the nights of partying in his soul. Indeed, it is interesting to note that the second word he formulated as a child seems to have been *beer*. It is not clear to me if James himself has an alcohol problem, although I know that he does like to have a glass of wine to "relax" at the end of the day. This is a remnant of the parental introject, embedded in his self. Are these moments of oneness with his parents and his past? Yes, I think so. Should he be called an alcoholic? I do not know yet how to answer this question. He has only discussed his drinking once, in a marital session years ago, and it was his wife who pointed out that he separates himself from her in the evening by this routine. At this point, the patient has no interest in discussing the topic of his alcohol use and so, given that it does not appear at this point to constrict his life in any dramatic way, I wait for more information, more disclosure. There is no need to push him in this regard. Because there is no alcohol crisis at hand, I am willing to wait, as part of the psychotherapy process itself, for the analysis to unfold in its own way.

Perhaps fitting hand in hand with their drinking is Robert and Nancy's preoccupation with work. It seems that neither of them ever has enough time to truly accomplish what they wish to get done. They never feel satisfied with what they have achieved. Thus we hear about Nancy's continual sewing sprees, but with the result that she never feels quite pleased with herself: "Like Grandmother Smith, she hasn't made anything perfect yet." We hear, week after week, about Robert's overburdened schedule, his sense that he can get nothing done, his feeling that "the weeks go by and he wonders if he will every get caught up." Even on a Sunday when he has planned to be away from business, he cannot keep himself from washing the windows while his son Thomas, then 3½, watches nearby. He never seems free of his work; he is enslaved to *doing*. There is no balance in Robert's nature, no time for reflection and formlessness, except when drinking. In that mode, he can relax and stop the compulsion to work.

Working seems to be a family trait. Indeed, when Robert and the family visited his parents, he spent the weekend working on the house with his father, rather than stopping to play games with his sons or simply to socialize with other relatives. Indeed, this compulsiveness has been passed to James and his brother who, as James put it, "like our parents, [are] still looking for the worthwhile thing to do." The trouble is there is never a stopping point, there is never a moment to enjoy what they have accomplished, to smile at themselves, to feel a break from the ever-enslaving work. A child whose parents are preoccupied with other tasks that are prioritized as more important than being with him will undoubtedly experience himself as unimportant and as a burden. His very existence is minimal compared to the important work his parents must accomplish. Therefore, he is most loved when he can be ignored, dismissed to play with his toys alone, or put to bed for the night – that way, the parents' work can proceed without interruption. This, I think, was part of the "psychodynamic oxygen" that James breathed from the beginning of his life, and part of why he struggles so with human relationships. Through the psychotherapy, there is finally some worth to his own personhood and some value to his existence. It feels strange, uncomfortable, and impermanent.

James's psychotherapy process is ongoing. The task lies in helping him allow moments of attunement, moments when he feels connected and valued, while working to lessen the inner detachment he has acquired from his childhood experiences.

The emphasis of the twentieth century, including Freud's influential perspective on the human condition, has been on self-reliance, separateness, and individuation. The "oceanic feeling" was not embraced as a healthy aspect of object relations, but was, along with dependence and merger, relegated to the category of infantile regression. Now, as we are nearing the twenty-first century, it is time to invite these crucial aspects back into our relationships and into our child-rearing philosophies. It is time to combine elements of both merger and individuation, dependence and separateness into our lives. The indissoluble bond cannot be dissolved, despite the century-long attempt to discourage its existence. The indissoluble bond cannot be broken.

2

SYMBIOSIS REVISITED

The [invisible] bond is like a magnetic force which attracts a baby to his mother and a mother to her baby. It is a field of emotional relatedness through which others may pass without ever being touched. However, anyone who understands what it is like to be a baby or a mother is able to see it.

Louise J. Kaplan, *Oneness and Separateness*

PARADIGMS ARE CONSTANTLY in search of new truths, shifting from one set of ideas to another. Kuhn (1962) believes there is no absolute scientific truth, only observable, albeit gradual, changes in scientific theories. He details a chronology for the development of new paradigms. Each model is an attempt to problem solve, to answer questions about the mysteries of the world in which we live. Each model offers an alternative possibility to the one before, comprehensive enough to gain loyal adherents and to sway converts from the dominant theory. Each paradigm stresses one specific truth, either ignoring competing views or de-emphasizing the importance of other concepts. The prevailing paradigm affects greatly all areas of scientific inquiry and influences the general public as well. As a case in point, the current emphasis on separation-individuation, a term first coined by American psychoanalyst and researcher Margaret Mahler, with echoes of Freud, left the lifelong significance of merging phenomena and the importance of attachment out in the cold.

There was an atmosphere of the foundation of a religion in [the weekly Wednesday meetings]. Freud himself was its new prophet who made the theretofore prevailing methods of

psychological investigation appear superficial. Freud's pupils —
all inspired and convinced—were his apostles. . . . Freud
began to organize his church with great energy. He was serious
and strict in the demands he made of his pupils; he permitted
no deviations from his orthodox teaching.

Max Graf, *Reminiscences of Professor Sigmund Freud* [1]

The disdain that Freudian theory holds for dependent, infantile feelings
can be found in many of Freud's theoretical premises and beliefs. First and
foremost is the idea that the newborn is completely narcissistic or self-
invested; there is no object relationship between infant and mother. He
views the baby as struggling with inchoate impulses that have been
discharged into a part object (such as the breast). Only over time does the
baby expand part objects into whole objects. As Freud indicates, it is only
from "repeated situations of satisfaction [that the baby has] . . . created an
object out of the mother" (1926, p. 170). In his seminal paper "On
Narcissism" (1914), Freud postulates that the baby lives in a state of
infantile narcissism, thinking only of himself. Thus, the baby is one with
mother because he cannot conceptualize an external other. The baby
experiences a sense of infantile omnipotence in which he believes that the
entire world, including the breast, is his doing. This stage is left as the child
experiences his helplessness and separateness, which occurs to him
through the frequent moments in which his impulses are not gratified.
The child builds ego structure and learns to manage his sexual and
aggressive impulses through the various psychosexual stages. In the oedipal stage, for example, the child views his father as a threat to his erotic
longings for his mother. Castration anxiety surges forth, which dispels the
child's wishes to claim mother as his wife.

Freud's developmental schema was the first to overlook the inherent
powerlessness that children, including babies, primarily feel. It is not
grandiose self-reflection that enables a boy to wish longingly for his

---

1. Ernest Jones, in his 1959 memoirs, disagreed with this comparison
between psychoanalysis and a new religious group. He wrote that "it was a pretty
obvious caricature to make [that Freud was 'the pope of the new sect; his writings
were the sacred text . . .'], but the minute element of truth in it was made to serve
in place of the reality, which was far different (p. 205).

mother, but rather a realistic understanding of his limitations *as a child* that causes him to long for adulthood and the love between a man and woman. Consider Freud's analysis of Little Hans, his only case involving any direct contact with children. Entitled *Analysis of a Phobia in a Five-Year-Old Boy* (1909), the material focuses on Hans's fear of horses. This fear significantly inhibited his movements since he lived in a city surrounded by horses. Ostensibly, the case gives Freud adequate proof of the oedipal complex. He feels that Hans had displaced his fear of his father into his fear of horses, viewing the horse as a father-symbol because of its powerful size and large penis. As well, the boy had become frightened that horses could bite off his finger, a symbolic representation of castration anxiety. In his only interview with the child, Freud comes to the conclusion that, to Hans, horses even resembled his father: the black strap around their mouths was like his father's mustache, and the blinders on their eyes were similar to his father's glasses.

Hans had been a precocious child, and his doting father, Max Graf (both he and his wife had formerly been patients of Freud's), had kept Freud up to date on Hans's early childhood escapades prior to the phobia. For the clinical data and case material, Freud relied on direct correspondence he received from Graf regarding his son's ongoing development and difficulties. In fact, Freud only met with the child once, conducting the bulk of his interpretations and interventions through meetings with Graf. As Freud indicates, his narrative almost exclusively utilizes the direct observations of Hans's words and behavior as recorded faithfully by his father. Hans's fear of horses seemed to have erupted suddenly when he was 4½ years old. As he went to the park with his nursemaid one day, he became frightened and asked to be taken home so that he could be comforted by his mother. The next day, Hans's mother took him out herself, only to find that again he was extremely anxious and fearful. He told his mother that he was afraid he would be bitten by a horse. Thus began six months of correspondence, interpretations, and interventions proposed by Freud and enacted by Graf. They felt that the primary stressor was the birth of his baby sister Hanna a year and a half earlier. Hans had been quick to notice how "small" her "widdler" (Hans's word for penis [p. 53]) was, although he consoled himself by adding "when she grows up it'll get bigger all right" (p. 53). Also in connection with the birth, Graf told Freud that Hans had been told "naturally . . . that the stork [was] going to bring a little girl or a little boy" (p. 52). Although Hans has difficulty believing this fact, the idea was presented as truth. At Freud's insistence, the parents finally "enlightened Hans up to a certain point: [they] told him that children grow inside their Mummy, and are then brought into the world by being pressed out of her like a 'lumf,' [Hans's word for excrement] and that this involves a great deal of pain" (p. 126). Immediately following this discussion, six months after his phobia began, Hans was freed of his fear.

Many analysts have presented their concerns regarding this case. Glenn (1980) comments that Freud allowed the father to tell misinformation to his son on two occasions, first, that the stork brings children, and second that girls have no "wee-wee makers" instead of having a different kind of "wee-wee maker." Slap (1961) notes that neither Freud nor Graf made any mention of the impact that Hans's separation, due to a tonsillectomy operation, may have had on his impending fears. And Rieff (1959) notes that "Freud's great case study of infantile sexuality . . . seems as much a study of infantile intellectuality. There is clever Hans tracking down the mystery of how babies are born, despite the frustrating lies of his parents and the baffling intrusions of a professor who likes to collect his stories" (p. 92).

Bowlby (1973) dispels any notion of oedipal anxiety. For him, the issue is separation anxiety. The boy had been replaced by a younger child, taken out of his parents' bedroom, and only allowed closeness with his mother when his father was out of town. Indeed, I would add that perhaps part of the child's increased masturbatory activity was due to his increased anxiety about being separated from his parents' bedroom, as well as his sense of freedom that he could now have access to his body in private. Bowlby notes that the mother threatened her child with abandonment and castration; these ideas came from her, not from him. I would add that the stork story did not at all prepare the little boy for what he saw when greeting his mother and new baby sister just after her birth. Freud describes the incident as Graf had relayed the story to him: "[Hans] did not look at his mother, however, but at the basins and other vessels, filled with blood and water, that were still standing about the room. Pointing to the blood-stained bedpan, he observed in a surprised voice: 'But blood doesn't come out of *my* widdler' " (p. 52). The parents had only told Hans that a stork had brought the baby, and yet he was exposed to items from the birthing scene. This certainly would have been difficult for the little boy and may have indeed left a worry inside him regarding castration and a concern for his own "widdler."

Bowlby believes the separation anxiety was caused by threats and fears of abandonment that the little boy had suffered at the hands of his mother, who told him, on more than one occasion, that "she won't come back" (p. 85) because he had been "naughty." Bowlby argues that the primary issue in this case is the child's fear of separation from his parents. In fact, the parents did later divorce, and each remarried (other spouses). Hans introduced himself to Freud fourteen years later and told him that, as a consequence of his parents' divorce, "he lived by himself; but he was on good terms with both of his parents; and only regretted that as a result of the breaking-up of the family he had been separated from the younger sister he was so fond of" (p. 182). Therefore, his anxiousness at age 5 was based in reality—his family was, quite literally, in danger of separation.

Little focus has been placed on the nature of the interactions between Hans and his parents. The case record cites incident after incident of threatening and punitive behavior, primarily by his mother. It is she who threatened him with castration, and it is she who threatened to leave. She also "threaten[ed] to beat him with a carpet-beater" (p. 120), and Hans tells us himself that she actually "whack[s Hanna] on her bare bottom" (p. 111). In fact, simultaneous to the crystallization of Hans's phobia was his mother's warning "not to put his hand to his widdler. When he woke up [from his nap] he was asked about it, and he said he had put it there for a short while all the same" (p. 65). A few months later, Hans told his father, when asked, that he no longer "put[s his] hand to his widdler any more" although he "still [wants to]" (p. 71). His father was unhappy that he still had the desire to touch himself and responded with the threat that "this evening you're going to have to wear a sack to sleep in" (p. 76). It is not clear if this punishment was actually carried out. Hans had originally increased his masturbation activities concurrent with being separated from his parents' bedroom, half a year after his sister's birth. Although this activity could indicate a further link to heightened sexual energy and erotic longings for his mother, it can also be viewed as an indication of heightened separation anxiety. Hans attempted to self-soothe, to console himself in the absence of parental love. It must be remembered that Hans had spent his first four years in his parents' bedroom; therefore, his frequent attempts to return to their room was understandable. He told his father, in fact, that he sought entry to their room when he was frightened.

By looking to Hans himself for the answer to his phobia, an entirely different conclusion can be drawn. The little boy told his father that his fear began when he and his mother witnessed a horse, which was pulling a bus, fall down: "it gave me such a fright, really! That was when I got the nonsense" [Hans's word for his phobia. (p. 90)]. The horse lay down on the ground and kicked its feet. "It gave me a fright *because it made a row with its feet*" (p. 90), Hans added. Then the horse died, making the reality of this fearful moment all the more understandable. Freud interprets this death as further proof that the horse symbolized Hans's father and the boy's murderous wish be rid of his romantic rival. Freud also connects the horse's row with children who stamp their feet when holding onto urine. Graf spoke with Hans about this connection. The boy agreed that he also has occasions to "make a row," saying that "when I'm cross, or when I have to do 'lumf' and would rather play" (p. 94). His father noted that Hans was prone to temper tantrums when angry and that, "in the very early days, when he had to be put on the chamber [to make 'lumf'], . . . he used to stamp his feet in a rage and kick about, and sometimes throw himself on the ground" (p. 94). Hans was always prone to constipation, so much so that "aperients [i.e., laxatives] and enemas [had] frequently been necessary" (p. 95). One can safely assume that a small child did not willingly submit either to swallowing foul-tasting laxatives or taking enemas; the entire experience of elimination was overloaded by parental severity. Just as they forced bodily compliance against his will, they also ignored his self-determination, which stimulated narcissistic rages. This was a child overwhelmed by parental dominance.

Seen in this light, Hans's fear of horses can be interpreted in another way. He knows these majestic animals are powerful enough to pull people, furniture, and wagons. And yet, they are slaves to the adults who drive them, who use whips to control their speed. Graf notes that his son was "often . . . very much terrified when drivers beat their horses" (p. 118), and Freud also mentions that "long before the phobia [Hans] had become uneasy on seeing the horses in a merry-go-round being beaten" (p. 149). Horses also are not toilet trained—their "lumf" and urine are excreted right outside their bodies onto the street, to be cleaned up by other people. Rather than fantasizing the horse as symbol for his father, Hans may very well have been identifying himself with these animals, who should be so strong and powerful but are really enslaved to others. He actually told his father that he himself was a "young horse" (p. 97), but Graf is too enamored of the oedipal interpretation to shift his perspective. Hans might have felt that he, like the horses, was under the control of more powerful others, and he might have fantasized that both the animals and himself were free to move about as they wished. Alternately, he might have enjoyed seeing that horses have the freedom to eliminate whenever and wherever they chose. No one forcefully controlled their bowel movements, and no one demanded that they be cleaned after defecation. When he saw the horse fall down and kick his feet in the air, he might have felt a tremendous identification with his own sense of powerlessness. Standing next to his mother, whom he both loved and feared, he may have felt frightened for the horse as well as for himself. When the horse died, in identification he died too—a prospect so terrifying that he could not stand even to see another horse again. What if yet another Hans-horse succumbed to the will and the whip? He could not bear to witness another act of brutality by overpowering adults. The world does not grant equal power to all living things: children and horses have few moments of free will in a world surrounded by "whackings," whips, castration threats, and "carpet beatings."

The ways in which both father and mother talk with Hans, threaten him, lie to him, and dominate him have gone unnoticed by other analytic reviewers in part, perhaps, because when seen in the context of the Victorian era, these were incidents of normative abuse. Instead, what has been underscored, time and again, is Hans's fear of his father because of a *fantasized* erotic longing for his mother. Yes, the concept of oedipal rivalry is based on the child's realization of his placement in the family: he cannot usurp his father's role and become his mother's lover. But in the Freudian schema, it is assumed that the child has an unrealistic sense of *grandiosity*. He believes himself equal to his father's power. In this conceptualization, it is only through the parental threats of castration that the child deflates his grandiose omnipotent self and relinquishes his erotic longing for his mother. My view is that the boy felt powerless in the first place, and therefore the fear of horses was connected to his understanding that he was little, that he could be bitten by a horse, or "whacked" by his mother, or ignored in his rages. He was right—he was a little boy, and he had been lied to by these protectors.

Seen from this perspective, his fear that he could be bitten by a horse has a second meaning. He, as the horse, would have had some recourse against the aggressors in his life: he could have bitten them. Hans did mention to his father, albeit playfully, that he would like to "beat" his mother with the "carpet beater" (p. 120). In fantasy, the Hans-horse would have been powerful enough to fight back against his threatening mother and unempathic father. Since Hans was lied to by his parents, who were supposed to protect him, then he might not be safe in the larger world, a world that, in his day, was driven by horse carriages and wagons. The curative moment came not when Freud tried to convince him of his oedipal fears, but when his parents finally stopped lying to him and told him the truth (which he had always known, in some fashion) about how his baby sister was born. Again, another case of normative abuse; again, another case of childhood powerlessness, again; another case of alienation.

> My symbiotic stage of life was difficult: I must have been full of frustrated rage at the rejecting mother whom I greatly loved nonetheless. The arrival of my sister, Suzanne, four years after my birth only aggravated my sense of maternal rejection. She was very much a "wanted" child, and she awakened our mother's maternal instincts. . . . I believe it was my observations of my mother's loving interaction with my sister—and the way it contrasted with her interaction with me—that guided me into pediatrics and psychoanalysis and, more specifically, into my subsequent investigation of the mother–infant dual unity. I do not think it an exaggeration to say that my own mother and sister represented the first mother–child pair that I investigated.

> Margaret Mahler, *The Memoirs of Margaret S. Mahler*

Mahler and colleagues (1975) detail a developmental schema that proposes how, in healthy development, the child moves from a symbiotic orbit to becoming a separated, self-sufficient being. The emphasis in her work is on the importance of separation and on the dangerous consequences of continuing the symbiotic bond after infancy. Her work has been a prototype for many of our cultural and child-rearing philosophies, and the word *symbiosis* has taken on great significance to many other psychoanalytic authors as well as the lay public. Blos, for example, applies Mahler's four-step paradigm to describe the various stages of adolescence, and Searles (1961) has used her term symbiosis to develop different stages of the transference—symbiosis, ambivalent symbiosis, and so on. Her theory has become so well known that even a *New York Times Magazine* column (August 7, 1994) referred to the concept of separation-individuation as if it were a commonly accepted and verifiable truth. The author of the article, M. P. Howard, writes:

> I understand what [this mother] feels: a symbiosis that began during those 9 months when her body and her baby were indeed one and continued during those quiet moments when she nursed under the gentle light of a night lamp . . . [an] experience of perfect unity – of oneness with the universe. Mothering starts there. It starts with an attachment that ends isolation. *But at the cost of individuation* (emphasis mine). [p. 18]

Mahler's developmental schema began with the understanding that "psychological birth is not simultaneous with biological birth" (1988, p. 128). The first stage of life is termed "normal autistic phase" (p. 41), in which the baby is in a total state of primary narcissism. In adherence to Freud, this stage was one in which the baby makes no distinction between self and other; turning his head to find the breast is simply reflexive, as are his rooting, grasping, and sucking responses. This stage and the following stage of symbiosis, it should be noted, have since been refuted by more recent researchers, most notably Stern (1985). He argues that the infant is a distinct being even at birth, and therefore, psychological birth occurs simultaneously with biological birth. The second phase, beginning around the second month of life, is termed symbiosis. In the passage below, Mahler explained her choice of this term.

> Unlike the biological concept of symbiosis, it does not describe what actually happens in a mutually beneficial relationship between two *separate* individuals of different species. It describes that state of undifferentiation, of fusion with mother, in which the "I" is not yet differentiated from the "not-I" and in which inside and outside are only gradually coming to be sensed as different. [p. 44]

She believes that the infant sees himself as part of his mother, intertwined as a "dual unity within one common boundary" (p. 44). Of interest, she ties this feeling state to the oceanic feeling because of the sense of "boundlessness" (p. 44) that she imagined the infant feels during these first four to six months of life.

However, the original, biological meaning of symbiosis is in fact a more accurate representation of the early mother–infant experience. Mahler reverses the basic meaning of symbiosis to integrate her theory into the dominant Freudian perspective. Freud's infant is a totally self-absorbed, nonrelational being. As Greenberg and Mitchell (1983) note,

Mahler's shift is a compromise between Freud's theory of infantile narcissism, in which the baby is unaware of any external object, and the object relationists. According to Mahler, this fused state is both a relationship between mother and baby and a nonrelationship, since the two are counted as only one merged object. As these authors indicate, this accommodation enables Mahler to stay within drive theory while moving to incorporate the relationist model as well. The alteration of the meaning of symbiosis, however, is a major shift in the conceptualization of the mother–fetus and the mother–infant relationship. Despite Mahler's view that psychological symbiosis is an undifferentiated state, the fact remains that symbiosis *is* (as she herself indicates in the passage cited above) "a mutually beneficial relationship between two *separate* individuals." Using the term symbiosis for psychological usage does, however, require a shift from its biological meaning because the former is not meant to describe a relationship between two different *species* (although it could be argued that a baby is a different kind of being than his mother), but rather to describe an intertwined relationship between two separate beings.

In the initial aspects of the next phase termed *hatching* (p. 52), the baby begins to differentiate his own body self from his mother's and to realize that, at times, she is out of his presence. This stirring of separation overlaps into what Mahler termed *practicing* (p. 65), a phase that culminates in the toddler's achievement of walking. The ability to walk unattended serves as a metaphor for the child's "psychological birth experience" (p. 74) because locomotion symbolizes independence. Mahler postulates that part of the exhilaration of this age, in which the toddler feels "the world is his oyster" (p. 74), is due to the fact that he has managed to escape from the symbiotic fusion with his mother. In fact, that the children Mahler observed seem to take their first steps away from mother signified to her the oppressive nature of the symbiotic experience.

In the next phase, *rapprochement* (p. 76), the toddler realizes that he cannot survive without his mother's ongoing assistance. His narcissistic omnipotence has been shattered. He is ambivalent, clinging to his mother at some moments and pushing her away at others. Mahler stresses the importance of the mother's response to her toddler's confused wishes. If she encourages too much symbiotic reattachment, her child will have increased difficulty in continuing the process of self-individuation. As well, if she is unreceptive to his need for refueling, her child will be forced too rapidly into an individuated position that causes difficulties in later development. This I have seen on many occasions. Mothers, stressing the cultural importance of separation, will take away the bottle and insist on cups by the age of 1½, or refrain from assisting the toddler until his frustration is extreme. The rationale usually amounts to the fear that their child will never become independent: "I don't want him to get *too attached* to me/the bottle/the blanket," and so on. And yet, in many cases, these mothers are women who themselves are highly dependent individuals. One, for example, still calls her mother two or three times a day, spends every weekend with her, and relies on her mother's money for support. The other, a recovering alcoholic, had a mother who was never available to her.

In the fourth subphase, entitled *consolidation of individuality and the beginnings of emotional object constancy* (p. 109), the toddler is able to integrate formerly split "good" and "bad" objects into complete objects. This phase, lasting from 20 months to around 36 months, culminates with the child's solidification into a separated self, with consistent self-characteristics. As well, the child now is believed to hold a full, internal representation of mother so that he can easily tolerate increased separations from her actual physical presence.

The separation-individuation paradigm stresses the importance of disengaging from the symbiotic mother. The research supporting this paradigm was designed to study the separations and reunions of mothers and babies, not the process of their growing and changing attachment. In pursuit of separation and reunion, her study unintentionally heightened this struggle. For example, the physical layout of the observation rooms encouraged less one-to-one contact between mothers and children than would have occurred in a less stimulating environment. Bimonthly in-home visits were made to each participant's home, but the data were primarily collected during four-hour sessions held twice weekly in a group format. This is a significant alteration of the mother–child relationship and one that greatly changes the dynamics and interactions between any mother and child. The room was arranged so as to encourage a separation between mothers and babies—a countertop partition was placed between the children's play area and the mothers' "sitting area" (p. 23). The mothers' area was behind the children's toy section, and it was comfortable enough so that the women could "chat, sip coffee or read . . . from which they had a full view of, and free access to, the children" (p. 23). Mahler makes the comment that the room was set up to resemble a park playground, so that the mothers could sit together and talk while watching their children playing separately. In this manner, the mothers had the "opportunity to attend to whatever mothering [was] required of them" (p. 23). When the quarters became too cramped, the site was enlarged. In the new setting, one room was designated for the mothers and infants and another room created for the toddlers. At first, mothers quite naturally followed their toddlers as they moved between the two rooms, but in 1966, Mahler instructed the mothers to stay in their sitting area, because "this situation was too uneven, permitted too much intermingling" (p. 27) between different mothers with different toddlers.

The entire setting, therefore, promoted separation between mother and baby for four-hour periods, twice weekly. The mothers naturally formed a group among themselves and, rather than spending those hours in primary interaction with their children, were often engrossed in their own more stimulating conversations. The children, similarly, focused on other stimulation besides their mothers—the toys, the other adults, the other babies, and the like. Mothers were often called out of the room for individual, half-hour discussions with the researchers. Some mothers left their children at the observation room so that they could do laundry, pick up other children from nursery school, or do other errands. Mahler writes that "when the child was a bit older and had been at the Center for a while" (p. 24), his mother might leave him in the program alone for the entire morning. The research setting, therefore, resembled more of a day care center than a forum for observing mother–child pairs. The toddler room, in fact, became somewhat like a nursery school, complete with teacher—again, not a conducive setting for studying the mother–child relationship. It is not clear from the research report at how young an age the children were left without their mothers, nor is it clear exactly how the leavetaking was handled. The impression, however, is that mothers were instructed to simply leave the room, as unobtrusively as possible, so that the children could discover their mothers' absences at their own pace. Mahler cites one example in which a 2½-year-old "did not immediately notice [her mother's] departure" (p. 113) from the toddler room. It was only later, after she had completed some drawings that she wanted to share with her mother, that she looked—and did not find—mother. She called for her mother several times, but, when "no one answered her call" (p. 113), she soon she became reabsorbed in her drawings.

This research accomplished just what it had set out to find—a detailed observation of separation. It provided numerous opportunities for children to leave or to be left by their mothers and gave researchers a wealth of data regarding these incidents. But that is not an accurate reflection of the nuances of each mother–child pair, nor is it an accurate representation of how the two interact when apart from others. That mothers were stopped from following their young toddlers is an excellent example of the problem. Mothers naturally follow, or as Mahler terms it, "shadow" (p. 79) their 1- and 2-year-old children, with good reason: they might fall, get lost, have trouble negotiating socially with another child, and the like. In this study, the mothers were encouraged to let the children manage on their own. One- and 2-year-old children require parental assistance, which these mothers, and their children, knew. Thus the natural inclination of mothers to follow, and, similarly, the natural response of the children to return to their mothers in the other room.

Mahler's bias against the quite natural attachment behavior of mothers with their 2-year-olds can be found in her further discussion of the child mentioned above, who had accepted her mother's departure so easily. This mother–child pair had seemed, to the researchers, to flourish in the earlier symbiotic and practicing period. The researchers felt this mother was "patient, understanding, and consistently emotionally available in the first *two* subphases, and when developmentally appropriate — so we thought at the time — she slowly encouraged her daughter's developing independence and autonomous functioning" (p. 115). But on the day that the mothers were told to stay in the infant room and refrain from shadowing their children into the toddler room, this mother had difficulty and only "reluctantly heeded the principal investigator's carefully explained request" (p. 115). The researchers felt that this mother made herself too available to her daughter in the later phases of development, thereby discouraging individuation.

Artificially separating mothers from children assisted the researchers in collecting the data they had set out to find. But the underlying message transmitted to mothers, however, was that it is often best to ignore their wishes to be closely attentive to their youngsters; that it is best for children to be left to try everything on their own first without the anchoring or the watchful eye of maternal protection. Since the observational playgroup met with such frequency and for so many years (sometimes younger children of the same family joined as well), it can be assumed that some of the mothers were themselves attached to, and influenced by, the study's overall tenor and gestalt. Mahler herself notes that these women must have felt supported by the researchers and the

other mothers, indicating the impact of these biweekly meetings. Therefore, it can be assumed that the bias of this study against attachment needs
influenced these women in the raising of their children.

Mothers who wanted a closer relationship with their children were
termed symbiotic or even parasitic. For example, another 2-year-old girl
had become oppositional regarding the release of her bowels. She had
adamantly refused to defecate for several days and was in obvious distress.
Ostensibly, she was reacting to the recent birth of her baby sister. She
tried, at the playgroup, to continue holding onto the feces, but finally
could wait no longer. She asked a research observer to read her a book
while she tried to defecate. As it was quite painful, she soon cried out for
her mother to come in, dismissing the observer. Mahler's footnote to this
incident reads: "as soon as the pain gets unbearable, the symbiotic mother
is the only one who is invoked to help in the painful delivery of the stool"
(p. 84). Why is the mother labeled "symbiotic?" She is called upon, quite
naturally, when her daughter is in acute distress. There existed a healthy
indissoluble bond between mother and daughter, who, despite having had
a recent period of stormy relations, were beginning to reconnect through
this incident. The mother was able to care again for her daughter, to
protect and soothe her. Why should the child have preferred any other
individual to help her instead?

Mahler's emphasis on individuation at the expense of merger phenomenon has its roots in her earlier work on infant psychosis. The
separation-individuation study, in fact, began as a way to understand
better the development of these abnormalities in psychotic children. She
and her colleagues were intrigued with such questions as "What was 'the
ordinary way' of becoming a separate individual that these psychotic
children could not achieve?" (p. 9) It was her long-standing belief that
psychotic children never left the "symbiotic mother–child common mem-
brane" (p. 10), remaining in an infantile state of primary narcissism that
left them boundary-less and identity-less. Therefore, in the background of
the separation-individuation paradigm was the idea that the early mother–
infant relationship must be rejected in a phase-specific manner so as to
avoid psychosis. Certainly, psychosis involves identity distortion and
confusion. But I do not think that the normal infant is born into a
psychotic state of merger. If we assume instead that the baby is born, as
Stern (1985) says, in an emergent self-state, then there is no need to view
the earliest months of life in such a pejorative way. The baby and mother
have moments of intense, empathic attunements that serve to bring them

ever closer to a state of oneness—but a state of fusion is an impossibility, which the two are not expecting to achieve. The premise, therefore, that moments of oneness, so often a part of the early mother–infant relationship, is something to move away from developmentally, skewed the rest of the study. It is no wonder that the observers saw only the dangers of attachment and not the joy; it is no wonder that the separation-individuation paradigm focused on the importance of leaving mother behind.

In a rather curious observation, Mahler notes that the young toddlers seem to take their first steps away from mother, indicating their wish to disengage from the symbiotic union. She herself seems surprised by this observation, noting that it runs contrary to popular belief. She cites the following passage from Kierkegaard (1846) to illustrate what she found to be a romantic but scientifically unfounded idea.

> The loving mother teaches her child to walk alone. She is far enough from him so that she cannot actually support him, but she holds her arms to him. . . . Her face beckons like a reward, an encouragement. Thus, the child walks alone with his eyes fixed on his mother's face, *not* on the difficulties in his way. He supports himself by the arms that do not hold him and constantly strives towards the refuge in his mother's embrace, little supposing that in the very same moment that he is emphasizing his need for her, he is proving that he can do without her, because he is walking alone. [p. 85]

But the truth may very well be that, in her sample, the toddlers walked away from their mothers simply because the overall gestalt at the center, as well as the observational room itself, focused on separateness and discouraged primary mother–child involvement. Certainly, if a mother is drinking coffee and talking with other mothers, her child may very well decide to take matters into his own hands. He is excited by all the toys that lie across the room and may very well decide to go after them on his own. As well, since mothers could drop their children off at the center and often had to leave the room for extended time periods, the children may very well have decided to fend for themselves.

Mahler stands corrected: Kierkegaard's image is indeed the more usual. In most cases, the child walks toward a loving other, is bolstered by this encouragement and excitement, and they both experience a mutual thrill in the accomplishment of this new developmental milestone.

Similarly, Bowlby (1973) feels that walking does not signify a move away from mother. In the toddlers he watched, he found that they were more apt to experiment with their newfound walking skills when their mothers were nearby and stationary. Of course, his bias is to view the process of walking as an extension of attachment behavior, and not as a sign of longed-for independence. Bowlby feels that the child realizes his unsteady gait is so inefficient that he usually asks to be picked up if the mother begins to walk away, so that he will not be left behind. It is not until the *end of the third year* that the child lessens his demands for being carried, which is simultaneous to his increased proficiency in walking and therefore simultaneous to his ability to stay close to his mother on his own.

In summary, merging moments are too important in human relationships to be relegated to a phase-specific entity. Mahler emphasizes the process of self-and-other differentiation and, in the process, continues the Freudian bias against fusion, oneness, and the oceanic feeling. It seems more accurate to describe the conflict in childhood and throughout the life cycle as a pull between attachment and individuation. The phrase separation-individuation emphasizes the need to move away from the "regressive" ties to the symbiotic mother. That the entire paradigm emphasizes separation actually proves just how powerful the maternal–child relationship and the feelings of attachment and merger really are. Mahler emphasizes the toddler's omnipotent view of the world as under his control. To the contrary, I view the child as ever cognizant that he is rarely in charge, that he is in actuality quite small and powerless. It is because of his ever-conscious state of littleness that moments of self-sufficiency, moments when he achieves something by himself—sitting up, walking, saying his first words—are so momentous and exhilarating. There is an innate drive toward maturity that surfaces no matter what kind of maternal environment surrounds the child. The emphasis need not be on separation and autonomy because infants are born to grow, mature, and develop. Spitz's work showed the dramatic results of babies and young children who were thwarted in the achievement of their physical milestones simply because the total environment was so unloving and cruel. Mahler herself is so "impressed" (p. 208) by the inherent maturational processes of the infant that she writes "we regard[ed] *individuation* as an innate given, which reveals itself with particular force in the beginning of life and which seems to continue during the entire life cycle" (p. 208).

It stands to reason, then, that if individuation is an inherent function of infantile maturation, it need not be emphasized as a developmental process requiring so much external manipulation. The issue is not separation or individuation, since these processes are naturally occurring in the infant's maturational makeup. Rather, what is most crucial to early childhood is the development of empathic connections, of intimate relatedness. The emphasis in our current child-rearing philosophies needs to shift from emphasizing separation to encouraging the development of empathic, accurate attunements that heighten moments of oneness, assist in the internalization of positive self-regard, and lessen psychic distress.

Paradigms are constantly in flux, and as Kuhn (1962) explains, society influences theoretical conceptualizations just as scientific beliefs affect social trends. Americans have always prided themselves on their rugged individualism, instilled in part by their courage in leaving their parents, grandparents, friends, and even children in pursuit of their own destiny in the country with "streets paved with gold." One might wonder if Mahler and other American object relationists, such as Kernberg and Masterson, were influenced by this cultural element in their emphasis on separation and individuation. Similarly the paradigm is now shifting, and the view by more recent generations of Americans, whose roots in this country are many layers deep, is moving away from the idea that separation is the key to healthy development. In recent years there has been newfound interest in the mystical and the transcendent. Spiritual retreats, massive fund-raising efforts such as "We are the World," and community spirit are in vogue. The communications revolution has made moment-to-moment contact with others a reality, thereby creating immediacy among peoples of different cultures and continents. The Internet computer system has revolutionized relationships to be even that much more immediate.

Other American psychoanalysts have already been shifting from a view of the primacy of separation. Certainly Searles, Sutherland, Kohut, and Seinfeld have written about the importance of symbiosis. Buie (1981), in fact, presents a discussion similar to the one I am proposing. He writes that merging should not be taken "literally, as if somehow there really were a genuine intermixing, blending of one person's personality with another's" (p. 285). This is a subjective experience, as Buie points out, because we scientifically know that "human beings always remain separate, both physically and psychologically." The symbiosis of infancy is not unique, therefore, and simply results from the dependent and helpless state of the neonate.

And yet despite this shift, there remains even today an insistence on separation by many psychoanalysts. For example, Ogden (1986) quotes Fain (1971) as believing that some infants are "addicted to the *actual physical presence* of the mother and [can] not sleep unless they [are] being held" (p. 184). Fain believes that mothers actually "interfere" with the baby's attempts to find autoerotic soothing devices, thus causing the infant to be "fully dependent upon the actual mother as object" (p. 185). What is nursing, if not a dependence on "actual mothers" for the life-sustaining nutrients that breast feeding provides?[2] Infants, of course, *do* need their "actual mothers."[3] To suggest that infants should be separated from their mothers, that they need not be nursed or rocked to sleep, is normative abuse. Furthermore, addiction is more frequently caused by too much separation than by too much attachment.

Bowlby believes that the psychoanalytic insistence on separation may be partially due to the fact that analysts are parents too. They have also been children and if attachment or merger is as crucial to development as separation, then much of what these individuals were raised with or what these individuals taught their children, would have been somewhat fallacious. As Bowlby (1973) states:

> Clinicians are often themselves parents, and so are likely unwittingly to identify over-readily with another parent's viewpoint. Parents may be thought of as experienced and sensible; the patients, by contrast, are young, and seen, perhaps, as inclined to exaggerate

---

2. Recent research has only begun to identify the wide range of nutrients, proteins, and hormones found in breast-milk. For example, a *New York Times* article of May 24, 1994 (Angier 1994) mentions that researchers have discovered the presence of oxytocin, a hormone associated with "affiliative impulses," and speculate that this "may help initiate the onset of a loving bond between mother and infant." Other ingredients provide antibodies to protect against infection when the baby's own immune system is still undeveloped; numerous other hormones, growth factors that help in tissue expansion; and natural opioids that may help form the baby's brain and affect his behavior are also found in breast milk.

3. The term *mother* denotes whoever is the primary caretaker. Nursing can still be continued, by using the breast pump, even if the mother herself is unable to be with her child every moment; in this case, the mother remains linked to her child, even when physically separated from him, via the pump. The point here is that whoever is caring for the baby does so in a way that is not oriented to a detached style of parenting.

or even fabricate. . . . Furthermore, parents may be respected citi-
zens, perhaps acquaintances or even friends whose account the
clinician is reluctant to question. . . . Pervading the scene, more-
over, and influencing all parties is the time-honoured command-
ment "Honour thy father and thy mother." [p. 320]

Greenberg and Mitchell (1983) have noted that the tendency of
analysts to accommodate their new theories to those of Freud may be due
to the attachment of analysts who, through their own analysis and the
analysis of these analysts, have a lineage that dates directly to Freud or one
of his early disciples. Even the August vacation, time honored in analytic
circles so much so that a popular novel, entitled *August*, was written about
a patient's experiences during her month-long separation from the therapist, stems from Freud. His month-long hiatus (a common European
practice), in which he traveled, visited with friends, or wrote theoretical
material, has been long instituted into the annals of psychoanalytic
doctrine. Today, not only do many analysts follow suit but also many of
the major psychoanalytic seminars are purposely held during this month-
long break. Even in analytic circles, attachments and loyalties are powerful.

I celebrate myself, and sing myself,
And what I assume you shall assume,
For every atom belonging to me as good belongs to you.

                                    Walt Whitman, *Leaves of Grass*

The British object relations school bases many of its formulations on
the concept of merger. For the most part, they stay close to the Freudian
conceptualization of merger as an infantile phenomenon, but argue that
its occurrence in later stages of life is a normative, albeit regressive,
process. It is clear that these authors have highly idealized merger as the
root of all relationships, a unique and unparalleled experience between
mother and child. There is a cultural norm in Britain of separating
children from their parents, including the long-standing reliance on the
British nanny and the use of boarding schools for even latency-aged
children. Bowlby, in fact, studied what he felt were the pathological results
of the normative practice of separating young children from parents

during what might be month-long hospitalizations. Idealization often occurs in response to longing and to loss, that is, absence makes the heart grow fonder. The idealization of the merger concept, found particularly in the picture of the fused mother–infant couple, may in fact have come from these kinds of prolonged, normative separations. This concept was developed in personal communication with Gracine Bueti, C.S.W., a psychotherapist in private practice at the Katonah Center for Psychotherapy in Katonah, NY.

Balint (1968) believes that merging is a facet of relationships even before birth. A primal interconnection exists between the fetus and the environment, in which the "environment and individual penetrate into each other, they exist together in a 'harmonious mix-up'" (p. 66). He adds:

> An important example of this "harmonious interpenetrating mix-up" is the fish in the sea (one of the most archaic and widely occurring symbols). It is an idle question to ask whether the water in the gills or in the mouth is part of the sea or of the fish; exactly the same holds true about the foetus. Foetus, amniotic fluid, and placenta are such a complicated, interpenetrating mix-up that its histology and physiology are among the most dreaded questions in medical history. [p. 66]

Balint gives the example of breathing to demonstrate how basic the "interpenetrating harmonious mix-up," or merging, is to all of life. Air is inhaled in order to breathe, oxygen is removed, and the air is exhaled with increased carbon dioxide. No notice is made of this exchange, and no recognition made of ownership—the air seems to belong, simultaneously, both to the individual breathing and transforming the particles of air and to the external environment. He emphasizes the importance of seeking out and enjoying symbiotic experiences. "The aim of all human striving," he writes, "is to establish—or, probably re-establish—an all-embracing harmony with one's environment, to be able to love in peace" (p. 65). Balint believes that opportunities for merging are often denied in the early mother–child dyad, leading to the pathology of the basic fault. Individuals who suffer from the basic fault are missing a wholeness in their personality and often feel empty, lost, and alienated from others. He uses the term *fault* because many patients described their subjective self-experiences with exactly this word. The patient felt he had "a fault, not a complex, not a conflict, not a situation" (p. 21). Further, the patient felt that someone had wronged him to cause him this fault; he had been "failed or defaulted" (p. 21). The basic fault occurs early in the relationship between mother and child, leading to a preverbal condition that is rooted deep in the personality structure. Even with treatment, Balint believes that these individuals could never quite heal the structural split of the fault. However, through merging moments of "harmonious oneness," which he believes occur throughout life, the individual becomes able to feel more content and whole.

In maturational development, the infant feels a oneness with the environment around him, viewing some objects as though they are part of himself. These objects Balint terms primary because of the primitive quality of their relationship to the individual throughout his life. Primary objects, such as mother, are symbolized in other forms as well—water, earth, air, and fire—and provide individuals with soothing moments reminiscent of early infancy. If, however, the individual has experienced too few merging moments in infancy or cannot regain similar experiences in later life, he will withdraw into his own world, into a state of secondary narcissism. Objects who are unable or unwilling to connect at this level of intimacy are frequently coerced or "conquered" by the individual to become cooperative. In this "conquest," Balint differs from the Winnicottian concept of object usage in which the object must be destroyed in order to survive. Balint feels that the object must remain intact, but "tolerate being taken for granted for a brief period, that is, to have only identical interests" (p. 75) so that a fusion state can be established into the relationship. He views this process as crucial to healthy relationships because "this unio mystica, the re-establishment of the harmonious interpenetrating mix-up, between the individual and the most important parts of his environment, his love objects, is the desire of all humanity" (p. 74).

Although it is most common to find these moments in interpersonal relationships, they can also be found in religious experiences, artistic creations, and even during certain phases of analytic treatment. Balint believes that these intense experiences can appear to the outside observer as states of narcissistic withdrawal, when in fact, for the individual, they are states of intense connectedness: "For these very brief moments the individual may truly and really experience that every disharmony has been dispelled, he and his whole world are now united in undisturbed understanding, in completely harmonious interpenetrating mix-up" (p. 75).

Balint stresses the nonregressive aspects of merging even in mature, healthy relationships and postulates that these moments enhance, rather than interfere with, emotional development. However, he views these moments as experiences in which there is no distinction between self and other: the mother and fetus are one, just as the nursing mother and child are one. The pregnant woman has been idealized as the prototype for maternal love and devotion—she appears, from outside observation, to be at one with her baby inside. Outsiders are excluded from this "interpenetrating mix-up" and are left only to imagine what the two are feeling. The nursing child too seems so blissful in his mother's arms. As they are intertwined in developing the newness of their relationship, the rest of the world is pushed away. Perhaps the exclusionary quality of the mother-infant relationship has been idealized in part to help those who have been left out of this intense love affair (husbands, other children, and so on) cope with their newly acquired secondary status. It is more accurate to view the mother–child relationship as two separate beings who are focused on breaching the fault and discovering immersion. Seen in this light, the joy of merging moments is all the more glorious, unique, and mystical.

I hear and behold God in every object, yet understand God
    not in the least,
Nor do I understand who there can be more wonderful than
    myself.

Why should I wish to see God better than this day?
I see something of God each hour of the twenty-four, and
    each moment then,
In the faces of men and women I see God, and in my own
    face in the glass,
I find letters from God dropt in the street, and every one is
    sign'd by God's name,
And I leave them where they are, for I know that
    wheresoe'er I go,
Others will punctually come forever and ever.

                    Walt Whitman, *Leaves of Grass*

Fairbairn believes that the earliest months of infancy are spent in a continuous merging state of absolute dependence on maternal care. The infant remains in a state of merger similar to his in utero experience, so as to "preclude his entertaining any thought of differentiation from the maternal body, which constitutes his whole environment and the whole world of his experience" (1943, p. 275). The infant relates to his mother as though she is a part of him, a phase he terms "primary identification" (1941, p. 34). This identification is "the cathexis of an object which has not yet been differentiated from the cathecting subject" (1941, p. 34). The infant relates to this cathecting other through the relational paths available to him, which include sucking and seeing. He experiences himself either as being one with her or seeking to be at one with her. Individuals are object-seeking from birth and use the erotogenic zones to feel intimate and intensely connected with others. Fairbairn, like Bowlby, views separation anxiety as the "earliest and original anxiety" (in Guntrip 1969, p. 128) and places infantile dependence, not the Oedipus complex, as the basic cause of all psychopathology. He views the infant as having a wholeness in the internal self and sees the splitting of the self into various internalized objects as caused by the twentieth-century push for early infantile individuation and autonomy.

Consider, for example, Fairbairn's view of thumb sucking. The baby does not seek satisfaction from his thumb simply because his mouth is in need of erotic gratification, but "because there is no breast to suck. Even the baby must have a libidinal object; and, if he is deprived of his natural object (the breast), he is driven to provide an object for himself" (1941, p. 33). The baby does not have more access to his mother's breast because of current cultural norms that stress the importance of helping him quickly find self-soothing techniques and that de-emphasize the overall importance of mother–infant attachment. Fairbairn compares thumb sucking with masturbation: both are autoerotic activities that compensate for lack of contact with the loved, external other.

In Fairbairn's developmental schema, the individual moves from his infantile attachments through a transitional stage while continuing to develop differentiated and interconnected relationships. In the final stage of mature dependence, individuals are able to shift between giving and taking, to have "cooperative relationships with differentiated objects" (1946, p. 145). In maturity the person still experiences moments of oneness, but this is a oneness of reciprocity. What prevents many people from achieving the stage of mature dependence is the fear that, in giving up their infantile attachments, they will not find new or more loving relationships. They fear that relinquishment of the old will only bring isolation and loneliness.

Fairbairn presents a view of the human drama radically opposing Freud's. Mankind's natural orientation is to be immersed in relationships, whether they be in internal or external contact with others. Alienation from others necessitates a withdrawal into psychic relationships with internalized objects. Hedonistic behavior occurs only secondarily to emotional deprivation; ego fragmentation occurs to assuage the painfulness of alienation. Fairbairn and, more recently, Seinfeld (1991) pay particular attention to the pathology of the schizoid. According to Guntrip, Fairbairn views this individual as "always . . . rushing into a relationship for security and at once breaking out again for freedom and independence: an alternation between regression to the womb and the struggle to be born, between the merging of his ego in, and the differentiation of it from, the person he loves" (1969, p. 36).

Seinfeld utilizes Fairbairn's theory of the tripartite inner split to describe and detail techniques aimed at making therapeutic contact, even with schizoid patients. For Seinfeld (1991), "the essence of the schizoid position is that the child transfers his relationships with external objects to the inner realm. The schizoid position serves separation/individuation by enabling the child to become less dependent upon the external world" (p. 242).

These individuals seem to live in a deadened state, having split off their wish for loving and caring relationships. To Seinfeld, at the core of the personality is an inner emptiness. The hunger that exists in all individuals and motivates them to seek and to continue seeking out loving others has been "frozen." These patients experience themselves as "thing-like" and view other objects, including non-human objects (work, food, money, clothing, drugs, alcohol, and so on) as thing-like also. The goal is to continually be in control of these outside "things," to avoid any intimate contact. Seinfeld feels that the empty core is in a continuous state of hunger, but a hunger that can never be satisfied. He details a kind of therapy in which the analyst must be active, involved, and continually trying to "make contact" with the patient, so as to "awaken" the patient from his deadened state. In his work Seinfeld (1991) "endeavor[s] to find a way into the patient's inner world, where [he] can be used as an anchor to find a path to the outer world. In this process the patient does not usually lose the therapist internally. If the therapist can reach the inner self of the schizoid patient, there is hope for emotional rebirth and object-related individuation" (p. 216).

I am in agreement that the therapist must actively help these patients become connected and, in fact, to continually question their usual "out-of-contact" manner of relating. However, Seinfeld's emphasis, like Fairbairn's, is on the importance of regression to phases of symbiosis or merger, whereas I am of the opinion that these moments are naturally occurring, lifelong possibilities and are never phase specific. Furthermore, although I am in total accord with the idea that patients may feel dead inside, I do not think of them as empty. Patients are full, although often filled with what Seinfeld and Fairbairn have called bad objects; they are never empty or vacuous.

A stone, a leaf, an unfound door; of a stone, a leaf, a door.
    And of all the forgotten faces.
Naked and alone we came into exile. In her dark womb we
    did not know our mother's face; from the prison of her
    flesh we come into the unspeakable and
    incommunicable prison of this earth.
Which of us has known his brother?
Which of us has looked into his father's heart? Which of us
    has not remained forever prison-pent? Which of us is
    not forever a stranger and alone? . . .
O lost, and by the wind grieved, ghost, come back again.

        Thomas Wolfe, Prologue to *Look Homeward, Angel*

Guntrip (1969) agrees with Balint and Fairbairn on the importance of interdependence throughout life. He focuses his attention on the pathological states of regression, however, while stressing that not all regressions are dangerous. "Regression is a flight backwards in search of security and a chance of a new start. But regression becomes illness in the absence of any therapeutic person to regress with and to" (p. 86). Guntrip demonstrates that healthy regressions occur daily in our lives, including, for example, the need to sleep. "Every night in sleep we return to a symbolic but material substitute for the womb. . . . Waking and rising is a rebirth. This healthy regression . . . has its instinctive basis in the impulse to flee or escape from further strain to where we can recuperate in safety" (p. 96). Although some restorative regressions occur in solitude, Guntrip suggests that most nonpathological regressions are those that involve other object relations. In these moments, it is likely that merging is experienced as a return to the womblike state. Guntrip views these moments as protective and restorative, leading to improved functioning and re-unification of the ego.

Guntrip focuses on the regressive withdrawal that is seen particularly with schizoid patients. He uses the womb to symbolize the security and protection that have been absent in the schizoid's daily relationships. Experiencing only depriving relationships, the ego flees back into itself, into "the very deepest level of the unconscious [where] there remain[s] some buried memory of this original 'oneness,' and the patient goes in search of it when he breaks down into a profoundly regressed illness based on a fantasy of a return to the womb" (p. 266).

The ego returns to an earlier time of security, seeking the womb for protection and rebirth into a hopefully more loving environment. Guntrip calls this portion of the ego the *regressed ego* and includes in it both the split-off portion of the libidinal ego and the unmet potential of the "true self." He is unsure, however, if phenomenologically "the regressed ego feels itself to be 'frozen in cold storage' (frozen in fear perhaps) or whether it feels hidden in the deepest unconscious in the warmth of a hallucinated intrauterine condition" (p. 74). Either way, this regression to the womb denotes a pathological and powerful disconnection from all relationships. In this state of "ego weakness," the ego is so structurally impaired that the individual feels too helpless and vulnerable to remain involved in any human relationship. The roots of this impairment lie in early infant deprivation, in which there is a splitting of the infant ego. Throughout life, then, "the vital heart of the self is lost, and an inner 'deadness' is experienced" (p. 97). In fact, the regression itself is crucial because it serves to preserve or restore the ego, to provide recuperation and rebirth. According to Guntrip (1969), "The ultimate characteristic of the regressed ego is dependent passivity . . . of the intrauterine state which fostered original growth and can foster recuperation. Nature heals in a state of rest. That is the goal" (p. 79).

This withdrawal to a womblike state is dangerous not because of the regression itself, but because of the possibility that the individual will remain so desirous of the comfort he finds in this passive world that he will resist returning to the complicated world of relationships. Rather than return, he may choose death. The schizoid can become so comforted by his withdrawal that he refuses to reconnect once again with others. He may confuse this passive state of withdrawal with death and become pulled in, ever closer to suicide. Guntrip believes that, in these moments of regression, the individual himself may not know which path he would rather choose, feeling torn by the hope for rebirth and the wish for death. Therapeutic contact during these periods may be the only possible way for the schizoid to avoid suicide, by providing a connective link to the patient while he experiences the depth of his regression. I have found, like Guntrip, that suicidal patients are often hoping for a release from their intrapsychic pain, rather than actually seeking to die. One patient (Dan, mentioned in Chapter 9), was *more* frightened of contact with me during these suicidal states of being. He was worried that this might be the "one time" in which I would empathically fail him, and so he stayed away even from me because he was protecting our loving, therapeutic relationship. He remained involved with me, internally, but could not trust that even I would not fail him, and then he *definitely* would have had no reason to live.

Guntrip clearly idealized the womblike state, seeing it as a restorative haven that can evoke a rebirthing process. I would argue that the womb may not always be heavenly; it can in fact be a particularly powerless or frightening place. The case of Kristin (in Chapter 8) makes this quite clear, for even in utero her mother was unwelcoming and hateful. Indeed, babies born addicted to crack or heroin or infected with the HIV virus would have a hard time agreeing with Guntrip's masculine and yet poetic view of the fetus. We can view the fetus's experience in the womb as both warm and cozy, and dangerous and scary. Furthermore, I take issue with Guntrip's view that attaining oneness is, first of all, *ever* possible, even in utero, and second, that moments of oneness are regressive. I am arguing here, that in order to embrace empathic attunements more fully, we must start to seek them out more regularly. We must insist upon having these miraculous moments inside our loving relationships and inside our psychotherapy offices. When moments of oneness become normative ones, expected in the daily course of life, then there will be no need to label them regressed.

Infant Sorrow

My mother groan'd, my father wept,
Into the dangerous world I leapt;
Helpless, naked, piping loud,
Like a fiend hid in a cloud.

Struggling in my father's hands,
Striving against my swaddling bands,
Bound and weary, I thought best
To sulk upon my mother's breast.

William Blake

Bowlby, a British clinician and researcher, took another route to formulate his developmental theories. He studied both young children and primate behavior. He started first with juvenile delinquents, agreeing with Winnicott's view that their stealing behavior is symbolic of an impoverished relationship with their parents. On noticing that these children all had had significant separations from their mothers, he began his quest to examine attachment/separation issues in childhood. In the late 1940s and 1950s, he studied young children who were hospitalized and thus separated from their families or whose mothers were hospitalized (most commonly, to give birth to another child). At that time it was not unusual for hospitalized children to undergo long-term stays with only weekly visitations from their parents. The thinking was that outsiders, such as parents and other siblings, could be germ carriers and might bring infections to the hospital should they have unlimited, daily contact. Bowlby's assistant, James Robertson, researched the effects on the children of these lengthy separations. The results of these studies, as well as of numerous others, convinced Bowlby that attachment was primary for human beings and that our society too readily encouraged separation.

In three lengthy volumes entitled *Attachment* (1969), *Separation* (1973), and *Loss* (1980), Bowlby presents his concepts. What is now known as attachment theory stems from the basic ideas detailed in these books. First, he chose the term *attachment* to indicate an ongoing process of intimacy (or perhaps love). He (1969) writes,

It is . . . extremely misleading for the epithet "regressive" to be applied to every manifestation of attachment behaviour in adult life, as is so often done in psychoanalytic writing where the term carries the connotation pathological, or at least, undesirable. . . . To dub attachment behaviour in adult life regressive is indeed to overlook the vital role that it plays in the life of man from the cradle to the grave. [p. 208]

Second, all human beings are inherently driven toward attachment. Babies are born with a capacity for clinging, known as the Moro response, which instinctively causes them to try and grab their mother if she moves too quickly. They stop crying when provided social interaction, and they babble and coo more intensely if responded to by an other. Bowlby (1973) states:

> For not only young children . . . but human beings of all ages are found to be at their happiest and to be able to deploy their talents to best advantage when they are confident that, standing behind them, there are one or more trusted persons who will come to their aid should difficulties arise. The person trusted provides a secure base from which his (or her) companion can operate. And the more trustworthy the base the more it is taken for granted; and the more it is taken for granted, unfortunately, the more likely is its importance to be overlooked and forgotten. [p. 359]

In this regard, Bowlby's theory sounds similar to Winnicott's *relative dependence*, Fairbairn's *mature dependence*, and Kohut's *selfobjects*. What is different is Bowlby's bias toward the importance of attachment and his detailed analysis of the dangers inherent in the cultural overindulgence of separations. Three distinct stages of distress occur whenever a young child is unwillingly separated from his mother. First, he *protests* loudly and insistently, trying with all his might to return mother to him. Later, he seems to *despair* her loss, but continues to evoke her image, unable to completely distract himself from her absence. Later still, he seems to have disconnected from her and to be emotionally *detached* from her. Should the separation be brief, the child does not remain detached; he will thereafter become more clingy, however, and hypervigilant in watching that she does not leave him again. One of the interesting aspects of Bowlby's observations is that mothers, as well as the general population, often misread the detached child as being an independent, self-assured baby. To Bowlby, the child who has had moments upon moments of overtaxing separation may give the appearance of perfection while, underneath, he is moving to a more detached state of being. Bowlby believes this to be true because the child seems unrelated and uninterested in the attachment figure who previously was so important to him. Now, the child moves to all but ignore his mother when she is around, no doubt out of both anger and fear of the separations to come. Bowlby correlates the stage of protest with separation anxiety, despair with grief and mourning, and detachment with defense. He believes that these three responses are phases of a single process, that of attachment behavior.

Attachment issues reverberate throughout life. An individual's belief in the availability of responsive others is based on the accumulated minutiae of attachment responses received in "infancy, childhood, and adolescence. . . . Whatever expectations are developed during those years tend to persist relatively unchanged throughout the rest of life" (Bowlby 1973, p. 202). Bowlby demonstrates that separations can also occur without actual physical partings. Even parental discipline that simply threatens the child with separation is enough to cause insecure attachment. Bowlby's example was that parents in those years often told their misbehaving children they would be sent away to an orphanage if they did not obey. Another common kind of threat used even today has the theme, "If you don't behave I'll leave you right now." This second type has many variations, which certainly do "work" in that the child usually becomes immediately cooperative. For example: "If you don't get your shoes/ coat/hat on this minute, I'm leaving without you," or if the child is not ready to leave a particularly enjoyable place, the mother often says, "Well, I'm leaving now. Bye-Bye, see you later." Or to curb unruly behavior, "If you don't behave better, you're going to go to your room." Over time, these threats are shortened to simply "You want to go to your room?" Again, it is not the use of these threats in and of themselves that is dangerous, so much as it is the cumulative quantity of their use, the number of times each and every day that they are used to bring about good behavior.

The importance of this idea should not be overlooked. Even the threat of separation is enough to cause a child to experience separation anxiety, to move into the stage of protest. I would go further and add that many moments of even normative abuse cause a separation, though not in actuality a physical separation, between mother and child. This separation leads to detachment, which adds to the development of the false self. For example, when the mother calls her child "selfish," "bratty," or "ugly," a barrier is raised by the child to protect himself from his hurt. He detaches from the separation she has made, the separation caused by her unempathic words. One patient described the subjective feeling state of what I would call being detached as "living behind a plexiglass window pane." His mother was a highly anxious, stressed, yet successful businesswoman and his father a high-powered executive in a major computer firm. Although the patient was quite bright, he had had tremendous difficulty learning to read. He was continually pushed by both his parents to learn his letters and spelling, being told that he was "lazy," "dumb," "rebellious." (In fact, he was dyslexic – undiagnosed because, in those years, the condition had not yet been discovered.) The pressure became more and more intense, with his mother often screaming at him to "study, study, study." He took to hiding in his room so that he could avoid contact. Now an adult, the patient chose a career that immerses him in reading and writing. He is also five years in recovery from heroin addiction. He described the window-pane as

> a place I can hide myself in. I can see out, I can observe, participate in, and seem like part of life. But I never can quite touch others or feel touched by them. I can't break through the plexiglass no matter what I do, and I feel the glass surrounding me like cellophane wrap. Inside of me is always this voice that says, "Don't say what you feel, it will only make things worse." And that's essentially how I live, and that's what I think keeps the plexiglass in place. I wish I could just experience raw touching.

Bowlby (1973) believes that the kind and quality of mothering directly affects the attachment experience. Mothers who "in general respond to calls for support and protection" (p. 204) are more likely to provide a "secure base" (p. 183) for their children, a base in which feelings of love and connectedness abound. Children who are not provided a secure base form "insecure attachments." These children fall into one of two categories, which resemble Fairbairn's exciting/rejecting object relationship: either they are ambivalently or avoidantly attached. The ambivalently attached child continually tries to get mother's attention, becoming clingy, demanding, and needy. Alternatively, the avoidantly attached child develops an "I don't need you" stance with the world, believing he can rely only on himself. This stance is built out of anger and despair, but the anger is never expressed outwardly. Instead, the child (like the patient above) simply walls himself in and away from others. Another patient, the third of five children who were closely spaced, felt an intense loneliness throughout her childhood. She was praised for being so quiet, so resourceful, and for never causing any "trouble" in the family. As an adult, she remains painfully reclusive despite frequent attempts to break through her self-imposed isolation chamber. Even in her psychotherapy, she is often secretive and avoidant, believing that I would prefer a "perfect patient" to the "crazy woman" who lives underneath.

> I stop myself all the time from telling you what I'm really feeling. It's not even conscious, it's just so ingrained inside of me. I remember telling myself as a little girl to accept the truth—I would just have to take care of myself because no one else was there for me. And I've lived my life that way. I really do feel that I'm all alone. If I did tell you all the things I think about, then I'm sure you'd find me crazy. And then, you'd send me away anyway, so you see, I'd still be all alone.

A large number of research projects are based on the conceptualizations that emanated from Bowlby's attachment theory. The most famous and widely used is Ainsworth's Strange Situation. In this experiment, a child and his mother are first observed together, playing with some toys. Then a stranger, the research assistant, comes in to join them, and soon after, the mother leaves. The child and the stranger are observed together, their interactions watched and coded. Finally, the mother returns, and the way her child responds to her is crucial to the study. Does he avoid her? Does he cling to her? Is he angry with her for leaving, or had he forgotten about her? The results indicate whether the child is securely, anxiously, or avoidantly attached to his mother. And, surprisingly enough, these results seem to hold true for these children during many follow-up studies. The way these children were observed relating to their mother has been an accurate predictor of the way they later relate to friends, teachers, and life in general.

In *Becoming Attached* (1994), Karen comments that

> the lack of a secure base would seem to leave one struggling with a profound and painful loneliness. The person with a largely ambivalent style knows it's there and is driven nuts by it, as if on fire and convinced he can never put it out. The avoidant person is dissociated from it. But both are haunted by loneliness, and I would speculate that for that reason the two attachment styles seem prone to certain types of addiction, the ambivalent becoming addicted to people, the avoidant to work, power, acquisition, achievement, or obsessive rituals. Ultimately, the power their loneliness has over them shows up in surprising ways. [p. 384]

Very often, the two styles of insecure attachment go together. For example, an addict in pursuit of the drug is in a state of desperate need. He looks like a craving, dependent child in pursuit of the rejecting mother. Simultaneously, he is the "I don't need anyone" individual who ignores his wife's pleas, spends his children's inheritance, and completely avoids all intimate contact. In sum, the addict may in fact operate on both sides of the attachment continuum, all in pursuit of the security he never had. The two sides of insecure attachment do not equal the whole of a secure base. Inevitably, the inner loneliness returns: the wall of detached painfulness remains sealed.

Bowlby extensively reviewed the psychoanalytic literature for its emphasis on separation anxiety. In many cases, this aspect of human nature had been sorely neglected. He pointed to Freud's early work that emphasized only the instinctual basis of the mother–infant relationship as part of the long-standing avoidance of attachment concepts in analytic theory. However, he also highlighted a passage from Freud's later work (1938) that stated that the infant's powerful tie to his mother is "unique, without parallel, laid down unalterably for a whole lifetime, as the first and strongest love-object and as the prototype of all later love relationships— for both sexes" (quoted in Karen, 1994, p. 95).

In Bowlby's opinion, children incorporate actual, lived events into their psyche—they do not fantasize. He is more than opposed to Klein's construction of a childhood world of phantasy. To demonstrate the point, Bowlby reviews Freud's analysis of the Schreber case (1973, pp. 174–177), noting that this case was instrumental in the psychoanalytic under-standing of paranoia and paranoid symptoms. Daniel Paul Schreber was born in 1842, the second son of a famous physician and teacher. By 1884 Schreber had become a judge, but shortly thereafter began developing psychiatric symptoms that eventually led to a nine-year psychiatric hos-pitalization. In 1903, he published the memoirs of his illness, which was of great interest to psychiatrists. Many of the entries concern his torturous experiences at the hand of God, which he perceived as "miracles." The following passage, quoted by Niederland (1974) from Schreber's memoirs, demonstrates the kind of hallucinations he imagined: "Hardly a single limb or organ in my body escaped being temporarily damaged by miracles, nor a single muscle being pulled by miracles either moving or paralyzing it according to the restrictive purpose. Even now the miracles which I experience hourly are still of a nature to frighten every other human being to death" (p. 75).

Freud utilizes only the material in Schreber's diaries to undertake his analysis of the paranoid personality. He hypothesizes that delusions of persecution are attempts to deny and alter the unacceptable thought of homosexual love through the defense mechanism of projection.

What Bowlby included in his argument that reality alone causes pathology is the fascinating reanalysis of this case by Niederland (1974), who studied the published works not only of Schreber but also of his father. The senior Schreber was a well-known orthopedic physician who published almost twenty books on orthopedics and child-rearing advice throughout his life. One of his most popular books, entitled *Kallipaedie or Education to Beauty Through Natural and Symmetrical Promotion of Normal Body Growth*, focuses on specific techniques for raising moral, well-behaved, and physically superior children. Throughout the book, he advises parents and educators to stress obedience, proper posture, and continuous supervision of every child. To assist in the attainment of these goals, for example, he invented iron braces for children, ages 2 to 8 years of age, to wear during the day and night to ensure perfect posture. The device used during the day, Niederland describes, consisted of "iron bars fastened to the chest of the child as well as to the table near which the child was sitting; the horizontal iron bar pressed against the chest and prevented any movement forward or sideward, giving only some freedom to move backward to an even more rigidly upright position" (p. 77). To ensure proper posture during sleep, Schreber recommended the use of a thick belt which, as Niederland describes, "was fastened to the bed and ran tightly across the child's chest, thus keeping his body posture straight as well as supine throughout the night" (p. 77). By correlating these devices with the delusional "miracles" that the psychotic Schreber son imagines are continuously being afflicted upon him by God, Niederland is able to demonstrate that this man's paranoid illness was grounded in reality; his psychosis, then, was a direct result of his traumatizing childhood experiences.

More important, however, for the discussion of normative abuse is the reality that one hundred years ago, child-rearing practices such as these were not at all uncommon. In fact, Niederland notes that Dr. Schreber's writrings were "prompted by a missionary zeal to spread information on physical health and body building everywhere so that a stronger race of men would result" (p. 59). Even Dr. Schreber's biographer Ritter (1936) proudly points to the physician as a philosophical predecessor of Hitler. Niederland, in reviewing the social mores of the late nineteenth century, observes that similar notions were widely held, in medical and nonmedical circles. . . . The popularity of Dr. Schreber's books proves the point . . . [P]ractices of mechanical restraint and corporal punishment . . . were given strong support by many authoritative physicians at that time. With due allowance to the *Zeitgeist*, it can nevertheless be assumed that the father's psychopathology as evidenced in his writings must have had a direct and massive impact . . . on the public who held his writings in high esteem for several decades. . . . [p. 57]

Normative abuse shifts with societal customs and traditions. What we would today consider physical abuse was viewed as normative one hundred years ago, and was not then considered abuse. Similarly today, if the detached, unempathic child-rearing practices viewed as normal in our culture would become socially dystonic, then some of the psychiatric conditions seen in our psychotherapy practices would be alleviated. The detached, alienated personality will have less opportunity to develop if parents, educators, and therapists understand and insist on child-raising techniques that emphasize attachment, interpersonal involvement, and intimacy. In this regard, just as the barriers to intimacy begin in the earliest relationship between parents and children, so do the opportunities for attachment and love.

3

THE ONENESS/SEPARATENESS PARADOX

> To believe your own thought, to believe that what is true for you in your private heart is true for all men—that is genius. . . . A man should learn to detect and watch that gleam of light which flashes across his mind from within. . . . Nothing is at last sacred but the integrity of his own mind.
>
> Ralph Waldo Emerson, *Self-Reliance*

WINNICOTT CHARACTERISTICALLY welcomes dialectics in his theoretical writings—for example, his idea that the child's capacity to be alone develops not by actually being alone but by being in the mother's presence. Another dichotomy exists between Winnicott's theoretical idea of a secret, true self and his belief that the baby is fused with mother in a complete merger state during the early months of life. Winnicott, whose writings are both eloquent and poetic, has left a paradoxical space in between these opposing positions.

Winnicott believes there is a secret, spontaneous self inside each individual, a spark that is the center of our own unique identities. "At the centre of each person is an incommunicado element, and this is sacred and most worthy of preservation" (1963a, p. 187). The true self comprises this "incommunicado element" and is the source of the individual's spontaneous needs, ideas, images, and gestures that, over time, have moved into the true-self arena because of external impingements. In the true self lives a creative spark, a powerful sense of being alive. To Winnicott, part of the true self can never be translated to others and must remain separate, known only to the self. "Although healthy persons communicate and enjoy communicating, the other fact is equally true, that *each individual is an isolate, permanently non-communicating, permanently unknown, in fact unfound"* (1963a, p. 187).

To help convey this spark of the true self to patients, I often show them a small glass prism, one of the many objects on my desk. I have also brought this object to the theoretical classes I have taught to convey this lovely, poetic image because I find that theoretical concepts can sometimes be better conveyed through symbols and metaphors. I hold the shining glass up to the light, and as the reflections bounce through its many-sided angles, I offer something like the following:

> You see, inside each one of us is a beautiful, reflective piece of ourselves. It contains our life's spark, our energy, our spontaneous, creative, and playful core. You might notice that this prism is chipped on a few sides, that it is not absolutely perfect. But that simply adds to its beauty, for what created those chips is important to retain. The light still reflects through, as it twists and turns brilliantly through every angle. And just as I have a secret, true self in me, so do you. But what has happened (and what Winnicott believed), is that when the demands of others impinge and overtake the true self, we learn to hide it, to cover it over. [I begin to cover over the sides of the pyramid.] Soon, there are no sides for the light to come in and bounce through; soon, there is only this tiny spark at the top that still remains, ever hopeful that you will release the rest of it from imprisonment.

> It is true that we can never share every aspect, every reflective glow of this inner self. Winnicott felt that if we were to do this, we would go crazy. But most of us shut out so much of our inner core, our inner light, because of fears based on the childhood reality that we would be laughed at, shunned, ignored, or hated. It is our job, in this process of psychotherapy, to help that inner self shine through, to release it from the imprisonment of falseness under which it has lived for so very long.

This moment has never failed to produce strong emotional results. It speaks to the lost, lonely, alienated inner core of so many patients I have treated. In most cases, patients are visibly moved. Dan, discussed in Chapter 9, welled up with tears and had to look away in silence. Other patients have asked to hold the prism, to play with the bouncing reflections, to finger the chipped ends of glass. Only on one occasion have I been with a patient who surprised me with the following response: "I don't think that's true about me. Maybe other people have this inner goodness that you're speaking about. Me, I've got nothing in there. There is no inner me that is sparkling, spontaneous, true. Don't get me wrong—I wish there were."

I asked him to tell me what he felt was inside of him. He replied, "Just shit." I recall being a little stunned by his answer, and then feeling terribly sad that no one had given him a sense, in any part of his being, of being loved or wanted. This patient had had a long history of drug and alcohol use, starting at age 12. He had stopped five years ago, after losing a large sum of money in a failed investment and being threatened with bankruptcy and divorce. Michael frequently suffered from depression and was oriented in a rather passive–aggressive style, as are so many alcoholics and drug addicts.

These few revealing moments from his childhood allow us room for speculation about the many other kinds of hurtful experiences he must have suffered. For example, when Michael was no more than 7 or 8, his mother angrily expelled him from the car, leaving him several miles from their home. She had become furious with him for something he had said or done that he does not now recall and had told him that she did not care if he ever found his own way home. As he watched her drive away, he nevertheless felt sure that she would soon come back for him, and so he decided to make her a little frightened too. He hid in the bushes, and sure enough, his mother finally did return. And yes, she was shocked when she did not find him there. He then came out of hiding and, upon getting into the car, received a welcoming of anger and slaps. A year or two before this incident, he had written a note to his parents saying that he was running away. Somehow, although he does not remember how, he was stopped. But that never prevented him from always, longingly, wishing he could escape.

Michael had never felt wanted by his mother. She had a "just-put-up-with-the-kid" attitude, never involving herself very much in his activities, interests, or thoughts. Not surprisingly, he spent much of his time watching television. Like so many other patients I have treated, he had never been made to feel excited about any talent, interest, or thought—any aspect of his being. He was never guided toward any career or given hope for the brightness of his future. He was never going to be a star; he was only supposed to plod along, day in and day out. Drugs made him feel alive—the sensation felt good, gave him something to be excited about, and gave him something to chase. It became his future.

Michael had virtually no access to his true self, and indeed it could be argued that his parents did in fact murder his sparkling, spontaneous inner core. The task of psychotherapy has been to help him shed the layers of deadness, what he calls the "shit" inside of him, and look for buried treasure. Before continuing with Winnicott's theory, I would like to emphasize again why I do not consider patients to be empty within, as has been conceptualized by other psychoanalytic writers. I view them as being detached, or numbed, from their inner selves. Having an inner core that has been made comatose by the daily experiences of normative, physical, or sexual abuse is different from having an empty self. The experience of being deadened inside implies that once, be it only at birth, there was an inner life. To convey to patients that they originally had a unique, inner spark that was paralyzed during their childhood is a more accurate, as well as a more hopeful, way to describe the inner self. Emptiness implies that nothing was obtained or retained inside the core self throughout childhood, adolescence, and even presently. Comatose implies that, although introjects have taken root and experiences have been codified, their accessibility, their freedom to be externalized and viewed in the psychotherapy process, has been buried alive. Keeping the inner self catatonic is an ongoing process, which is discussed more fully in Chapter 10.

According to Winnicott, a false self develops to protect the true self from being damaged or destroyed by maternal expectations. The false self provides an illusion of personality and gives the child an external face composed of his mother's wishes, expectations, and needs. The false self *falsifies* to gain love and admiration from mother. I would add that the false self actively *attempts to murder* any thought or feeling that does not fit into the maternal schema. There is a continuum to false-self development, with the most severe pathology found in those who cannot gain access to the true self. On the other end of the spectrum, a little false self is needed in even the most mentally healthy individuals because it provides appropriate socialization cues necessary for living with others.

The true self, that "incommunicado element," lives at the core of the self. And herein lies the paradox. For the true self to exist, it cannot be overtaken by, or merged into, mother. And yet according to Winnicott, the baby begins life in a period of "absolute dependence," a world in which he and his mother are merged in a "nursing couple" (1952a, p. 99). Even in utero, the mother and fetus form a union. Especially in the last few months of pregnancy, the mother becomes "preoccupied" with her baby. She becomes increasingly involved, indeed consumed, by this new life forming inside of her, and she begins to decathect from other relationships. Her world becomes her baby, and her focus is centered on responding accurately to her infant's gestures. This relationship continues after birth because *"there is no such thing as a baby.* . . . One sees a 'nursing couple'" (1952a, p. 99). Indeed, the infant is born into "an environment-individual set-up, [where] the centre of gravity of the being does not start off in the individual [but] . . . in the total set-up" (p. 99).

The mother provides numerous functions for her child, both environmental and emotional. Her provision of total care, her entire absorption into her baby's needs and gestures, is crucial to both his physical and psychic well-being. The baby does not only require feeding but also the bonding and attachment that feeding allows. The mother must emotionally bond with her child during the feeding; otherwise the whole process is deadened, apathetic, and cold. Bollas (1989) has grouped Winnicott's environment mother in terms of her functions. The mother, as "processor of the infant" (p. 213), is called by Bollas the *transformational object.* Rather than being an internalized object or a separate external object, the transformational object is actually a process—a continually interactive relationship, one that provides an environmental backdrop onto which all future scenes of life are played. The mother transforms and translates the environment for her infant by the way she feeds him, cuddles him, and cares for his physical being. Her approach in these daily tasks, whether hurried or angered, loving or anxious, is felt by her child and forms the background for all his later experiences of the world. Stern (1985) is in agreement here, as the infant can feel differences in the affective states of those around him.

I have seen the results when a mother who, overwhelmed by the care required for three older boys closely spaced in age, was unable to involve herself with her youngest son. He became my patient eighteen years later. He had been frequently fed by a bottle propped up through the crib bars, which his mother had remarked was "the most efficient way to do it." This was a young man who called himself "the angry youth" and who frequently became psychotic when enraged. Wrestling had helped him sublimate his aggression, but when he graduated from high school, he had no place to take his rage but into drugs and alcohol. From my perspective, he was truly unable to be soothed. Despite the many sessions we had together, he rarely allowed himself to be contained even momentarily. For the most part, he was never without his anger, detachment, and aloofness.

> There was a child went forth every day,
> And the first object he look'd upon, that object he became,
> And that object became part of him for the day or a certain
>   part of the day,
> Or for many years or stretching cycles of years. . . .
>
> His own parents, he that had father'd him and she that had
>   conceived him in her womb and birth'd him,
> They gave this child more of themselves than that,
> They gave him afterward every day, they became part of
>   him.
>
>   Walt Whitman, *Leaves of Grass*

I am breaking from Winnicott for a moment to detail Kohut's developmental schema, in part because he disagrees with Winnicott, Mahler, and the many other analysts writing within an ego psychology perspective on the very issue I have just raised. Kohut (1980) feels, as does Bowlby, that these theories all have in common the belief

> that man's life from childhood to adulthood is a move forward from a position of helplessness, dependence, and shameful clinging to a position of power, independence, and proud autonomy. . . [taking] . . . for granted that the undesirable features of adulthood, the flaws in the adult's psychic organization, must be conceptualized as manifestations of a psychological infantilism. . . . [As opposed to being symbiotic, the infant] is not dependent, clinging or weak, but independent, assertive, strong—it is psychologically complete so long as it breathes the psychological oxygen provided by contact with empathically responsive selfobjects and, in this respect, it is no different from the adult who is complete, independent, and strong only as long as he feels responded to. [pp. 480–481]

Kohut (1977) starts with the premise that there is a unique self state at birth, which is "a center of initiative and a recipient of impressions" (p. 99). He believes that one's internal structure is built upon the "transmuting internalizations" (1971, p. 49) of what he calls selfobjects, or merged objects, which provide cohesion and stability for the developing self. His developmental schema stresses the importance of interrelatedness and merging inherent in the self-selfobject experience. Throughout childhood, and indeed throughout life, the self internalizes selfobjects, or merged introjects, building psychic structure. The infant has basic narcissistic needs that must be fulfilled by his parents for healthy development. Like Winnicott, Mahler, and others, he believes the infant enjoys an early state of omnipotence in which he feels himself to be the master of the universe. As part of this omnipotence, the baby infuses at least one parent with projections of his own grandiosity so that he can feel safe and secure when merged in his or her presence. These infusions occur during moments of disppointment, when the perfection he experiences in his own world is temporarily disrupted. In these moments, the child seeks merging with the idealized selfobject for protection and comfort. The child's grandiosity is gradually toned down by the inevitability of parental failures. In the process of viewing his parents more realistically, he also gains a more realistic self-image. If, however, the child has been disappointed too often or has experienced too many empathic failures from his idealized parental figures, he will instead shift to relying on himself. Grandiosity and omnipotence return, while the child removes all imperfections from himself and places them into external objects. Kohut terms this style of being *pathological narcissism*.

As with Winnicott, there is much of Kohut's theory that I can embrace. I do feel, however, that there is one problematic area in his schema. I do not believe a baby or young toddler views himself as omnipotent, as a perfect being who is able, like a magician, to get for himself whatever he wishes. In a personal communication with Jane Spivack Brown, a psychoanalyst in New York City, she stated her belief, similar to mine, that babies and even young toddlers most resemble invalids. Babies cannot walk, they cannot talk, they cannot feed themselves, their digestive systems are undeveloped, and they have no bowel or bladder control. How similar this is to adult stroke victims or, to some extent, to mutes and paraplegics. One patient, a mother of three teenagers, recently had had a partial stroke. She told me that she now had a "perfect" understanding of what young children feel. She said the experience of trying to learn again how to put her mouth and tongue in just the right position to make the right sound for each word was incredibly frustrating. And to relearn to walk, to reprogram her legs to be under her command, was challenging, maddening, and humiliating. As she put it, "If I had a young child now, I would be a much better mother because I now know what they feel inside. It is humbling to see others do what you know you should be able to do, or want to do, but can't. I would have a lot more patience if I were mothering those children again."

For most of the day, every day, children feel their smallness—so much so that when they have a singular, autonomous achievement, they feel spectacular! The omnipotence that is so frequently described in the literature is no more than the child's moment of exhilaration, relief, and joy of self-accomplishment. This omnipotence can also be felt, paradoxically, when the child asks for and gets what he wants from a larger, more powerful other. I propose that the omnipotence that these writers attribute to children is actually a projection of parental feelings stemming from being made into a selfobject or what Winnicott termed a *subjective object*. As a subjective object, the other is commanded to do the infant's bidding. For Winnicott, this means that the infant feels merged with the external other to the degree that the object becomes the baby's *subject*. Similarly for Kohut, the selfobject is a merger between self and other, another term meaning the subjective object.

Let me give an example. The young child has already gone to sleep for the night, but he awakens sometime later and calls for his mother. But both parents are tired, and they too have gone to bed: it has been a long day. They feel that they should be "off duty" now—after all, he is supposed to be asleep. But he calls out, "Mommy, I want some milk, please!" How do the parents respond? Most of us would certainly give a try at either telling him to go back to sleep, compromising with a glass of water so that we do not have to go downstairs and become more fully awake, or ignoring his request. Some parents might become more forceful, out of their irritation at yet again being a subjective object. "No, you cannot have anything else now. You are in bed. If you had wanted more to eat, you should've had more at dinner. That's all there is to it. Now go back to sleep." The subjective experience, for the parent, is something like this: *I just can't believe it. I am so tired, I can't do another thing for that child. All day long, I am getting this, doing that. He is really a tyrant! He never gives me a break! He is so incredibly selfish!* And for the child, the subjective experience might be something like this: *I don't want to make Mommy angry. But I'm hungry. I can't get back to sleep. I wish I could go and get the milk all by myself!* And of course, the reality is that if he could have gotten it himself, if he could have gotten out of the crib and climbed down the stairs and taken the glass off the shelf and pulled the heavy refrigerator door open and picked up the large milk container and poured his own glass, he certainly would have done it. One patient told me that when she was 4 and 5, she frequently awoke earlier than the rest of the family. But no food was left out for her to eat, and so, quite resourcefully, she would walk to various neighbors' houses and have breakfast with them. It became quite a joke in the neighborhood that this child "had cereal bowl, will travel." What it taught her, of course, was that she was too burdensome at home, that she had to be self-reliant, and that she could not depend on her parents to provide for her.

The descriptions of children as omnipotent, narcissistic, grandiose, and selfish relate more to the feelings that parents may experience in the continual, demanding moments of child raising. Parents can become drained and can feel so powerless that they may even rage out of control. A screaming infant can be so upsetting that new parents sometimes shake their child—even to the point of death—in order to stop the incessant, wild cries. One patient confided in me that she had once, as a new mother, placed a pillow over her colicky baby's face in a moment of rage, exhaustion, and despair. She immediately took the pillow off, but she realized that it is moments such as these that lead some parents to murder.

Kohut believes, as does Winnicott, that the child must lessen his idealization of his parents in order to view them, as well as himself, more realistically. This process actually happens quite naturally, without the need for overt parental failures. Mother is idealized by her baby simply because of her size, her verbal ability, her mobility, her milk—in short, everything. In time, the child will learn to walk, talk, and refuse the breast. Having equalized these differences, the child sees other aspects of mother to admire—her worldly knowledge, for one thing. The child does not necessarily need to experience her failings in a more complete way in order for him to separate because, simultaneous to her actions, he has grown and has mastered many of the functions she had previously provided. As well, if mother and baby are well attuned, she will not lessen her ministrations until his level of frustration has matured to match her actions. For example, an infant demands an immediate response to his needs for food, comfort, involvement; an empathic mother responds quickly to as many of these requests as she can. When her child is older, she can explain that he must now wait before some of his requests are filled. He is now able to understand her communication and has developed the frustration tolerance to adequately handle her momentary refusals. These moments do not cause empathic failures or stimulate the separation process, because the child's frustration tolerance has increased concomitant with the frustrations placed before him. He has actually increased his own ability to cope with the disappointments of daily life; this dynamic cannot be, therefore, the overall cause of his ongoing separation from his mother. This shift in ideology is important to note because, in clinical practice, there is often the assumption that the patient will begin to separate from the therapist only when his idealization of the clinician lessens, as he sees the failings of this important other. I do not think it is so much a matter of the patient losing the idealization, which indeed may never occur, as it is the patient having gained a more empowered sense of self. As the patient grows, the need to utilize the therapist's power is not as intense; similarly, the toddler who nurses still enjoys this connection, but needs it less and can substitute other food or comfort if need be.

Kohut's emphasis on empathic attunement, both in parental–child relations and in psychotherapy, is certainly of tremendous value. Maintaining an empathic connection means being able to view an other's experience from that particular perspective. Freud calls this process "to feel oneself into another" (*einfühlung*) or empathy (cited in Wolf 1988). I view the process of empathy as part of merger phenomena, because one individual submerges or immerses himself into the other. Kohut (1973) writes that "empathy is a fundamental mode of human relatedness" (p. 704); it is the "accepting, confirming, and understanding human echo" (p. 705). Buie (1981), in his discussion of empathy, points out "that empathy may or may not . . . be associated with the illusion of merging closeness, and that empathy may begin in the infant's early experience with its caretaker and may be linked motivationally to fulfillment of yearnings for a merging quality of closeness" (p. 287). Because he views merger as a regressive, infantile phenomenon, however, he also adds that "to the extent that empathy remains linked with merging, its scope will necessarily be restricted" (p. 287). He bases this view on the idea that an infant does not have the capacity to attend to an other. However, the important dynamic here is that the child learns, via his mother's empathy, how wonderful it feels to be attuned. Then, over time, as he develops his intellectual and emotional capacities, he can begin to understand the feelings, via the empathic process, of others.

Jordan (1983) believes that daughters benefit greatly from having the same-sex primary nurturer because the mother, too, can more easily empathize with her female child. She cites Hoffman's 1977 study that found that females are more empathic than males and concludes that men tend to have more difficulty with the essential "surrender[ing] to affect and momentary joining with the other" (p. 3). Men and women are equally capable of cognitively noticing and labeling the affective states of others; the difference, however, seems to be that women are more compelled "to attend to [these] affective signals." In these studies, women "demonstrate more emotional attunement and responsiveness to the other's feelings — more feeling *with* the other" (p. 4). Jordan considers the causes of these sex differences to be rooted in early socialization cues, sex role identification, and early childhood experiences.[1] Cultural mores dictate that girls be more caring, loving, and attentive to the other, whereas boys are expected to distance themselves from feelings of pain, suffering, and hurt. Kaplan (1983) notes that women are "schooled in empathy" (p. 14), whereas men have greater difficulty experiencing affective aspects of empathy. Kaplan further suggests that the socialization and childhood experiences of male therapists cause them to have more difficulty experiencing the *affective* components of empathy, because in the male experience these components are less developed. Thus the psychoanalytic view that empathy is regressive; thus the emphasis in psychoanalytic theory on separation at the expense of merger.

Submersion of the self into the other is very much a part of mothering and part of being a subjective object. The mother must put aside her own wish to sleep, as in the case cited above, for attending (yet again) to her child's needs. Kaplan (1983) writes that "terms like regression, merger, fusion, and symbiosis belie the mother's sense of a mature self coexisting with this intense affective connectedness" (p. 15). She adds, and I agree wholeheartedly, that "theories which fail to recognize [that intimate attachment coexists with differentiation] cast mothering into an infantalizing and magical light, missing the complicated intellectual and emotional process that it is" (p. 15). Pregnancy is certainly an example of a woman's body being her own *as well as* an other's. No matter what her childhood experience has been, her nine-month pregnancy is an opportunity to prepare her for the artful negotiation between self-and-other coexistence. The empathic problem for women, in fact, may be that they have learned all too well how to immerse themselves into an other, but

---

1. While Jordan was concerned only with environmental factors, I would add that there are inborn, genetic differences between the sexes. Biological factors must be included as part of any gender comparison.

have too little practice with what Jordan termed self-empathy; they tend to devalue their own needs for the sake of the other. In Chapter 10, I discuss the ramifications of this kind of relating in more detail.

I agree with Kohut's overall premise that empathic attunements must dominate childhood experiences. I do, however, disagree with his position, and that of Winnicott, Freud, and others, that these moments of attunement create an illusion of the child's grandiose omnipotence. Rather, these moments of parental empathy serve to build confidence in the child's ability to assess his limitations realistically and to seek help without feeling powerless or shamed. The more opportunities for empathic responsiveness from mother, the more powerful and confident the child becomes, because in the interaction between the two, the child feels connected to and supported by a more powerful other. It is the interaction, the maternal assistance itself, that raises the child's self-esteem: he has been worthy of recognition and response. It is not that the child believes himself to be all-powerful—it is that he realizes his wishes and needs are being met by the most important external other in his world. It is from these moments of attentiveness that he has been made worthy. Inadequate attunement between mother and child, in contrast, is frequently the major cause of narcissistic rage. Kohut uses this term to refer to moments when the self feels its very existence threatened by other selfobjects. Wolf (1988) states that "the origin of the narcissistic rage must be sought in the childhood experience of utter helplessness *vis-à-vis* the humiliating selfobject parent. . . . the self's structure weakens in the absence of the needed responsiveness" (pp. 80–81).

The normalcy of childhood temper tantrums can be seen in this light. The child feels helpless in the face of an overpowering other. That temper tantrums are often at their peak around 18 months may indicate a connection to the difficulties a child experiences in language development. Children are just at the beginning stage of discovering a better way to communicate their wishes and yet are too unskilled to utilize their newfound linguistic ability. Children seem to have the cognition to understand language months before their mouths, tongues, and lips are able to form words. Unfortunately, a common, normative response to temper tantrums is for the parent to say, "I'm leaving the room now, and when you have stopped this behavior, I'll return." Or, alternatively, "Go to your room for a time-out." Some parents become even angrier themselves and answer a tantrum with, "You keep this up and I'll really give you something to cry [or be angry] about." These responses, all indicative of detachment behavior, are based on the belief that the child is manipulatively raging to evoke anger or guilt from his mother. Perhaps, instead, these moments are in fact the best time for mother to remain with her child, to indicate that, even in rages, even in anger, he is still loved. The message conveyed is that the parent–child bond, their intertwined relationship, does not stop even if the immediate emotion felt is anger rather than love. To abandon a child in his anger or rage may simply increase his sense of helplessness and powerlessness. Furthermore, mother can be helpful in calming her child's rage and in de-escalating the tantrum. If it were actually possible for a child to "know" how to "stop this behavior," he certainly wouldn't start it in the first place. After all, why would he wish to be screaming until hoarse, flailing arms and legs around on the floor until bruised?

For many children, these moments of narcissistic rage, which are essentially moments of terrifying helplessness, can be fairly frequent. For some children, these episodes carry over into a lifetime of narcissistic powerlessness. Let me cite two examples. The patient named Rebecca in Chapter 1 was extremely attached to her father. She was also his protector and confidante. At one point during her analysis, he was being threatened by creditors with lawsuits and possible financial ruin. Rebecca came into the session enraged: "If anyone lays a hand on my father, I will kill him." [As I did not respond but simply waited for more, she went on.] "He's a good man. This is all bullshit, trying to discredit him. They're just jealous. I mean it—I have my father's gun at home, and I can use it. And I am seriously thinking about blowing their brains out."

Certainly, I had many possible options about how to answer her. I could have chosen to discuss the wisdom of this course of action or to point out her wish to protect and save her father at her own expense. I might have even become alarmed, since she had mentioned a specific plan of violent action. But instead I answered with something like this:

I know that you are dead serious about being able to harm these people who are so angry with your father. And I believe you—you probably could kill them. I know that you have enough passion and enough of a conviction of the value of these killings that you could carry out the plan. [She looked surprised and pleased. I had acknowledged her rage and taken her seriously while all the same labeling her powerful. And powerful is what one wanted to be most of all—to be viewed as strong, not helpless.] But if you do kill them, then what? You will be sent to prison, I'm sure, and then what? Your father will have lost his special daughter, and you and I would have to continue therapy behind bars. That seems like a lot to lose.

She did move out of this rage and out of her homicidal fantasies. But I think what helped her the most was that I attended to her sense of helplessness and showed her the power in her passion.

A second incident was extraordinary. In one of the theoretical classes I was teaching, we had just finished discussing Kohut and the issue of narcissistic rage. In fact, I had offered the case example of Rebecca as a strategy for therapeutic intervention. A student came in the very next week and asked to speak to the class as a whole. She told us this story:

Last week, a few days after class, I was abducted by a kidnapper at gunpoint, in the garage of the hospital where I work. He got in the car with me and pointed his gun at my head. He drove, and I sat next to him, holding onto my rosary beads with all my strength. I started remembering the idea of narcissistic rage, and the point being how powerless the person feels, beneath it all. So I told him that I knew he could hurt me if he wanted to, that I really believed that he was dangerous. The man liked this—he liked that I took him seriously. I told him that I believed he could indeed hurt me, but that I thought he was a good person—that he really didn't want to use his power to harm me. I kept talking to him like this, in sort of an Eriksonian hypnotic chant, and it really calmed him down. Soon, he put the gun down and just drove. After a while, he asked me if I was a mother. "Yes," I said, "and a grandmother. Do you want to see a picture of my daughter and grandchildren?" He did, and he said,"I bet you are a wonderful mother. I wish I had had a mother like you." At some point, I was able to convince him to let me out of the car, that he could keep the car and that I wouldn't call the police. He did let me go. I then flagged down a police car, and they chased him all over town. I later learned that they did finally catch him, about a half hour after he had let me go. I thank God we talked about narcissistic rage in this class. Seeing this guy as feeling humiliated, powerless, like a young child, made the difference, I believe, between my life and death.

On Another's Sorrow

Can I see another's woe,
And not be in sorrow too?
Can I see another's grief,
And not seek for kind relief?

Can I see a falling tear,
And not feel my sorrow's share?
Can a father see his child
Weep, nor be with sorrow fill'd?

Can a mother sit and hear
An infant groan, an infant fear?
No, no! Never can it be!
Never, never can it be! . . .

William Blake

I return now to Winnicott and his belief that the infant has no conception of what constitutes his own person and what does not. In this stage of absolute dependence, the infant so clearly exists in a state of oneness with his mother that he cannot distinguish between what is hers and what is his. The infant lives in a world of "undisturbed isolation" (1952b, p. 222) because the environment has not impinged upon him. When the environment responds accurately to his gestures, he has no need to be disturbed from his self-state. In this early stage, the infant believes he has created the world both inside and outside himself. His gestures are so adequately responded to by his mother that when the breast he hallucinates does indeed appear, he feels omnipotent. This Winnicott (1945) termed "a moment of *illusion*" (p. 152), the moment when the child creates the breast in synchronicity with his mother's ability to respond to his asking for it. In this moment, the baby experiences satisfaction from his own creation and enjoys his omnipotent power over the world. These omnipotent moments provide the baby with faith in himself and the world around him. In these moments, "the baby creates the object, but the object was there waiting to be created and to become a cathected object" (1971, p. 89). It is hoped that this "moment of illusion" becomes many moments, soon leading to what Winnicott terms the area of "potential space" (1971, p. 41). For Winnicott, the illusion that the child has created the breast that feeds him is a crucial developmental step, which occurs before the child's later disillusionment that in fact it is his mother who presents, and controls, the breast. This reality is left unchallenged by the mother, who agrees to share her infant's view of his omnipotence until, over time, he gradually forms a more realistic understanding of himself and the environment around him. Ogden (1986) also discusses this Winnicottian paradox, suggesting that perhaps the moment of illusion would be better described as the illusion of "invisible oneness" (p. 173). The illusion, he feels, is not of omnipotence but of need; the mother so well provides for her baby that the infant experiences no needs. Ogden does not answer the paradox of Winnicott's oneness/separateness dichotomy, however. "The mother must shield the infant from awareness of desire and separateness, *and* the mother must safeguard the infant's opportunity to experience desire and the accompanying knowledge of separateness" (p. 175).

Although I wholeheartedly agree with the idea of healthy infantile omnipotence, I think it originates in a different way. The breast does not just magically appear to the infant because he wished for it. Does not the infant convey his wish by some movement, be it his fingers groping toward the beloved object, his head turning and trying to "root," or his vigilant and loud crying? I suggest that the infant knows to search for the breast outside of himself *precisely* because he knows it is not his own; he knows that he must find it. He is certainly aware that an other is providing the breast for him, and what may be experienced subjectively as his omnipotence is that he has been able to *get that which he has wished for*. He has been heard—in essence, his prayers have been answered.

As to whether it is the infant who experiences the mother as a part object, or the mother who experiences herself that way, or even both, is hard to say. Stern (1985) states that the infant quickly learns to consolidate the human form into one being, a process developed by watching the many functions that his mother performs. She soon is integrated from separate functions into the same object that diapers, soothes, and cuddles. I can certainly recall the earliest days of breast-feeding my children, during which I felt that I was nothing more than a "big breast" for them; there were moments when I wondered if I meant anything more to them than the milk I carried.

In the Winnicottian schema, the baby then begins to expand what is termed the capacity to believe in others, simpatico with moments of illusion. Indeed, his relationship with his environment mother is predicated on the idea that she will be available and responsive to him. If she is, then the infant increases his ability to feel more stable and to believe in the world around him. If, however, the child experiences his mother as inconsistent and too often abandoning, he will experience his entire environment—indeed, all his object relations, both in his inner and external world—in a rejecting and unsoothing manner. Again, I would argue that the infant would have no need to believe in anyone but himself if the moment of illusion occurs as Winnicott has described. Over time, the infant's capacity to believe is expanded to encompass more and more moments of his life. Failures in maternal responsiveness can lead to a profound sense of distrust in both other objects and the larger world. The kind of psychic oxygen the infant comes to know is directly related to the kind of environmental mothering he has received. This experience is so profound that it often remains his frame of reference for experiencing the world as a whole. Winnicott feels that a child whose spontaneous gestures are not responded to is a child who comes to distrust his belief not only in the external world but also in himself. He loses faith in his own capacity to create his world and to have it respond as he would like. He also loses the capacity to believe in others, which greatly impacts his conceptualizations about the world and what he can expect from it for the rest of his life.

All the cases presented in this book describe individuals who have had tremendous distrust in themselves and in the world around them. There has never been anyone for them to believe in: moments of attunement, of receiving that which they asked for, have been all too rare. They have become hopeless, resigned to the fact that, as one of my patients put it, "God visits other people on my street, but He never comes to me." I recently received a phone call from a former patient, Mary, who periodically calls me to "touch base" and remain attached. I had treated her six years ago when she was hospitalized with a severe drug problem, serious depression, and a committed wish to die. I asked her what had inspired her commitment to recovery. She answered that she began to want recovery from the beginning of her hospital stay. She will never forget that, in the admission interview, a nurse began to cry as Mary told the sad facts of her life—for example, the sudden death of her newlywed husband and the diagnosis from doctors that she would never be able to conceive. Mary said that it was the first time she had felt that anyone "felt bad for me." She began to feel like living, because she experienced so many "caring staff members who were interested in me. When you think you don't have any value, and they see something in you, it makes a difference." She was a talented artist, and her art work was displayed in the hospital—she was being "paid attention to." I asked her why she remains in touch with me, to which she answered, "You helped me save my life. I am indebted to you. And besides, I call you so that you won't get discouraged with others who may not make it, so that you can feel good about your work." What also "saved" her was an unexpected pregnancy, which she conceived while hospitalized—not only contrary to medical prediction but obviously against hospital rules! Becoming pregnant signified that she had not been forsaken by God. Now married with two additional children, Mary said, "Some people keep using drugs, even when they have children, but I was determined not to do that to my kids. I had been given a gift, finally, and I wasn't going to damage that." I answered her with, "Well, I guess you knew what you needed more than I did." To which she replied, "Not me—God."

my mind mine

my mind mine
is ready for digging.
won't you come inside?

my mind mine
is open to giving its gems,
whether precious or no:
fool's gold—perhaps
silver—not likely, or
copper—too dull, unrefined.

for my mind mine
reaps only unfinished what you
with your tools can define

yet you, come inside, you with your unique You,
and dig out all here.
combine it, my alchemist,

to make it a sum of
my mind mine and yours.

Karen B. Gural

I am particularly drawn to Winnicott's (1971) area of *potential space*, which is a "third area of human living, one neither inside the individual nor outside in the world of shared reality" (p. 110). He conceptualized this space as follows:

> This intermediate living can be thought of as occupying a potential space, negating the idea of space and separation between the baby and the mother, and all development derives from this phenomenon. This potential space varies greatly from individual to individual, and its foundation is the baby's trust in the mother *experienced* over a long-enough period at the critical stage of the separation of the not-me from the me, when the establishment of an autonomous self is at the initial stage. [p. 110]

Winnicott believes this area exists because "with human beings, there can be no separation, only a threat of separation; and the threat is maximally or minimally traumatic according to the experience of the first separatings" (1971, p. 108).

The idea of potential space between mother and baby is rooted in the psychoanalytic concept of a fusion state in infancy. The space is actually a continuation, albeit an invisible one, of the intense connection between mother and child. The theoretical concept of potential space does not, however, answer the paradox of the untouchable true self and the fusion state of babyhood. The idea of potential space addresses the idealized notion of a continuous, merged relationship between mother and child, but it does not fully address the reality of their actual distinctions. Even in infancy, and perhaps even in utero, separation is an inherent self-state. The potential space that develops between mother and baby depends on their mutual interactions, on their combined efforts to bridge the separateness that underlies their relationship. For some, the space created is unsatisfying because it is too vacuous, whereas for others, the area is too smothering. The infant is boundaried, and from the beginning of his life has some idea that he is asking a larger, more powerful other to provide him the breast (and everything else) that he desires.

These days, mothers are told to allow "demand feeding," rather than scheduling the infant for four-hour feeds. Still, despite this recommendation, many mothers who attempt to breast feed are given contradictory advice from their pediatricians. I myself was told not to feed my daughter in less than two-hour blocks. But how can that be considered demand feeding? How does the infant experience those times when he cries for the breast and gets a pacifier instead? I soon ignored this advice because my daughter was insistent in her demands for more frequent nursings. But had I not done so, it would have been even harder for her to experience here what Winnicott sees as the moment of illusion, because even in those first few days the breast was not always given when she asked for it; she had some concept of boundaries between herself and the breast.

How often it happens in the very early months of a baby's life (and indeed, to some degree throughout childhood) that his mother is left to guess just what his cries mean at any given moment. Does he want to nurse? No? Does he want a new diaper? A change in position? Want to sleep? No? Too hot? Too cold? Too noisy? Some child experts believe that a mother can distinguish among four basic cries of her baby: the cries of pain, hunger, loneliness, or anger. I personally never found that to be the case, except for recognizing a cry of pain, which was always immediate, intense, and unrelenting. As for the other cries, I only knew that I needed to soothe my babies in some way—and quickly. I wanted to find out what they wanted as fast as possible so that I could limit their frustration and avoid creating in them the feeling of alienation, detachment, or disconnection. I recall these moments as being inordinately frustrating for me and at times feeling as though I had totally failed my babies because I was unable, as Winnicott suggests, to gratify them with the exact item they wanted on every occasion. Yes, on the whole I, like most parents, was able to provide for them what they wanted most of the time, but I know there inevitably were times, especially early on, when I could not. Their response was either to give up the asking or compromise for something else. For me, the magic never came from the perfect attunement of being a fused nursing couple. On the contrary, I was always awed at the way we worked together to understand their cries and at the way *they* helped *me* to bring to them what they wanted.

Stern (1985) provides a theoretical underpinning that is in consonance with my own mothering experience. At birth, the baby has what Stern terms an emergent self, which becomes more crystallized by the age of 2 months. Based on current clinical research, he makes the point that the infant doesn't know what he doesn't yet have. In other words, comparing an infant to a 1-year-old is not useful, so contrasting our self-conception with an infant's self-state is fallacious. However, it is amazing the kind of knowledge a young baby quickly attains. For example, an infant only days old can distinguish his own mother's milk from another's milk and at 3 weeks can distinguish among different shapes, moving his arms and legs in response to stimulation. Stern uses the term emergent self-state to indicate that the baby is continually learning and emerging into a more fully integrated being. Furthermore, the infant knows the difference between lying separately in his bassinet and being embraced in his mother's arms. He is not lulled into believing that he and the greater, external object are one.

Between 2 to 6 months, the baby organizes himself into what Stern called a *core self*, with four key self-experiences. In Stern's (1985) terms, these are self-agency, meaning a sense of control over one's actions; self-coherence, meaning a feeling of the self as a physical whole with boundaries; self-affectivity, meaning an experience of feelings; and self-history, meaning a sense of continuity with the past and past moments. The infant knows that a specific action, such as kicking at a mobile, was generated by his own foot. The infant can distinguish, at 3 months, a picture of his mother from that of other women and can differentiate sounds that are coming closer from those that are moving farther away. The infant knows how to smile, cry, and coo, indicating the ability to evoke different affective states. As further evidence of this self-experience, it has long been common knowledge that babies recognize, and respond to, the feeling states of their parents. So it is that parents who are arguing in front of their baby may soon find their child crying or wailing in affective tones that match their own emotional tenor. And fourth, indicating an ability to retain a self-history, babies have exceptionally good memories and will remember incidents, such as kicking the mobile, at a later date.

Stern (1985) goes on to write that "this sense of a core self is thus an experiential sense of events. It is normally taken completely for granted and operates outside of awareness. . . . Sense of self is not a cognitive construct. It is an experiential integration" (p. 71).

The Winnicottian area of potential space is an area infused with primitive creativity, which later extends to all cultural phenomena, such as the areas of "play and of artistic creativity and appreciation, and of religious feeling, and of dreaming, and also of fetishism, lying and stealing, the origin and loss of affectionate feeling, drug addiction, the talisman of obsessional rituals, etc." (1971, p. 5). Winnicott (1952b) believes that "we adults use the arts and religion for the off-moments which we all need in the course of reality-testing and reality-acceptance" (p. 224). It is a special space, in which the true self shines brightly, reflected into an other's bright light. Incorporating Stern's ideas, it can be a moment of oneness between mother and baby that is simultaneously a moment of connection between two very separate selves. Stern believes these moments occur fairly frequently between baby and mother, but similarly, he does not call them mergers because this implies a total fusion between self and other. Even an infant in the first six months of life experiences merger as "a way of being with someone [else]" (Stern 1985, p. 109). Stern explains that mergers

> are simply the actual experience of being with someone (a self-regulatory other) such that self-feelings are importantly changed. During the actual event, the core sense of self is not breached: the other is still perceived as a separate core other. . . . The self-experience is indeed dependent upon the presence and action of the other, but it still belongs entirely to the self. There is no distortion. The infant has accurately represented reality. [p. 105]

In the next year and a half, from 7 to 18 months, the child embarks upon the domain of what Stern termed *intersubjective relatedness*. Because the child for the most part is primarily preverbal during these years, the world that he shares moves in three spheres: sharing joint attention, sharing intentions, and sharing affective states. Stern proposes that intersubjective relatedness is a basic psychological need, going beyond the benefit of enhancing security and attachment. He views a continuum of opposite poles that spread between a sense of "cosmic psychic isolation, alienation, and aloneness . . . [to] the feeling of total psychic transparency" (p. 136). Indeed, I would agree, having witnessed so many patients with drug and alcohol problems who suffer greatly from being near either end of this pole.

The last domain, the last sense of self to be incorporated into the total self, is the acquisition of a verbal self. Stern (1985) views language acquisition as a sharing of mutually understood meanings.

> Every word learned is the by-product of uniting two mentalities in a common symbol system, a forging of shared meanings. With each

word, children solidify their mental commonality with the parent and later with the other members of the language culture, when they discover that their personal experiential knowledge is part of a larger experience of knowledge, that they are unified with others in a common culture base. [p. 172]

Teaching language to a child is indeed a mutual process. Each new word or phrase is a result of merger, of a moment of mutual understanding and oneness. Very often, in fact, it is the mother who must bend herself and become a subjective object in order to communicate with her child. Mothers must do so because children first begin to speak by using their own idiosyncratic process, by symbolizing more familiar words and easily pronounced phrases for more difficult expresssions. Instead of saying car, the child says "toot toot"; instead of saying rabbit, the child says "hop hop." These idiosyncratic words are understood by mother and left to develop, in due time, to the more standard language. In the meantime, mother is expected to serve as translator. Even between herself and her toddler, she repeats what he has just said to reassure them both that she has understood. When another person is added to their conversation, she will inevitably translate all the words that are simply her own child's adorable "secret" language and give the correct rendition. A potential space develops in the language acquisition process as both mother and child creatively mold joint understandings.

A child's vocabulary is based primarily on his parent's choice of words, as well as his total environment. One child learns the language of anger, whereas another is taught the silence of emotional secrecy. One child is taught how lovable he is, being told continually "I love you" or "I am so proud of you," whereas another child hears only criticisms. One child may be told he is a "darling" and a "sweetie," whereas another hears only "jerk," "little beast," or worse. The language a child hears is fused into his being; it codifies his experience. Stern makes the point that language is inevitably imperfect, that whereas one word explains, another limits. A "beautiful" sunset does not describe the detailed hues, the sparkling ocean, the red ball of fire. How incomplete the experience if the acquisition of language is limited, emotionless, or cruel. Because psychotherapy is a verbal process, part of the work itself is to increase the patient's development of a more expressive and complete language. So many patients come to treatment without the language of anger, love, or sadness. This seems to be especially true of alcoholics and drug addicts, who need to be taught the experiential degrees of feelings. Primarily, they have a limited vocabulary and cannot verbalize the distinctions between irritation and frustration, anger and rage, or even dislike and hatred. For many, the minute they have experienced irritation, they swing into rage (which no doubt they learned from their parents).

Psychotherapists must be ever cognizant of the fact that the language of emotions is one we know well but one that our patients may not, especially since it is primarily through language that an area of psychotherapeutic space develops. It often happens, for example, that a patient who has become highly affected by or involved in his therapy begins to imitate certain key phrases of mine or certain inflections reminiscent of my voice. Sometimes in reverse, I have found myself incorporating specific words or phrases that are characteristic of certain patients. This incorporative process indicates to me that language, like all other aspects of relationships, is influential, in flux, and capable of being affected by merger moments.

Stern feels that the inevitable misunderstandings of the mother do not bring about ruptures of the infant's sense of parental omniscience. On the contrary, the child does not have the expectation that his mother should know his inner thoughts because, Stern feels, the baby understands that the two of them are separate beings. Misunderstandings simply motivate the child to learn more and to speak better. Although I agree that misunderstandings serve to stimulate increased language development, I feel it necessary to underscore how *frustrating* these momentary lapses in understanding can be, for both mother and toddler. The child, feeling he has adequately communicated his wish, is crestfallen by the realization that he has not been understood. Although he tries again and again, he may be unable in each instance to communicate his internal thought. In the process of language development, he is a long-standing beginner. Even as he begins to control his mouth and tongue muscles, he still needs more practice until he is understood. This process can add to a sense of isolation, alienation, or detachment. Furthermore, a child who has many caregivers (i.e., day care during the day, parents at night) has to *start all over again* so that the idiosyncratic nature of his beginning speech is understood. There is no consistent translator to bridge the lingual gap. And that, again, is not only frustrating but it can also lead to a pervasive sense of aloneness. An expressive passage from Wolfe's *Look Homeward, Angel* (1929) details the alienation he felt as a child when caught between the preverbal and verbal world.

He was in agony because he was poverty-stricken in symbols: his mind was caught in a net because he had no words to work with. He had not even names for the objects around him: he probably defined them for himself by some jargon, reinforced by some mangling of the speech that roared about him, to which he listened intently day after day, realizing that his first escape must come through language. He indicated as quickly as he could his ravenous hunger for pictures and print: sometimes they brought him great books profusely illustrated, and he bribed them desperately by cooing, shrieking with delight, making extravagant faces, and doing all the other things they understood in him. . . . The situation was at once profoundly annoying and comic: as he sat in the middle of the floor and watched them enter, seeing the face of each transformed by a foolish leer, and hearing their voices become absurd and sentimental whenever they addressed him, speaking to him words which he did not yet understand, but which he saw they were mangling in the preposterous hope of rendering intelligible that which has been previously mutilated, he had to laugh at the fools, in spite of his vexation.
.... [He crawled to a pile of alphabet blocks.] Holding them clumsily in his tiny hands, he studied for hours the symbols of speech, knowing that he had here the stones of the temple of language, and striving desperately to find the key that would draw order and intelligence from this anarchy. . . .

I find the Winnicottian area of illusion, an almost felt space between two people who are intertwined inside one relationship, an extraordinarily compelling vision. Considering the view that separateness coexists with oneness, however, I am suggesting a revision in the form and purpose of the transitional realm. In reverse, the area of illusion still exists as beautifully and poetically as Winnicott had imagined, but with a different psychoanalytic mission. In order to detail this different mission, we must first review the theory of transitional objects and space.

Winnicott (1971) views the transitional process as the "infant's journey from the purely subjective to objectivity" (p. 6), a process that involves his growing ability to discriminate between objects that can be and cannot be placed under his omnipotent control. This process is achieved through the child's gradual disillusionment in his own powers as he moves from a stage of object relating to object usage. In the first stage, the child views others as subjective objects, meaning objects under his control. He gradually moves into object usage, in which objects become separated and differentiated from his being, a process achieved by his realization of those objects that are truly outside of his omnipotent control. The child learns the difference by attempting to destroy most of the objects around him: those that survive cause him to realize that they are not controlled by him, as described by Winnicott (1971): "The subject says to the object: 'I destroyed you,' and the object is there to receive the communication. From now on the subject says: 'Hullo object!' 'I destroyed you.' 'I love you.' 'You have value for me because of your survival of my destruction of you.' 'While I am loving you I am all the time destroying you in (unconscious) *fantasy*'" (p. 90).

Important to this stage is the child's development of transitional objects, which are objects that serve to bridge his subjective experience with objective reality. These objects are the child's first "not-me" possessions, meaning objects that exist both under his control while also being separate, rather than merged, into him. Winnicott believes that the transitional object symbolizes the breast, which is the object of the first relationship. As with the breast, the object is seen as controllable through magical thinking, although later it can be manipulated through physical means. The milk in the breast is taken internally, and yet the breast itself remains external to the infant. Thus, the breast is itself part of the transitional realm because it stays both inside and outside the infant's self.

I would like to revisit the concept of the transitional object from another perspective. We begin with the very different assumption that the baby starts life in an emergent state of being and that he knows he is boundaried by his skin. He therefore knows that the breast is not his, but his mother's. If 3-week-old conjoined twins know the difference between sucking their own and their sister's hand, then a baby knows he is sucking a foreign object that belongs to the big, and it is hoped, loving, body that smells so good and holds him so protectively. He drinks in the milk and then, and only then, does it become his own. The breast and its milk belong to his mother. It is when she allows herself to become a subjective object, *under his control*, that he is granted what I am calling an *immersive moment*: a moment of connection, when two separate beings merge into a space of oneness.

I am suggesting a change in the term and definition of transitional object. For Winnicott, the transitional object is an object that helps the child separate *away* from mother. It is an object that the child picks, but one that is supported and loved by mother as well. I would like to offer the term *immersive object*, because such an object also serves to keep the child *close to* mother, to keep him intimately connected to her while she is gone. Bowlby also suggests a change in the term so as to indicate that the attachment process is still continuing, albeit without mother's physical presence. He prefers the term *substitute object*, because the inanimate object is a substitute sought out because of the mother's absence. He (1969) notes that "a much more parsimonious way of looking at the role of these inanimate objects is to regard them simply as objects towards which certan components of attachment behaviour come to be directed or redirected because the 'natural' object is unavailable. Instead of the breast, non-nutritive sucking is directed to a . . . blanket or cuddly toy" (p. 312).

The importance of these objects is to keep the child from feeling overwhelmed by a sense of aloneness, separateness, and alienation. Indeed, if the child felt, as the general psychoanalytic perspective has argued, that he and mother were already merged, then these objects would not be needed.

I agree that these transitional possessions are used as substitutions for the real thing, but, like Fairbairn, Bowlby and others, I am cautioning against the societal insistence that infants quickly seek such substitutions for mother. This cultural norm stresses the importance of the child quickly developing self-soothing techniques, which serve to shift the baby's primary attachment from mother to his tiny self. However, these replacements for mother can actually lead to a lifetime of separateness and can increase the individual's sense of detachment. One of the most important functions of mothering is to become the object of attachment for her child so that he places primary importance on human relationships and not on inanimate objects. The mother helps build her child's foundation for a lifetime of attachment between the infant and the world of human relationships. It is somewhat surprising to read that Bowlby (1969) does not feel that a substitute object, such as the pacifier or blanket, necessarily "bodes ill for a child"(p. 310), particularly if used in conjunction with satisfying relationships. He goes on to say, however, that "presumably it would be possible for the whole of a child's attachment behavior to be directed towards an inanimate object and none towards a person. Such a condition, were it to last any time, would almost certainly be inimical to future mental health" (p. 311). Bowlby does not specify at what point the pacifier or blanket becomes a primary attachment object. I would caution that parents very often shift their babies too early to these inanimate substitutes because of cultural sanctions and that the importance of what Bowlby terms "non-nutritive" sucking has been underestimated. In fact, he seems to have made a cultural accommodation to prevailing social customs that rely on pacifiers and blankets in his downplaying of "non-nutritive" sucking. Whereas at many other points he uses examples of primitive societies and of primates to strengthen his theoretical ideas, in the case of "non-nutritive" sucking he uncharacteristically sanctions the tremendous difference between Western norms, other cultures, and primate behavior. Bowlby (1969) notes that

> in the simplest societies, in which an infant may spend most of the 24 hours in contact with his mother, non-nutritive sucking and also clinging are directed toward the mother's body, as they are in all species of non-human primates. In other societies, on the other hand, including our own, non-nutritive sucking may come during the early weeks of life to be directed toward a dummy or a thumb. [p. 309]

To downplay non-nutritive sucking is to misunderstand the dynamics of nursing. First, nursing keeps the mother close at hand, furthering the mutual attachment process—she cannot leave her baby if the baby is continually sucking on her breasts. And second, the non-nutritive sucking stimulates hormonal activity in the brain to increase the milk supply; it is therefore nutritive! From the infant's perspective, the act of sucking is a positive reinforcer, because even when milk does not appear immediately, the baby learns quite quickly that the more he continues to suck, the more the milk will flow. How very different, then, is this sucking on the breast from sucking on a pacifier. There is no response from a pacifier because the milk can never appear; sucking on the pacifier is non-productive and non-relational.

Why is there an intersection among sucking, continued physical contact, and increased milk? Perhaps because these long, extended nursing periods are important to both mother and baby. For the mother, it has been shown that nursing increases hormones that actually provide additional loving, caring feelings for her newborn. As well, the extended sessions help her become accustomed to her new role as subjective object without sacrificing her self but rather willingly sacrificing self-needs for the tiny, helpless other. For the baby, these periods provide comfort from his more usual self-state of separation. In these moments he receives both physical and emotional comfort.

Why, then, is it that mothers are routinely advised to get the baby to adjust to pacifiers or to using his thumb? Unfortunately, because in our society, the child must not be made to be *too dependent* on mother, so that the child can learn, early on, to soothe himself. In our society where mothers all too frequently must return to work, where day care is provided for babies 2 weeks old, children must learn quickly to cope with their separateness. They must not become overly attached, because there is little room in our culture for a primary attachment to just *one* more powerful other.

These two chapters have revisited the mother–infant relationship. I have presented the idea that the opposite of attachment is detachment, not separation, an idea similar to what Surrey (1983) terms *relational-detachment*. We are not merged at birth, attempting to "hatch" from symbiotic union into a forever blissful state of self-reliance. The baby begins life in a separated self-state, but with the knowledge that he is not alone. Even the fetus is both separate and connected to his mother. There is no total state of fusion in which the baby believes he and mother are one, just as there is no completed state of individuation. Those who attempt total separateness are those who have become detached, alienated beings. The yin-yang[2] of humanity is not separation-individuation but attachment-separateness. For too long, we have focused on the maleness of separateness, with the result that we have skewed the harmony of humanity. We need to encourage the femininity of attachment so that our patients, our children, and our society can become whole.

---

2. Yin–yang is the Eastern concept of balance. In this view the world is comprised of complementary forces or principles that cannot be separated: both exist simultaneously. For example, yin contains all the feminine, the earth, and darkness, whereas yang is made up of maleness, heaven, and light. The two are believed to proceed from the Supreme Ultimate, and as one increases the other decreases. Yin–yang is believed to be the accurate description of the processes of the universe.

4

THE IMMERSIVE MOMENT

Loving does not at first mean merging, surrendering, and uniting with another person (for what would a union be of two people who are unclarified, unfinished, and still incoherent—?), it is a high inducement for the individual to ripen, to become something in himself, to become world, to become world in himself for the sake of another person. . . . This advance (at first very much against the will of the outdistanced men) will transform the love experience, which is now filled with error, will change it from the ground up, and reshape it into a relationship that is meant to be between one human being and another. . . . And this more human love (which will fulfill itself with infinite consideration and gentleness, and kindness and clarity in binding and releasing) will resemble what we are now preparing painfully and with great struggle: the love that consists in this: that two solitudes protect and border and greet each other.

Rainer Maria Rilke, *Letters to a Young Poet*

THE AFFECTIVE EXPERIENCE of igniting an empathic connection between two separate beings is the magic of love, the holiness of spirituality, and the miracle of humanity. That two beings, separated by a lifetime of unique experiences, can "feel themselves into the other" is truly extraordinary. A 1960s *Star Trek* television episode comes to mind, in which Captain Kirk, dangerously hurt in battle, is restored by the touch of an empathic healer. She puts her hand over his many wounds and absorbs each one into her self. She winces as she takes them in. Using her powers of healing, she is then able to erase these injuries from her own body. (It is interesting to note that the word *heal* derives from the Anglo-Saxon *haelan*, meaning to make whole.)

Moments of oneness often begin in the ordinary moments of everyday life. The distinguishing feature of such moments is that both individuals feel a completed communication of understanding, that they have joined together past their separateness. This is not to suggest that both individuals have become intertwined to form a completed understanding of the other, but rather that at least *one* aspect of at least *one* of them is now fully understood. In psychotherapy, it is the therapist who engages his empathic abilities[1] to understand the patient. The patient is not, for the most part, delving into the mind and heart of the analyst. In this moment of understanding, the area of "potential space" between them enlarges. I prefer the term *area of immersion*, because space implies distance. The area of immersion is created through moments of oneness that are important to deepening the sense of connectedness and closeness between two people, such as the patient and therapist.

Bollas (1987) uses the term *aesthetic moment* for what I call moments of oneness. I am suggesting the shift in nomenclature because the experience is one that brings people closer together into a more immersive, connected feeling-state. These moments can occur whenever the individual feels a "deep subjective rapport with an object" (Bollas 1987, p. 16) that re-evokes an early, infantile feeling-state. This experience can occur in any kind of object relationship, including such activities as listening to poetry or opera or viewing a beautiful landscape. Bollas ties the aesthetic moment to the transformational processes of infant and mother. Her style

---

1. According to the Moore and Fine (1990) definition of empathy, it "is an essential prerequisite for the practice of psychoanalysis. In the analytic situation empathy derives in part from the analyst's evenly suspended attention and the developed autonomy that is part of his or her work ego. Analysts do not view empathy as a mystical or transcendent experience. . . . Empathy, therefore, is a temporary, partial ego regression in the service of the analytic process" (p. 67). Perhaps analysts do not experience every empathic moment as particularly mystical. But the patient, who may have *never* felt understood or connected to an other, usually does. In fact, the general public's view that analysts read minds relates to the empathic and interpretive aspect of the analytic process. It is *exactly* this affective connection that makes empathy so powerful. The therapist may also feel a deepening oneness with his patient. Is this mystical or transcendent? Not in the sense that it comes from a kind of magical outer body experience. Yet it is mystical and transcendent in the sense that it is a moving experience for patient and therapist, that it literally *moves* them closer in intimate understanding.

of caring for her child and his perception of her nurturance form perhaps the first experience of the human aesthetic: "[This] is the most profound occasion when the nature of the self is formed and transformed by the environment. The uncanny pleasure of being held by . . . any object rests on those moments when the infant's internal world is partly given form by the mother since he cannot shape them or link them together without her coverage" (Bollas 1987, p. 32).

Thus, the merging experience is more than a matter of feeling held and safe. It is a moment of transformation, an occurrence of change. While I was vacationing in Hawaii, for example, a most unexpected aesthetic moment, or moment of oneness, occurred. We were on the beach at sunset, and like many other tourists, we were simply watching the glorious orange fireball descend through the clouds. It was a magnificent sunset, with sparkling rays splintering out of the sky, a golden reflection shining on the ocean below. To have been inspired by the beauty of nature was soul-satisfying enough. But then a most amazing moment occurred. Someone, somewhere, or maybe it was everyone everywhere, at the same moment, began to clap. And suddenly, all the way up and down the beach, the tourists, the children, and the locals clapped in awe of this beauty. We were swept away by an immersive moment, a moment when our separated lives were intertwined by the spectacular sky. The moment passed, the sun sank below the ocean's end, and the oneness was gone. Couples, families, and residents walked on down the beach, returned to our separated lives.

A leaf, a sunbeam, a landscape, the ocean, make an analogous impression on the mind. What is common to them all—that perfectness and harmony, is beauty. The standard of beauty is the entire circuit of natural forms, the totality of nature; which the Italians expressed by defining beauty ["the many in one"]. Nothing is quite beautiful alone; nothing but is beautiful in the whole. A single object is only so far beautiful as it suggests this universal grace. The poet, the painter, the sculptor, the musician, the architect, seek each to concentrate this radiance of the world on one point, and each in his several work to satisfy the love of beauty which stimulates him to produce.

Ralph Waldo Emerson, *Nature*

Lemkow (1990), in her book entitled *The Wholeness Principle*, con-
ceptualizes a "drive" toward unity or wholeness. She believes, as do I, that
the twentieth century has focused almost to exclusion on our separateness
and individuality rather than on our unity. She makes the point that a
shift back to unity has recently begun. There is an "obvious interdependence and interaction of peoples, and of our physical, ecological, social,
moral (human rights, for example), economic, security, and other conditions" (pp. 158–159). She sees the drive toward unity as a new philosophy
that is beginning to impact the natural sciences as well as the general
public. She notes that there is a "present reorientation of science revolving
about the problems of wholes and wholeness, whereby science is, for
instance, increasingly substituting organic models for mechanical models,
and shifting from structure-oriented to process-oriented thinking" (p. xiv).

She quotes passages from other scientists and philosophers to demonstrate her concept of wholeness. From Arthur Koestler, in his 1973
book entitled *The Roots of Coincidence*, she quotes:

> In the growing embryo, successive generations of cells branch out
> into diversified tissues, which eventually become integrated into
> organs. Every organ has the dual character of being a subordinate
> part and at the same time an autonomous whole. . . . The individual
> self is an organic whole, but at the same time a part of his family or
> tribe. Each social group has again the characteristics of a coherent
> whole but also of a dependent part within the community or
> nation. . . . The Principle of Complementarity [I believe he is refer-
> ring to the yin–yang principle] ascribes to subatomic entities a dual
> nature. [p. 107]

In the following passage Lemkow writes in a vein similar to my own
perspective, which is that moments of oneness are often found in the
ordinary interweavings of our daily lives. Similarly, her thoughts are
reminiscent of Bollas's aesthetic moments. She writes that "the experience
of unity" can occur in many settings, from being with a loved one to
enjoying nature, a painting, a poem, a play, or music.

> Before a beautiful landscape, for example, one may suddenly, spon-
> taneously, feel *it* to be a unity, and invariably this is accompanied,
> consciously or unconsciously, by a feeling of *oneness* becoming *whole*

and *at one* with nature. The landscape naturally comprises a myriad components, such as numerous trees and shrubs, perhaps some animals, perhaps man-made structures, certainly the varying contours and textures of the land, the configurations of color and pattern of land, sky and water. Yet all these meld into a unity that includes the experiencer. And as we well know, this is invariably refreshing, even bliss-making. [p. 217]

Indeed, some individuals are able to feel a powerful union with nature in an intensity they do not experience with other human beings. James, mentioned in Chapter 1, is one such person who has found that connections within the natural world are more easily accessible and less painful than seeking oneness in a loving other. Similarly, many detached individuals find nature a particularly powerful healer, as do many alcoholics and drug addicts. In fact, it is a useful technique to encourage recovering patients to explore, enjoy, and experience the natural beauty of the world. One patient, for example, became an avid skier, hiker, surfer, and biker. After many years of recovery, he even took an extended trip into the Grand Canyon as part of a "spiritual quest" (his words). Inside the vast canyon, he found a sense of oneness he had not experienced throughout his many years of sobriety. Associations to Balint's basic fault apply in this case, although the canyon's beauty helped heal his internal void.

> To see a world in a grain of sand
> And a Heaven in a wild flower,
> Hold Infinity in the palm of your hand
> And Eternity in an hour.
>
> William Blake, *Auguries of Innocence*

Love, as the song says, is a many-splendored thing. Although this book is not a detailed analysis of the condition of being in love or of loving, it seems clear that one emotional aspect of love is the intensity of feeling totally and completely understood. The affective component to feeling understood is the immersive feeling-state, a feeling in which the separated self is joined by an other.

As it is my intention to present not only the theoretical concept of immersive moments but also to evoke the affective experience that always accompanies these moments, I have incorporated various poems to help convey the power of immersion. Matthew Arnold's poem "The Buried Life" describes the struggle, even between lovers, of reaching the inner hidden core of each self. Presented below is an excerpted passage from his poem, written more than 100 years ago.

> Alas! is even love too weak
> To unlock the heart, and let it speak?
> Are even lovers powerless to reveal
> To one another what indeed they feel?
> I knew the mass of men concealed
> Their thoughts, for fear that if revealed
> They would by other men be met
> With blank indifference, or with blame reproved;
> I knew they lived and moved
> Tricked in disguises, alien to the rest
> Of men, and alien to themselves—and yet
> The same heart beats in every human breast!
>
> But we, my love!—doth a like spell benumb
> Our hearts, our voices?—must we too be dumb?
>
> Ah! well for us, if even we,
> Even for a moment, can get free
> Our heart, and have our lips unchained;
> For that which seals them hath been deep-ordained! . . .
>
> And long we try in vain to speak and act
> Our hidden self, and what we say and do
> Is eloquent, is well—but 'tis not true! . . .
>
> Only—but this is rare—
> When a belovèd hand is laid in ours,
> When, jaded with the rush and glare
> Of the interminable hours,
> Our eyes can in another's eyes read clear,

When our world-deafened ear
Is by the tones of a loved voice caressed—
A bolt is shot back somewhere in our breast,
And a lost pulse of feeling stirs again.

I have always been surprised at the scarcity of psychoanalytic literature dealing with countertransferential feelings of love. It has generally been agreed that patients will fall in love, transferentially speaking, with their analyst. But rarely in analytic literature has the analyst discussed his own attachment, his own intimate feelings, toward his patients. Peck (1978) writes that psychotherapists seem to be "embarrassed" by the subject of love. He attributes the psychoanalytic community's difficulty with this emotion to two main factors. First, he points to the confusion in society between romantic and genuine love, which brings confusion to the psychotherapy office as well. He also believes that the emphasis of the psychoanalytic community on being seen as a scientific methodology, complete with all the rigors of measurable objectives, leaves the affect of love outside the treatment setting. Weinstein, in Lasky and Silverman's book Love (1988), has also written about the exclusion of love from the psychoanalytic literature. He quotes Tauber as writing: "I have thought for a long time that what strongly blocks us is a profound unease in dealing with love, affection and tenderness in our work; we have acknowledged the need to deal with anxiety, hate, rage, etc. but are unclear about and evasive with love, affection and tenderness" (p. 192).

In the same source (1988), Freud is quoted by Marie Bonaparte as saying, "One must never love one's patients. Whenever I thought I did, the analysis suffered terribly from it. One ought to remain completely cool" (p. 193). As Weinstein points out, "This type of thinking led to the consequent conceptualization of the neutral, accepting, and relatively unresponsive analyst" (p. 193).

In the practice of psychotherapy, particularly when treating detached and addicted individuals, however, it is particularly important to analyze the loving emotions that surface in the stirring of the immersive process. These patients are people who have never been taught to feel; these are people who have never felt wanted and loved. A therapist who remains neutral is essentially repeating the "sins" of the patient's past; active involvement is necessary to keep the patient interested and to help him feel alive. The female patient I described in Chapter 3, who continues to keep in touch with me despite the completion of her therapy many years previously, had explained that it helped her to think of me, to imagine what I might tell her in moments of distress. I had asked her if she kept in touch with another therapist who had also been instrumental earlier in her recovery. She said, "No, because he never returned my calls or letters. I once went to a reunion at the hospital because he had promised to be there; he didn't show up. That really angered me. I remember him telling me once that 'only the ones in trouble call back.'" This therapist had conveyed the prevailing concept that separation is maturity and connection is immaturity. This patient and I talk together probably no more than two or three times a year, and yet she has derived a great deal of comfort from her internalized relationship with me. She could tell herself to "stay straight," for example, and get through a strong drug urge by imagining her next conversation with me in which she could say, "It's now been seven years." To be told by her other therapist that keeping in touch could only mean that she was having difficulty impresses upon her the view that self-reliance is the key to success. And that is a reincarnation of what her parents had always insisted upon.

A second example comes to mind. A cocaine addict whom I had treated for several months in the hospital had remained in contact with me after his discharge. In our last conversation, he seemed to be in greater distress than in our previous phone contact. I had a sense, in fact, that he was struggling with intense urges that might indeed overwhelm him. When, after several weeks, he had not called to check in with me again, I decided to contact him instead. He was very moved by this gesture, this act of concern. I remember him saying, "You were thinking of me? With all those patients to be involved with, and you were worried about me? I can't believe it—you still care about me." The truth was that he had begun to use drugs again, but my phone call—my reconnection to him—was experienced by him as so powerful that he admitted to the relapse, asked for rehospitalization, and has been sober for the past eight years. Every year, on the anniversary of another year of sobriety, he calls to tell me about his past year, and he often recalls that the time I called him had changed the way he viewed himself. He was a person to be cared about; he was a person who had impacted an other's life.

Peck writes (1978) that "it is essential for the therapist to love a patient for the therapy to be successful, and if the therapy does become successful, then the therapeutic relationship will become a mutually loving one. . . . If the psychotherapist cannot genuinely love a patient, genuine healing will not occur" (p. 175). Weinstein, in Lasky and Silverman (1988), refers to Spotnitz (1985) as saying that "to give too little of any kind of feeling because the analyst has too much is a technical error [and quotes him]: 'The patient is entitled to whatever feelings – positive or negative – are needed to resolve his resistance to mature functioning. . . . These feelings should be a source, and tool, of communication'" (p. 193).

It is my wish to make connections – intimate, immersive, and powerful – with patients, to develop an affective bond in which the dynamic interpretations can be made most safely. To stay silent, to respond only intellectually, keeps the psychoanalytic dyad from creating that powerful immersive arena. As Seinfeld (1991) states, "I understand love to mean that the therapist reaches the inner self of the patient, causing him to feel cared for and valued in his own right" (p. 207). It is the affective component of a psychoanalytic interpretation that embraces the patient, not the intellectual communication. Zuckerberg, in Lasky and Silverman (1988), puts it this way: "In loving our patients, I believe we are healing. Therapeutic cure rests on a unique human connection, one that is accurately empathic, accepting, and reliable" (p. 157).

Lifting merger out of the prevailing view that it is an infantile, phase-specific phenomenon may help clinicians free themselves to explore more fully the affective experience of feeling themselves into the other. For example, although much of M. Scott Peck's book *The Road Less Traveled* is relevant to my thoughts on oneness, he also holds to the theoretical position that merger is the essence of infantile experiencing. He stresses the difference between romantic love, in which two people are regressively merged into one, and genuine love, in which two mature individuals are separated but are one. He believes that the self must become boundaried before it can transcend itself in a non-pathological way. What I am suggesting is the exact reverse: the self is boundaried from the beginning and it is only in ongoing fusion experiences that healthy separateness can exist. Freeing merger from the chains of infantilism may release the immersive process and deepen the clinical work. Clinicians, like their patients, may find it a mystical, and loving, connection.

>>> The face of all the world is changed, I think,
>>> Since first I heard the footsteps of thy soul
>>> Move still, oh, still, beside me, as they stole
>>> Betwixt me and the dreadful outer brink
>>> Of obvious death, where I, who thought to sink,

Was caught up into love, and taught the whole
Of life in a new rhythm.

Elizabeth Barrett Browning, *Sonnets from the Portuguese*

Love is frequently experienced as a salvation for each partner. Freud views this conception as an idealization, meaning an unrealistic evaluation of an other. It may very well be that the initial idealization of a lover turns out to be an overevaluation, a euphemistic hopefulness, but there may be aspects of one's lover that are realistically worthy of admiration. Part of the transformative experience lies in the power of immersive moments. In these moments, the individual does indeed feel transformed, enhanced by the other. Bollas (1987) proposes that the individual searches for transformational objects and transformational moments throughout his life. In adult life, fusion is sought "not to possess the object; rather, the object is pursued in order to surrender to it as a medium that alters the self, where the subject-as-supplicant now feels himself to be the recipient of envirosomatic caring, identified with metamorphoses of the self" (p. 14).

For Bollas, the importance of the aesthetic moment is its ability to change the subject through a process similar to and hearkening back to the early maternal–infant dyad. He makes an important point: we are programmed, as it were, to expect an other to save us, to bring us relief, comfort, and protection. And these expectations of others do not die in infancy, but remain part of our everyday life: "I think we have failed to take notice of the phenomenon in adult life of the wide-ranging collective search for an object that is identified with the metamorphosis of the self" (pp. 15–16).

Infants idealize their mothers in a realistic way, as well as in an overesteemed manner. They idealize her walking, her talking, her feeding. When they themselves can do all of these things, then they no longer need to idealize these aspects, but instead can idealize something else in her. Older children idealize other aspects of their parents, and adolescents idealize teachers, peers, and celebrities. It is not necessarily the case that these idealizations are "unrealistic": a teacher may indeed be worthy of admiration; a basketball star is indeed talented and has an enviable lifestyle. The unrealistic aspect of idealization comes into play when the entire person is considered in an overesteemed way, rather than just the particular quality that is so highly admirable. In some cases, these individuals may very well have estimable qualities, but the entire person has, certainly, his own human flaws. An artist or musician, for example, has talent that is certainly enviable. A lover who is competent in areas uncomfortable for the other can also be realistically idealized. Eigen (1981) believes that, whereas Freud viewed idealization as pathological and defensive because it is "unrealistic," he himself feels that "ideal moments of a dual union may be regenerative and not primarily defensive. Undefensive and defensive use of ideal states completely intermingle in actual living" (p. 430).

The poem "Mirror" well describes the idealization process inherent in a loving relationship and exemplifies that admiration can be inspiring rather than destructive.

> Love is the mirror
> Whose shimmering light, gently diffused,
> Reflects the loved one's image,
> Hiding imperfections. Sharp angles
> Melt to curves; the stature heightens
> Within this temperate glow.
>
> This magic lens encompasses
> Not only form and face
> But marks the living soul
> Within its ardent sphere,
> Transfiguring at subtle pace
> Homeliness to queenly grace,
> Commoner to peer.
>
> Center this bright mirror
> To glimpse inherent good.
> But should some human frailties
> Obscure the pleasant view,
> Then let Love be the optic beam
> To hold the focus true.
>
> Nan G. Rody

A therapist, too, can be idealized without this idealization being attributed to a defense against devaluation. The therapist offers the patient insights, observations, and suggestions that the patient has been unable to attain on his own. This is not an unrealistic evaluation: therapists are trained to empathically attune to others, to analyze dynamic conflicts, and to provide ego supportive anchoring. I well remember one patient's description of our empathic oneness. In response to an analytic interpretation, she often felt a strange sensation overcome her entire body. The feeling would start first in the back of her head, and then move down her neck and spine, traveling out of her body through her arms and legs.

> It's a feeling of bricks tumbling down. I can't really explain it, but it feels as though part of my brain, which has been rigidly segmented, has been freed; part of the wall has come down, and I feel relieved, lightheaded, and opened up. Then it travels down into my body, and I feel a kind of chill, a tingling sensation sort of like the bricks keep falling down throughout my body. It always happens when you tell me something that makes me feel you truly understand me, that you are saying things to me that I never dared to voice myself but have always felt. It's an incredible sensation.

Indeed, the power of our affective connection caused a physical release of disconnection inside her; part of the walls of her inner detachment were melted away.

Psychotherapists are, for many patients, a transformational object. Since we have been trained to provide patients with the knowledge, affective stability, and insight to help them be transformed, it might be better to argue that, when we are no longer used in a transformational way, the therapy has either become stuck or is at the point of completion.

> The meeting of two personalities is like the contact of two chemical substances: if there is any reaction, both are transformed.
>
> Carl Jung, *Modern Man in Search of a Soul*

Out of my experience . . . one fixed conclusion dogmatically emerges . . . that we with our lives are like islands in the sea, or like trees in the forest. The maples and pines may whisper to each other with their leaves . . . . But the trees also commingle their roots in the darkness underground and the islands also hang together through the ocean's bottoms. Just so there is a continuum of cosmic consciousness against which our individuality builds but accidental fences, and in to [sic] which our several minds plunge as into a mother-sea or reservoir.

William James, *Memories and Studies*

Bollas (1987) places the aesthetic moment in a humanistic realm, although he offers the idea that these moments can "evoke in us a deep conviction that we have been in rapport with a sacred object" (p. 31). The reasons for this are twofold: one, because the moment is experienced as having been created by the object, and two, because these moments cannot be predicted or controlled. It is the very element of surprise—what he terms "uncanny"—that makes the object feel it is the "hand of fate." These elements are also at the root of the spiritual experience, whether felt in communion with nature, religion, or the arts. The outcome of the aesthetic moment is the immersive experience, which explains the power of prayer and faith.

Many individuals seek exactly what he describes—a transformative object—in their relationship with their God, their unique form of spirituality. I prefer to use the term *spirituality* rather than religiosity because spirituality does not connote any particular belief system or ritualistic ceremony. Rather, it conveys an underlying affective component that Freud terms "religious energy." This powerful feeling is at root a moment of oneness, in which the oceanic feeling of transcendence is experienced. In these moments of complete understanding[2] with an other, transcendence occurs: the individual has a feeling of being transformed and of being overcome by an other's presence. This feeling can occur while absorbing nature's beauty, feeling a divine presence, or imbibing a lover's essence. Indeed, the root of the word spirit is from the Latin *spiritus*, meaning breath, courage, vigor, and soul. It comes from the root *spirare*, meaning

---

2. Of interest, *Webster's Unabridged Dictionary* (1983) quotes the following passage from Job (32:8) as pertinent to the definition of *understanding*: "There is a spirit in man, and the inspiration of the Almighty giveth him understanding."

to breathe. To breathe in? Or out? The spiritual moment is one that occurs both inside and outside an individual's self-state. How similar this idea is to Balint's (1968) merger, in which he offers breathing as a perfect example of the "interpenetrating harmonious mix-up." Winnicott (1945), too, refers to spirituality and breathing in his conceptualization that "the subject of illusion is a very wide [area] that needs study; it will be found to provide the clue . . . to mysterious phenomena . . . . Somewhere here, too, is the interest in breath, which never decides whether it comes primarily from within or without, and which provides the basis for the conception of spirit, soul, anima" (p. 154). In an immersive moment, the individual has *gone beyond* his self to join with an other. The spirit, or breath, is taken in by the other as it is released from the self, and vice versa, the breath is taken back as it is released from the other.

Spirituality, like love, is another emotion rarely explored by psycho-analysts except to reiterate Freud's view. He writes about the dangers of religion in *The Future of an Illusion* (1927), in which he states that religious doctrines "are not precipitates of experience or end results of thought; they are illusions, fulfillments of the oldest, strongest, most urgent wishes of mankind; the secret of their strength is the strength of these wishes" (p. 30).

The French writer Romain Rolland wrote to Freud in response to this book, stating that he felt Freud had missed the point, that there is something about a particular religious feeling-state that is comforting. Freud discusses the major points of Rolland's letter in the beginning of his next book, *Civilization and Its Discontents* (1930). Referring to Rolland as "a friend whom I so much honour" (p. 12), Freud quotes Rolland's view that he was never without "a sensation of 'eternity,' a feeling as of something limitless, unbounded—as it were, 'oceanic' " (1930, p. 11).[3] Rolland be-lieves this feeling to be the source of "the religious energy" that is manipulated by religious institutions to inspire their worshipers to carry out the organization's needs and demands. In a sentence similar in thought to a passage written by Albert Einstein, quoted later in this chapter, Rolland states that "one may . . . rightly call oneself religious on

---

3. According to Masson (1980), Rolland came to the idea of the "oceanic feeling" while researching material for his biography of Ramakrishna, the nine-teenth-century Bengali saint. Ramakrishna, in turn, had been affected by older Sanskrit texts that tied spiritual experiences with the sea. (For example, one portion of a Sanskrit text reads "You are an infinite ocean. The universe is a wave.")

the ground of this oceanic feeling alone, even if one rejects every belief and every illusion" (p. 12).

Freud found himself struggling to analyze and understand the root of this feeling-state. He admits having never experienced this sensation, but "this gives me no right to deny that it does in fact occur in other people. The only question is whether it is being correctly interpreted and whether it ought to be regarded as the 'fons et origo' of the whole need for religion" (p. 12). Küng (1979) makes the important observation that Freud was an atheist *before* he developed psychoanalysis. It was not psychoanalysis, therefore, that shifted him away from religion; rather, his atheism was a background for psychoanalysis. Küng (1979) observes that "this too is what Freud constantly maintained, that psychoanalysis does not necessarily lead to atheism. It is a method of investigation and healing and can be practiced by both atheists and theists" (p. 75).

I discuss the oceanic feeling at this time to demonstrate just how deep is the bias in psychoanalysis against this feeling-state, as well as against religion. The fact that Freud states that he had rarely felt this sensation of a powerful connectedness to others and to the larger world around him is quite telling. (It is rather surprising as well—he seemed to have found temporary soul mates in various men—Fliess, Jung, and the like. Perhaps it was that he experienced discomfort in merger experiences.) Freud's stated inability to resonate with this feeling may provide additional clues about why he focused so little attention on the mother–infant relationship or why he so strongly dismissed the idea of ongoing, mature interdependence. Perhaps he, too, had had moments of normative abuse as a child, which had forced him into a position of omnipotent illusion. After all, he came to the idea of the oedipal complex in part through his own self-analysis, perhaps indicating a denial, or repression, of his own childhood powerlessness. In this context, Miller, in *Banished Knowledge* (1990), quotes a letter from Freud (*Complete Letters*, pp. 230–231) to Fliess in which he describes his father: "unfortunately, my own father was one of these perverts and is responsible for the hysteria of my brother (all of whose symptoms are identifications) and those of several younger sisters. The frequency of this circumstance often makes me wonder" (p. 55).

Freud (1930) concludes his analysis of the oceanic feeling with the acknowledgement that, indeed, this "sensation of eternity" does exist for many people. He speculates that "the part played by the 'oceanic feeling,' which might seek something like the restoration of limitless narcissism, is ousted from a place in the foreground. The origin of the religious attitude can be traced back in clear outlines as far as the feeling of infantile helplessness" (p. 20).

In connecting the oceanic feeling to religion, Freud attempts, as he had in *The Future of an Illusion*, to demonstrate the infantile nature of religion. Although most analysts have interpreted his material in this manner—thus the thrust for so long in psychoanalysis to ignore, debunk, or repudiate religious feelings—Freud's analysis of this feeling-state simply traces its origins to the beginning of life. He states that, although this feeling is simply a "shrunken residue of a much more inclusive—indeed, an all embracing feeling which corresponded to a more intimate bond" (Freud 1930, p. 16) between mother and infant, he also feels that some of this "ego-feeling" *may remain throughout life*. It may "exist . . . side by side with the narrower and more sharply demarcated ego-feeling of maturity . . . . In that case, the ideational contents appropriate to it would be precisely those of limitlessness and of a bond with the universe . . . the 'oceanic feeling' " (p. 16). Freud, therefore, admits that the oceanic feeling does not necessarily diminish with maturity, and that it is found during moments of intense love, in the bonding between mother and child, and in moments of religious devotion. Indeed, in a later passage in *Civilization and Its Discontents*, he refers to the sexual relationship of the faithful, marital couple as an indissoluble bond.

Like Rolland, Freud most objects to the tendency of religions to exploit this feeling-state, to tie the individual to the church rather than to let the individual evoke this feeling wherever he would like. W. Earl Biddle (1956), as cited in Gay (1987), reiterates this perspective. Biddle states that "when the truth in Freud's discoveries is brought to light it will be found that they do not conflict with religious principles. To the contrary, Freud discovered that man is by nature religious and that the concept of the Supreme Being is *experienced* in childhood" (p. 93).

What is important to convey here is that, despite Freud's own words that those with a certain "maturity" may also incur the oceanic feeling, many psychoanalysts have continually focused on what they view as the "infantile" nature of religion. Freud's opposition is primarily to the rituals, the dogma, and the ceremonial aspects of religion. Yet the authors of one psychoanalytic dictionary, Moore and Fine (1990), state that the term *oceanic feeling* was originally used

to describe an *alleged* mystical source of rich beneficent energy . . . .
Experiences of the oceanic feeling in adult life are manifestations of

extreme regression, typically following a sense of having been abandoned or of being threatened by abandonment. The experience resembles a neurotic symptom insofar as a defense against the threat of overwhelming aggression coexists with a gratification, that is, the illusion of narcissistic bliss. [p. 133, emphasis added]

It is time that psychoanalysts stop "view[ing] themselves as knights of modern science locked in noble combat with the destructive forces of ancient religious superstition and irrational but authoritarian dogma" (Peck 1978, p. 207). It is time that the oceanic feeling takes its place as one of the most powerful, evocative, and human of feelings. Rolland, in a 1931 letter to Freud, echoes this sentiment. He writes,

Since the appearance of my "oceanic works," letters have come forth from all corners of the earth (and also from your Austria), like a gushing of waters that had previously been dammed. . . . And that is why I believe that, in history and in action, one must always count on these invisible forces that act in secret when they are not made manifest by explosions in broad daylight . . . . It would be dangerous for the philosopher and the man of action to ignore them. [translated in Parsons 1993, p. 385]

Küng (1979) has argued that classical analysis released sexuality but repressed religiosity because the " 'personality' was totally dissolved into processes, the 'spirit' was scorned as a philosophical phenomenon" (p. 154). He "plead[s] not for a religious psychotherapy or a psychotherapy only for the religious, but rather for a therapy that takes the phenomenon of religion seriously as one of the specifically human forms of expression" (p. 155). It seems, unfortunately, that Freud's view has been so powerful that the majority of analysts have not challenged his perspective. The fact is that human beings are capable of experiencing the oceanic feeling, a feeling that is first felt in moments of oneness between mother and baby. In these moments, the infant has felt his separateness, asked for something *beyond his own meager abilities to obtain*, and is gratified by the other. Be it nursing, cuddling, diapering, or stimulating, he has discovered an other's powerful presence that responds, protects, and loves. This exchange is powerful and affects the child's sense of himself and the world around him throughout his life. "Seek and ye shall receive," says the Bible. If there is an other ready to give, then the child becomes faithful in all things.

Despite this psychoanalytic ban on spirituality, a few authors have been willing to write their thoughts about this powerful emotional experience. Guntrip (1961) believes that "we cannot simply equate religion with immaturity and science with maturity as Freud wished to do" (p. 383). Rather, he feels that, similar to Fairbairn's category of "mature dependence," there exists a category of religious devotion that he terms "mature religion[, which] would express man's fundamentally dependent nature, in a relationship of emotional rapport with and reverence for external reality as a whole, immediate and universal, symbolized in a meaningful philosophy of life" (p. 384). Rinsley (1988) explores the conversion process, noting that when an individual "claims that God, Jesus or the Holy Spirit 'came into' him . . . he is utilizing language that is strikingly similar to the technical jargon by which the psychoanalyst describes the process of introjection. . . . For it is indeed the 'inner Presence' that makes us human, no matter by what title we label it" (p. 5).

I would add that the ability of an individual to *take in* the "inner Presence" is in direct correlation to what Winnicott terms *the capacity to believe*. If an individual has had little success with moments of transformation throughout his life, his ability to do so with a God representation will also be minimal. So often, recovering patients are terrified of the incorporative process. One patient who did feel comfortable placing me "inside her heart" would nevertheless not allow members of Alcoholics Anonymous, friends, or her sponsor inside. "You are different—you aren't quite real," she would say in response to my questioning. Other patients much prefer experimenting with a new God representation rather than allowing me inside, because they feel in greater control with a less tangible presence (see Chapter 9, for a description of John).

Meissner (1987) has written extensively on the issue of hope and faith. He draws a distinction between primitive regressive states and mystical experiences, highlighting his bias based on his own strong religious faith.

> In mystical states, we are dealing with a condition in which the self is subsumed by the loving presence of a divine object, which calls on the soul's capacity to reach beyond the boundaries of self, and to empty out the self in a loving embrace and absorption into the object. This transcendent capacity of the psyche to immerse itself in such a loving object relation need not be regarded as regressive; rather, it may reflect one of the highest attainments of man's

spiritual life and capacity. Such transcendent absorption in the love object stands in radical opposition to the psychotic self-absorption of the primarily narcissistic psychotic process. [p. 123]

Meissner's view assumes that the transcendent experience enables the individual to feel part of a loving, soothing, divine object. He does not address the individual who feels the divine object is perhaps powerful but vindictive, or omniscient but punitive. As well, he seems to suggest that the spiritual individual has reached a higher level of merging capacity than the non-believer, a view that discounts other forms of achieving these fused states, such as artistic creativity, unity with nature, or intimate interpersonal discussions.

Another author has applied the Winnicottian transitional arena to the God object. Rizzuto (1979) has devised a questionnaire that studies the kinds of God representations that individuals develop. Her data demonstrate that individuals create their unique God object based on childhood experiences, both the realistic ones with their parents and the fantasy states they would like to have. Rizzuto views God as a special transitional object, in part because, whereas other objects wear out their usefulness and are decathected over time, "He is always potentially available for further acceptance or rejection . . . . God, like a forlorn teddy bear, is left in a corner of the attic, to all appearances forgotten. A death, great pain, or intense joy may bring him back for an occasional hug or for further mistreatment and rejection, and then he is forgotten again" (p. 179).

Her findings did corroborate that, once the image of God is formed, this idiosyncratic representative does not shift or alter. "Like the teddy bear, . . . a good half of [the God object's] stuffing [is] from the primary objects the child has 'found' in his life. The other half of God's stuffing comes from the child's capacity to 'create' a God according to his needs" (p. 179). Rizzuto applies the mirroring aspect of parenting to components of the God representation, noting their similarity in the biblical phrase, "God created man in his own image." If parental mirroring has been inadequate, the child may internalize his sense of powerlessness and compensate by feeling himself "like God." If, on the other hand, the child experiences in the mirroring a powerful, idealizable other, he is more likely to transfer this idealization to his developing God representation. In her summary, Rizzuto (1979) compellingly writes:

To ask a man to renounce a God he believes in may be as cruel and as meaningless as wrenching a child from his teddy bear so that he can grow up. We know nowadays that teddy bears are not toys for spoiled children but part of the illusory substance of growing up . . . . Asking a mature, functioning individual to renounce his God would be like asking Freud to renounce his own creation, psychoanalysis, and the "illusory" promise of what scientific knowledge can do . . . . [p. 209]

Wright (1991), in a comparison of religion and psychotherapy, speculates that many of the clinicians who practice psychotherapy today would have been the clergy of yesterday. Both, he says, are concerned with issues of trust, love, caring, social values, and morals. Both are concerned with truth, healing, and wholeness; both are concerned with mental anguish, and both offer cures for emotional suffering. He warns that "theory has become theology, and the practitioners of the new order have become its high priests rather than its therapists . . . . In the end the therapist himself succumbs to a new tyranny of the real in the form of his theoretical beliefs" (p. 329).

The immersive moment is a spiritual, sacred moment. Whether it occurs in a psychotherapy session during a deepened, empathic connectedness, or with nature, or with a divine object is of no difference. Psychoanalysis means study of the soul; it is time to embrace the immersive moment as partner to insight. The job of psychotherapy is not to de-emphasize, defuse, or discharge these moments of oneness, but to encourage, heighten, and embrace them instead. Only then will we be helping patients in their recovery from their detached, alienated core.

I often ask patients about their relationship to a God of their own making, because I assume, as does Rizzuto, that all individuals living in a Judeo-Christian culture have a relationship of some kind with a God representation, even if that relationship only exists because of the cultural norm. Faced with the image of Santa Claus, for instance, everyone must have an explanation for, belief in, or dismissal of this evocative figure. For recovering drug and alcohol patients, the issue of God is even more complicated. The majority of such patients have channeled their transformational object purely into their drugs. They have little hope that other people, or even a God, can hold any salvation for them. Many of them, because of their traumatic childhoods, have felt forsaken by their God object and have turned away in anger, sadness, and shame. Others, whose God representation is punitive and vengeful, are frightened to awaken a relationship with this powerful other whom they imagine is bound to be angry with their many past transgressions. One patient who was trying to learn to trust his God as well as other people would continually tell himself, "God rules with an open palm, not a closed fist." God had haunted him, prior to recovery, and he needed to analyze this relationship, as he had done with his other object relations, so that he could lessen his shame and come out of hiding.

The most beautiful experience we can have is the mysterious. It is the fundamental emotion which stands at the cradle of true art and true science. Whoever does not know it and can no longer wonder, no longer marvel, is as good as dead, and his eyes are dimmed . . . . A knowledge of the existence of something we cannot penetrate, our perceptions of the profoundest reason and the most radiant beauty, which only in their most primitive forms are accessible to our minds–it is this knowledge and this emotion that constitute true religiosity; in this sense, and in this alone, I am a deeply religious man.

Albert Einstein, "The World as I See It"

Before Alcoholics Anonymous, we were trying to find God in a bottle.

Bill Wilson

Whereas the detached schizoid has become walled off from emotional connections with all others, the alcoholic[4] has found a successful substitute in his substance of choice. Alcohol, like all drugs, is a very powerful transformative object, infusing the user with an intensity that most human relationships could never match, let alone the detached,

---

4. Throughout the book, for the sake of simplicity, I often interchange the words alcoholic and addict. I am not attempting to distinguish, in these passages, alcoholic from addict, because the same overall dynamics apply to both kinds of substance abusers. In discussing specific patients, however, I always indicate whether the patient is a recovering alcoholic, addict, or both.

unempathic relationships that are the only ones that most addicts have experienced. Because of the paucity of loving relationships in their lives, these individuals are essentially starving for moments of oneness that can relieve them of their sense of powerlessness and alienation. And indeed they find it — in a substance, one that is extraordinarily powerful and that they can be fooled into thinking is under their own control. Bollas (1989) notes, similarly, that "the drug push[es] this passive and deadened person through the illusion of transformation" (p. 152). The addictive substance alters the emotional and affective state of the user. Paradoxically, the substance is both a separate object before ingestion and a merged object after its use. Like the breast, it is a distinct entity and yet its milk flows into, and is captured by, the user.

Balint (1968) similarly views the alcoholic as feeling a sense of harmony while intoxicated, a sense that "all's right with the world." He views the craving for this harmonious oneness as the basis for all addictions: the need to find peace and comfort somewhere. Ongoing experiences with merger, so important to the development of healthy, intimate relationships, have been either absent or so severely damaged that the only harmony an addict feels is in an intoxicated state of bliss. To use Balint's theoretical frame, the basic fault of the alcoholic can only be filled, albeit temporarily, with drugs and alcohol.

Guntrip (1969) views the schizoid as ever alternating between the painful world of reality and the retreat of his restorative, inner womb-haven. The addict has found an alternative haven in his drug, a haven that soothes his alienated soul and provides a sense of connectedness and fusion. Whereas the schizoid has the capacity to, in essence, soothe himself by creating a restorative retreat inside his self structure, the alcoholic cannot do so, and therefore must look to the alcohol to provide a safe retreat. So often, I have found that alcohol and drugs have actually *protected* a patient from suicide; the substances reduced the psychic pain, loneliness, and sadness that might otherwise have overwhelmed his fragile core. Freud, in a later section of *Civilization and Its Discontents*, also discusses the importance of addictive substances in aiding individuals to cope with "the suffering which may come upon one from human relationships" (p. 26), as well as the overriding, painful nature of life itself.

> Life, as we find it, is too hard for us; it brings us too many pains, disappointments and impossible tasks. In order to bear it we cannot dispense with palliative measures. . . . There are perhaps three such

measures: powerful deflections, which cause us to make light of our misery; substitutive satisfactions, which diminish it; and intoxicating substances, which make us insensitive to it. [p. 23]

Freud ties religion to these "palliative measures," no doubt as part of the illusions that serve as "powerful deflections." Freud places illness and war as two of the greatest sources of suffering and believes that "our relations with other men . . . [are] perhaps more painful to us than any other" (p. 25). He, too, notes the powerful effects of intoxication as a means to deaden the torments of life. And indeed, he was well aware of the power of addiction. Freud readily admitted that he was addicted to cigars and, according to Gay (1987), believed that they "greatly enhanced his capacity for work and his ability to muster self-control" (p. 169). In fact, it was this addiction that caused the cancer that later ravaged his palate and eventually took his life. Freud was unable, however, to stop smoking. Gay (1987) observes that "the pleasure that continued smoking gave Freud or, rather, his incurable need for it, must have been irresistible. After all, every cigar was another irritant, a little step toward another painful intervention . . . . Plainly there were depths to his mind that his self-analysis had never reached, conflicts it had never been able to resolve" (p. 427). Several years later, when he was too physically ill to continue smoking, he wrote to Lou Andreas-Salomé that he had "completely given up smoking, after it had served me for precisely fifty years as *protection and weapon in the combat with life*" (p. 573, emphasis added). Freud understood firsthand the power of soothing substances: he himself was unable to battle the struggles of life without the use of chemical agents.

Treece and Khantzian (1986) have written extensively about the self-medicating aspects of alcohol and drug use, proposing that these substances fill specific characterologic or affective deficits in the user. They believe that each kind of drug, hallucinogenic or narcotic, for example, offers the individual user a specific effect that is soon sought after exclusively. An individual who prefers heroin over cocaine is more likely to have difficulty regulating his aggression than tolerating depressive feelings. Indeed, recent findings demonstrate a correlation between attention deficit disorder and cocaine use, for example, indicating that the abuser has found a stimulant (such as Ritalin, a prescribed drug often given for the treatment of attention deficit disorder) that actually helps him feel less scattered and frenetic. I have also observed a qualitative difference in the personalities and histories of heroin addicts versus other addicts and alcoholics. I agree with these authors that opiate abusers do have tremendous difficulty tolerating and managing anger. The drug essentially numbs them out, makes them feel calm, soothed, and warm all over. One patient of mine described his high as if "a warm blanket was cuddling me, totally surrounding me all over."

In addition, these individuals seem to have a greater ability to tolerate, and indeed to demand, immersive moments in therapy and in their lives. They demand an intensity in the therapy that I have not experienced with most other patients, which I have come to realize is a result of their need to find transformational objects of the kind and quality that can match the opiate. The intensity of the drug relationship may be impossible to match in any human relationship—after all, an intravenous user experiences fusion with an object that gets "under his skin" in a way that no other relationship ever can. Liedloff (1975) speculates that heroin addicts may be searching for the continuation of an "in arms" period of infancy that had been insufficient. She too notes that "the feeling heroin gives is like the feeling the infant has in arms" (p. 129). She offers the idea that perhaps some addicts are able to stop using after they have attained enough of "the missed in-arms period so as to free [themselves] to move to the next emotional phase" (p. 130). As I have discussed earlier, complete merger with an other, even mother, is impossible; the heroin user experiences a merger more intense and penetrating than any other. These patients often have had a similar kind of mother — an overly intrusive and self-involved woman—or at least their experience of her was as overly enmeshed and clingy. One patient called his mother "my smother," another, "the human vacuum cleaner." Indeed, given that mother is the first transformational object, it is no surprise that later objects are expected to offer the same kind of intensity and power. Although this seems to be a direct contradiction to Liedloff's idea, it may very well be that these mothers never stopped the "in-arms" period, needing their children to remain infants so as to attempt a continual fantasy-state of merger.

Carl Jung, in a letter to Bill Wilson, January 30, 1961:

> What I really thought about was the result of many experiences with men of his kind. His craving for alcohol was the equivalent on a low level, of the spiritual thirst of our being for wholeness expressed in medieval language: the union with God . . . . Alcohol in Latin is *spiritus*, and you use the same word for the highest religious experience as well as for the

most depraving poison. The helpful formula is—*spiritus contra spiritum*.

reprinted in January 1968, *AA Grapevine*

Long before I had come across this quote from Jung, I too had thought about the double meaning of the word spirit. It certainly is no coincidence and clearly indicates that alcohol is as powerful a substance to imbibe as taking in the spiritual moment, the moment of oneness. William James (1901) observes that alcohol "stimulate[s] the mystical faculties of human nature," and the intoxication of alcohol is "one bit of mystic consciousness" (p. 297). Clinebell (1962) points out that the transcendent effects of mind–altering substances have made them symbols for the mystical effects of religion. Many primitive cultures believed alcohol was a gift from the gods, as, for example, the Incas felt about coca. The ancient Greek god of wine, Dionysus, was connected to the world of the afterlife. The American Indians still use peyote in religious ceremonies, just as wine is a sacramental object in both Judaism and Catholicism.

Thomas Wolfe, writing about his life through the character of Eugene Gant in *Look Homeward, Angel*, (1929), provides an informative description of his first taste of alcohol. There are several important aspects to this passage, not the least of which is the transformation of this detached, alienated man into a powerful, intoxicated drunk who feels he has had a spiritual awakening. For most alcoholics, the first episode is particularly powerful, one that may never be repeated in such intensity throughout the rest of their years of abuse. This phenomenon is so well known that it is called "chasing the first high." Wolfe's description is of one such powerful moment—a moment that transformed him forever. It occurred after his family allowed him a taste of a small drink before leaving for town.

> What he had drunk beat pleasantly through his veins in warm pulses, bathing the tips of ragged nerves, giving to him a feeling of power and tranquility he had never known. . . . He took a water tumbler and filled it experimentally with equal portions of whiskey, gin, and rum. Then . . . he began to drink the mixture slowly.
>
> The terrible draught smote him with the speed and power of a man's fist. He was made instantly drunken, and he knew instantly why men drank. It was, he knew, one of the great moments in his life—he lay, greedily watching the mastery of the grape over his

virgin flesh, like a girl for the first time in the embrace of her lover. . . . In all the earth there was no other like him, no other fitted to be so sublimely and magnificently drunken. It was greater than all the music he had ever heard; it was as great as the highest poetry. Why had he never been told? Why had no one ever written adequately about it? **Why, when it was possible to buy God in a bottle, and drink him off, and become a god oneself, were men not forever drunken?**

He had a moment of great wonder—the magnificent wonder with which we discover the simple and unspeakable things that lie buried and known, but unconfessed, in us. So might a man feel if he wakened after death and found himself in heaven.

Then a divine paralysis crept through his flesh. His limbs were numb; his tongue thickened until he could not bend it to the cunning sounds of words. . . . Behind his drunken body his brain hung poised like a falcon, looking on him with scorn, with tenderness, looking on all laughter with grief and pity. There lay in him something that could not be seen and could not be touched, which was above and beyond him—an eye within an eye, a brain above a brain, the Stranger that dwelt in him and regarded him and was him, and that he did not know (emphasis added). [pp. 411–412]

Wolfe came from an alcoholic family. Although some of his family later denied the extent of alcohol abuse, Wolfe viewed his father and at least one older brother as alcoholics. His parents had an estranged relationship and eventually lived apart in two separate houses. He, by all reports, was a man of excess—a huge binge eater who frequently overindulged in alcohol and cigarettes. One biographer (McElderry, 1964), wrote that "to Wolfe, a bar was always a friendly place. He cashed most of his checks at a liquor store because he could never remember to get to the bank during banking hours. On many occasions he drank excessively, getting himself into petty quarrels that embarrassed him and often his friends" (p. 127). McElderry noted that Wolfe was breast-fed until the age of 3½ and slept in his mother's bed until age 9. Reading about his mother in the portrait of her as Eliza Gant, it seems that she, too, was a "smother" kind of mother. She was pained by every one of his autonomous milestones, refusing, for example, to cut his baby curls until he was 7. That he breast-fed into toddlerhood is one thing, but that he slept in her bed until age 9 indicates a strong regressive pull, no doubt encouraged by her, to remain a baby. Mrs. Wolfe is quoted in Nowell's 1960 biography of Wolfe, explaining her relationship with her youngest son:

> He being the baby I kept him a baby. . . . I think we just weaned Tom off by the other children laughing at him and talking to him about being just a baby. He still nursed. But it was a habit with him, that was all: he didn't really need it. . . . Tom . . . had beautiful curls, beautiful brown hair. . . . I kept it curled every day. It struck him around his shoulders. He often said they called him a girl because he had curls and wanted his hair cut off. I told him, "Oh no, I want to keep it long, you know." . . . So I kept putting him off until it had to be cut off. . . . But the sad part to me—my baby was gone—he was getting away from me. [p. 23]

According to Nowell (1960), "this abnormally prolonged infantile relationship affected Wolfe's entire character and life. He was always trying to escape from it, and yet was always reverting to it, either with his mother herself, as in his early years, or to substitutes for her, as in his later ones" (p. 23). Mrs. Wolfe's speech was always overdone, flamboyant and exaggerated. In reading Look Homeward, Angel, I have the impression that her voluminous chatter served more to distance Eugene and push him into hiding than to bring him closer to her. His self-portrait gives poignant clues to the making of a detached, false self and to the powers of the spirit of alcohol.

The dynamics of addiction are multitextured, but there is a thread that weaves through the pain-colored blanket. The children who become addicts are children who have experienced *too little* omnipotence and *too few* merging moments. This lack plays out in one of two ways. In the first, the mother is unempathically distant and controlling; the child is expected to attune to her needs. Whether because of normative, sexual, or physical abuse, the child rarely experiences a sense of his own power. He lives in his own isolation chamber, a daily experience similar to that of James in Chapter 1 who was crying while being strapped to a mattress. The detached self develops and stops asking for help because, as Winnicott notes, he has failed to develop an adequate capacity to believe in others. Feeling disconnected, he turns to himself for protection and comfort; feeling alienated, he tries to forget that which he does not have. He develops only the capacity to believe in himself, not in others. He asserts himself as though he were a powerful being so that he can shield himself from the humiliation of looking for help that never comes his way. And he assumes, falsely of course, that he can control the substance that he begins to take into his body. It is a worthwhile price to pay—and for a while he remains in control. When the relationship shifts and he again finds himself under the control of a merciless drug, he returns to being the unwanted, powerless child. Unless he has the drug in him, he is alone again in his isolation chamber.

Paradoxically, another scenario is just as likely to lead to the same results. In this case, the mother is overly attentive, overly gratifying, overly involved. She rarely lets the child experience his separateness; immersion is all she will allow. He is so flooded with interpersonal contact that he, too, retreats inside himself to create the needed space. He is so constantly surrounded by her that he never feels his own omnipotence. Instead, he feels her presence as if it were his own. That is not immersion of two separate individuals, but dominance by one overpowering self. Although he may have developed the capacity to believe in others, he will have little capacity to believe in himself. And that is, of course, just as crucial. The detached self takes root in his outward presentation of self-assurance, but inside he is withdrawn and self-doubting. The drug experience provides relief from the separateness he continually has to keep; he can feel himself whole without having the smothering relationship of human objects. And again, this works until the drugs overtake him and he can no longer control the experience. Then, he has returned to the original scenario: he is a slave to an overpowering, demanding other.

> *Cindy*: Did I ever feel my mother was involved with me? Is that the question? *[Pause]* No, of course she wasn't. I was the youngest of five girls, and we also took care of my aunt's three kids from the time I was 2. My father was drinking in those years, and I don't think she really had time for anyone. I remember, as soon as I was old enough, spending my days outside with friends. Of course I never brought them home because who knew what kind of shape the house would be in? *[Pause]* An early memory? Watching my sisters go to school, leaving me home alone and seeing them come home, all buddy-buddy. I just wanted to be part of them; but always I was the little sister, the one who got laughed at and teased. It was my big sister who really raised me—thank God for her involvement or I would have had no one.

Matt: My mother? She was always there for me in many ways. She was a great mom. But you know something? To this day, I can't get her to stop hugging me and giving me kisses on the lips when she sees me. I tell her to cut it out, that I'm a grown man, but she says it's just how she loves me, how she'll always love me, and I have to get used to it.

Lauren: Since I was little, it was my responsibility to take care of the seven of us. Every year my mother had another child. In the beginning I didn't mind so much because she wasn't drinking and she was involved too. But then, when she began to drink, I was totally in charge. That was a lot to ask of a 10-year-old—I remember having to shave my brother's head because he had lice. You can't imagine what that was like, to hold a struggling 4-year-old and be his mother. My father? Drunk or working. I never really had a childhood.

Cathy, in her early thirties, always surrounded herself with others. Her mother, she remembers, was constantly around her, telling her what to think, feel, say, and do. She notices it now, because she watches her mother caring for other young nieces and nephews.

She constantly says—don't touch this, don't do that. And I've been remembering that she was always like this with me. And I know that's where I got the feeling, deep within me, that I'm bad. Everything I always did was "no, no, no." There was absolutely no privacy in my home. My mother would always walk into my room, no matter what I was doing, and think nothing of it. I always felt watched, and kind of like I was part of her. It was hard to go to college—now that I think of it, I called her every day, at least once or twice. For years I thought she was my best, and perhaps my only, friend. I told her everything.

Cathy also spent her college years high on drugs and continually in and out of various relationships. At this point, she uses drugs only when visiting with her lover, who lives several hundred miles away. The two continually, immersively, use the phone and the Internet computer system to stay in close contact. If several hours have gone by and they have not made contact, Cathy gets edgy. She realizes that she has repeated the "smothering" relationship between herself and her mother; she sees that she cannot live without these intense, frequent immersions. She has such fear of her internal self, such a belief that she is bad inside that she cannot bear to have a moment alone. She detaches from herself, fleeing into the embrace of an other, because she believes herself to be bad.

A woman in her late fifties, Beatrice came to therapy because her career had been endangered by recent office changes. This was devastating to her because she had spent her entire work life making her company one of the top twenty advertising agencies in New York City. She had sacrificed family, friends, vacations, and career opportunities in other cities to benefit this company, and now, after almost thirty-five years of work, she was being positioned out of power. Indeed, this was a devastating blow, but her reaction was more severe than what might have been expected. Through the therapy, we discovered that her extreme disappointment had its roots in her mother's continual disaffection and lack of interest. She was never loved, Beatrice felt, by her mother, who took great pains to perfect her own beauty, go to her social events, and attend charity benefits. Beatrice was raised by a series of nannies who, with the exception of one, never really loved her, but "put up" with her instead. She did have a younger brother who was the apple of her mother's eye, making Beatrice's unwantedness all the more painful. She was labeled "hellion," "rebellious," and "difficult" by her mother who never understood her interests. She remembers her father with love, but he was continually struggling to support the family financially and was hardly ever home. As in so many households, he left the emotional heart of the family to his wife and never intervened in his wife's parenting style. Beatrice remembers very little of her early childhood, except for two incidents. In one, her mother had been screaming at her for something she had done wrong and then flicked her with a fly-swatter, adding that she would not hesitate to use it again. In the other, after Beatrice had teased her brother, she had tripped and fallen. Immediately, she said to herself, "You are bad, bad, bad." Other than these, her memories began in adolescence. Beatrice had always longed for the mother she never had, the mother who might have taken her shopping and dressed her in pretty clothes, or the mother who would have sat with her and been interested to learn of her newfound attraction to boys. But most importantly, she longed to be noticed. The results of this longing have been imprinted into her character.

> I never miss anything. Even when I'm sitting here talking with you, a part of me is observing everything. I am noticing the paintings

behind you, the furniture to my left and right, the window behind me. When I go out, all my friends know that I have to sit in such a way that I can see what's going on all around me. I have to know — I can't allow myself to miss anything. *[K.B.W.: How does this affect your ability to be totally involved in a conversation with anyone else?]* Oh, I'm never totally involved. I'm always detached from it. While I'm thinking of what's going on in the conversation, I'm also watching everything around me, and while I'm doing that, I'm observing myself, how I am coming across, how much I've said that is really from the heart. Besides, usually I never disclose much about myself. I'm the good listener, the one who offers good advice and counsels my friends. *[K.B.W.: So again, no one pays attention to you.]* I never thought of it that way. No, no one does.

Over time, Beatrice came to see that she rarely, if ever, was "real," that she rarely, if ever, integrated her true self into her false mask. She came to focus on her detached self and would observe how she was walled behind her mask. A turning point in her therapy came when she demanded that we "not waste time," that she felt we were not getting to the deeper issues, to the heart of her self. She was able, in this session, to put into words her lonely inner self, her wish that I would help her smash through her walls of isolation. This, I have found, is a frequent request made by detached patients at a significant moment in the treatment when they have become painfully aware of just how isolated they really are. It is always an important moment, a moment when these alienated beings are asking for closer, more immersive contact with an other, with whom they are wanting to share their inner selves. Beatrice began to discover an inner deadness, a part of herself that was bored with life, bored with being so uninvolved with others. She began to understand her compulsion to shop. She then began to investigate activities in which she could become involved, community projects that could make her feel more outwardly connected. Her numbed self was beginning to thaw, as she was beginning to express her inner feelings. The process is far from over, but the point is that her detached self has begun to melt because of the immersive connection. The detachment had been caused by the uninvolved nature of her mother's relationship with her; the attachment has been formed by her sense of being important, interesting, and valuable. "I have never felt a sense of connection in my life, not until now. My friends and I joke that they have their Sunday church services for solace, and I have my therapy."

The alcoholic has perfected the mask of the false self. He plays the arrogant, self-assured, and self-confident individual to everyone around him; he has become so detached from his inner helplessness that even he believes himself to be strong and self-reliant. The most familiar comment for an alcoholic is "I can do it on my own." Numerous addiction specialists have observed the grandiose mask that prevails. Buxton, Smith, and Seymour (1987) have written that the drug addict has become "his/her own Higher Power" (p. 280), unable to listen to others and unable to accept any external assistance. Clinebell (1962) points to basic disturbances in the mother–child dyad in which basic trust was not established. The child who later becomes an alcoholic had no choice but to develop an early, and therefore premature, self-sufficiency. He writes that the child "had become his own mother, his own god" (p. 486). Rinsley (1988), applying Kohutian principles, feels that the child did not infuse early omnipotence into his parental figures, leading him to distrust their power and authority. "Such a failure of trust in one's original god-like parental figures finds later and tragic expression in a pervasive mistrust of any and all authorities . . . . [which characterizes] those trapped in . . . addiction" (p. 6). I would argue that the parents of these individuals have, in reverse, not provided adequate immersions for the burgeoning child to develop a healthy sense of competence and self-esteem.

In this perpetual state of infantile helplessness, the addict turns to substances that infuse him with power. The immersion with this transformative substance does what his parental relationship did not: the drug provides him with an internal power base. His false mask reads "self-reliant"; his inner core hides in helpless shame. In merging with the substance, the addict is seduced into believing that he is in control of the transformative power of the drug. He feels he is in control—powerful and omnipotent. The intoxication is experienced as a melting of his detached falseness, and for many, the experience provides a melting of social inhibitions and emotional repression. Many of these detached individuals, when sober, are shy and hesitant in social settings but, when inebriated, become the life of the party. There is indeed significance to the phrase, "sex, drugs, and rock and roll." For many alcoholics, the combination of these potent disinhibitors is necessary to achieve feeling states of union and oneness. Social anxiety is a common factor among recovering alcoholics, who often become painfully self-conscious in moments of daily conversation and at social functions. One patient compared the struggles he now has, in sobriety, with the ease of his manner when he had been drinking. His feelings are not at all unusual among those in recovery.

> At parties now, I never know what to talk about. Everyone else seems so at ease, able to project self-confidence and to discuss current events with such enthusiasm. I never had this problem when I was drinking. In fact, now that I think about it, I realize that I discovered early on that alcohol helped release me from my usual sense of awkwardness with others. It let me feel free to be like everyone else. I could go to parties without any fear, any sweaty palms or racing heart. I often drank the most *before* I even got to the party, just to calm my anxiety and fear.

Similarly, many alcoholics experience what I would call a sexual phobia, which has inhibited their ability to enjoy the immersive contact of love-making. Without the use of drugs or alcohol, these individuals are sexually frightened and frigid. This phenomenon, when examined in the context of immersive functioning, is highly significant. The intoxicant has been required, first, to release the alcoholic from his prison of detachment so that he can allow the tender touch of the other's love to penetrate his body. Many recovering substance abusers have been surprised to find that the freedom and abandon with which they had previously enjoyed sexual encounters have diminished and been replaced instead with a self-consciousness that inhibits and restricts their sexual performance.

> I used to have several sexual conquests in a week—all under the influence of cocaine. It was such a marvelous high—I truly thought I was the greatest lover since Don Juan! But now, even after nine years of sobriety, I still become anxious and a little fearful whenever the relationship I'm pursuing becomes sexual. I want the lights off, I don't want to look at her body or have her look at mine, and I often have trouble allowing myself to release into sexual ecstasy. It feels so strange to me, to have this kind of difficulty now, because when I think back on all those years of erotic love-making, it seems to me that I should still be that same person I was when I was using the drugs. Instead, I act more like an adolescent schoolboy who is awkward and completely innocent about sex. Part of me realizes that this whole thing is about making contact—intimate contact—with

my girlfriend. And that the reason why I don't allow myself to release with her is because I won't allow myself to feel so connected to her, so dependent and so bonded to her love.

For some, the disinhibiting qualities of drugs and alcohol allow them access to feelings that would otherwise have remained buried. Sometimes, these feelings are of love, joy, and romance, but just as often they are the repressed emotions of anger, rage, and hatred. What is immersive about these moments is not that they bring the user serenity and peace, but that they bring the individual in close contact with his true self and his buried feelings. Should these be feelings of betrayal, jealousy, or hurt, so be it. Should these be feelings of love or sexual attraction, then so it is. The intoxication, the transformation, is the melting away of the detached, false self. For a moment, the user can feel a transcendence to his *inner* self. Use of a drug also provides the illusion that the addict is still the master of his destiny, that he is in fact able to transform his own world into something quite unique and different. LSD, for example, provides the user experiences of tremendous transformation—room sizes and furniture shapes change dramatically, and sounds and physical perceptions alter significantly. For an individual who feels powerless in other areas of his life, this can be an omnipotent fantasy come true.

The alcoholic has found moments of oneness primarily through intoxication. Other people are too dangerous—unreliable, untrustworthy, or unempathic. If not in other human relationships, then why not turn to God? For most of these abusers, God is viewed in the same way as other object relations. He is seen as either unavailable because of the insignificance of the abuser, or He is feared because of His power. God is not experienced as controllable, therefore it is terrifying for the alcoholic to find comfort in prayer. The substance seems to be the only way out: it seems to be controllable (no addict starts using with the assumption that he, too, will fall under the drug's spell), and it is less frightening than God. Furthermore, because the effects of the substance mimic mystical experiences, the addict feels a temporary respite from his sense of existential alienation and can feel invulnerable due to the drug-induced creation of an area of immersion. For the moment, the individual finds relief from his detached core and from his alienated world. He can ooze with transcendence, wax philosophic about life, and enjoy relief from the prison of his soul. He has immersed himself into a powerful union, a union with an other who is extraordinarily transformational; all the while he can believe that he is the one in control and that he still is in need of no one.

[Alcohol is] the devil in solution.

Sir Benjamin Ward Richardson, *Ten Lectures on Alcohol*

5

UNLOCKING A DEAF HEART

The great source of terror to infancy is solitude.

William James, *The Principles of Psychology*

THIS CHAPTER DESCRIBES a detailed case analysis of Mark, a patient who had experienced such a paucity of immersive moments in early childhood that he felt continually disconnected from the world around him. Through a period of omnipotent immersions within the therapy, the patient became empowered and gave up both his need for addictive substances and his suicidal tendencies.

I had originally written some of this case material as part of my doctoral dissertation. As I was writing the dissertation, Mark began a psychotherapy session with thoughts he had been having about his treatment. He spoke of the "emotional connectedness" that he felt toward me, and told me that more than AA or anywhere else, his relationship with me had opened his heart and helped him feel "human." I recall being surprised that he had thoughts so very similar to the writing I was currently involved in, and so I spoke to him about these ideas. I went on to say that I had used his case as an example to demonstrate my ideas. He asked if he could read the dissertation when it was completed. I agreed, adding "as long as we talk about how this made you feel." Not only did we talk, but spontaneously, he responded with the letter that is now, with his permission, presented below. The letter, which is printed in italics, is almost entirely unedited and includes the titles he gave to various sections. It is split between different passages of my narrative, so as to simulate an ongoing dialogue. Usually, Mark is not one to reveal himself so fully and candidly. I am very grateful to him that he has allowed me to publish this letter in full. It is particularly valuable because in no way did I ask for this material, suggest he write it for the book, or sway him to my particular way of thinking.

Wright (1991) has offered the idea that each psychoanalytic theory is conceived out of the personality and life experiences of each theorist. In the same vein, the therapy between one patient and one analyst is very much a result of the idiosyncratic joining of two beings. It is understandable, therefore, that some of Mark's ideas are similar to my own, just as some of my thinking has been influenced by him. Mark was pleased that I wanted to include his thoughts—the inclusion of his case study in this book has made him feel valuable and significant. As he said, what a thrill "to be part of something that I didn't have to do anything but be human."

HISTORY

Mark, now in his mid-twenties, was raised in an upper-middle-class family that, to any outside observer, seemed to provide a loving, attentive, and stable home. His parents were devoted members of their local Catholic Church and were active in their small-town community. His older sister graduated high school with honors and won full merit scholarships to both her undergraduate and graduate Ivy League schools.

And then there was Mark. His mother once told me that she never believed he would live to see his twentieth birthday—a point of view that Mark himself shared and one that was based on a very troubling history. By the time he was 19, Mark had made more than five serious suicide attempts. These attempts were the result of a desperate feeling of disconnection from both his family and friends and a sense of being a "misfit" and a "crazy man."

When he was 1 year old, Mark became ill with a severe ear infection that was not treated. It resulted in a partial hearing loss that continues to be annoying to him. As a child, he would frequently complain that he did not hear the things his parents were telling him and that he could not make sense of his teachers' instructions in school. Both parents ignored his complaints and felt he was being deliberately oppositional. It was only when a routine school hearing test diagnosed his disability that they were forced to believe him.

Mark's partial deafness can be seen as a metaphor for his core sense of alienation. He always felt unheard in the family, as though he were living in his own separate world of emotional silence—indeed, even at the age of 1 year. How is it that his parents could have ignored what must have been a terribly painful ear infection? How is it that his cries went unattended?

Mark frequently had explosive temper tantrums as a child and soon began to head bang. He would bang until he felt pain or dizziness, and he sometimes used enough force to dent or bash in doors and wallboard. As Mark later described, this behavior evolved out of a frustration so deep that he was trying to bang it out of himself. Again, where were his parents? Why did they allow him to suffer so? Why did they not use their power, their strength, to stop him from such self-mutilations? I can only imagine that they felt, as many parents do, that he should have his tantrums alone. They might have said, "When you finish stomping and yelling and banging, then we will continue talking again." This is one of the reasons I have concerns about the use of time-out behavior modification techniques. If the child cannot control his aggression at the beginning of a conflict, what makes anyone think he can do so when separated in his room? Even physically stopping a young child from hurting himself is a far better course of action; the child learns that his parents love him and do not want to see him hurt himself.

In reviewing this case, I think that Mark's later turn to suicide was just an escalation of these early moments, moments when his painful self-abuse was not contained. Certainly, these self-abusive moments increased the vast psychic separation between Mark and his parents: there he was, banging his head in fury and frustration, knowing all the while there they were, outside, listening and not helping, watching from a *distance*, and never intervening. Mark has told me that one of the most familiar refrains he heard as a child was, "You figure it out for yourself." Although it can be encouraging for a child to develop his autonomous self, it is also just as important for parents to guide, in a non-intrusive way, the child to successful solutions.

At age 6, Mark destroyed the family typewriter with a hammer because he was frustrated at his inability to use it properly. He continued destroying property for several more years, including a brand-new bicycle. He had been thrilled with his new bike and had been riding it in the garage before school. The chain came off a few times and he kept fixing it. His parents told him to stop riding and get ready for school, but he wanted them to fix the bike. They refused, telling him they would do it after school. He exploded in a rage, in part due to the disappointment in his bike and in part because of his parents' response. As Mark terrorized the family, paradoxically, he also felt powerless inside because his tantrums never influenced his parents. Instead, he only became more alienated and separate.

He frequently stared for hours in his room at the blank wall next to his bed. He once wrote a few quotes on the wall to have an object to communicate with, but for the most part, he simply stared aimlessly into the white particle board. At other times, he would bang his head with heavy objects—wood or metal—and watch himself bleed while becoming numb to the pain. When he stopped feeling the pain, he would increase the blows; he wanted to find a way to feel alive. Again, where were his parents? They would see the blood on the sheets, the scars on his face. Perhaps because they had become so fearful of him, they made no comment about his behavior.

These incidents portray Mark's feeling that he was never seen or heard by his family despite his valiant attempts, which had serious implications for his psychological suffering. Winnicott (1971) has written that the baby needs an external mirror: "When I look I am seen so I exist" (p. 114). In Mark's case, he was not looked at; he did not exist. There was no external other to resonate against or to melt into. Rather, there were only hard walls and blank stares.

TRANSMUTATIONAL EMOTIONAL REGRESSION
PROVIDING A SOLID FOUNDATION FOR STABILITY[1]

*For starters, I **hate** [that for your book you gave me] the name Mark. Since it's **you** of all people writing this thing, I'll forgive you.*

*I found it interesting that throughout the work, you'd make comments about parallels or metaphors. This, for me as the case study in question, was rather intriguing due to the fact that these were comments about my own self and not a separate person. Possibly one of the strongest points in the piece was the paragraph [immediately above]. I have no idea who Winnicott is (most likely because I read **none** of the other sections of your paper, but I'll get into that later), but I find the point, There was no external other to resonate or to melt into, exceptionally insightful and personally helpful.*

---

1. The headings that introduce Mark's reflections in this chapter are his, and not the author's.

An incident that Mark recalled in great detail further exemplifies his alienation. At around the age of 4, Mark was outside playing while his mother was talking to a neighbor. He stumbled into a bee's nest, and when the bees took revenge he ran toward his mother's legs. The bees swarmed around him, furiously attacking his little body. But as he ran toward the safe harbor of his mother, she told him to run into the house, in effect, away from her. Mark ran into his bedroom and tried to shield his body with his arms while waiting for his mother to rescue him. She did not appear until after she had finished her conversation with her neighbor, and then, rather than hold and comfort him, she stayed outside the bedroom offering practical suggestions.

This was no doubt one of many instances in which, rather than providing comfort, she stayed outside his grasp, outside his imploring reach. Further, just as with her reaction to his rage, she did not use her presence as a transformative, soothing object for him to introject. He was given no ego protection to cope with his anxieties, fear, or fury. Having no powerful object to merge with, he was left struggling with these over-whelming emotions on his own. For Mark, his mother's hands-off manner indicated to him that his suffering would go unnoticed—just as his head banging was ignored, his deafness denied, and his inner world disregarded. He was psychically alone: there was no other to merge with despite the fact that there are continually moments in life that offer merging opportuni-ties. The infant who searches for the breast is just one example of searching for a powerful other who provides and protects. The opportunities for immersive contact are continual in life; they simply take alternative forms.

The less Mark was heard, the louder he screamed. He became even more oppositionally defiant, focusing on his parents' extreme religiosity. His mother was a devout Roman Catholic who attended daily Mass and took comfort in the many crucifixes that adorned her home. Mark was expected to adopt her beliefs wholeheartedly, to attend religious school weekly, and to pray in church on Sundays. However, he had absolutely no interest in prayer or in God and, at a very young age, began to assert these views to his parents. The three of them had frequent verbal and even physical battles as his parents tried to force him into conforming to their beliefs and to cooperate with their religious rituals. One interpretation I offered Mark concerned his incorporation of his mother's religiosity. Her object of attachment was Jesus; He was her savior. Mark had attempted, through his own sufferings, through his own multiple deaths, to become the Son that she would love. He had, in his own way, tried to break through the religious barriers that so distanced him from his mother. But he could not get through.

Mark began to feel crazier and crazier, because although he felt he was entitled to his own opinion, his family's disapproval and even censorship caused him further to doubt his inner self. Although he never adopted their belief system, he was never able to shake the inner belief that his ideas were crazy and bizarre. His sister was accepting of their views, and the church, the community, and even his own friends thought he had the "greatest" parents. He was sent to a psychiatrist who sat behind a desk in a dark room and spoke to him disapprovingly about his masturbation. Again and again, Mark found himself misunderstood by whomever he came in contact with. Again and again, his inner self burrowed deeper to avoid the pain. His detachment grew stronger and more resilient.

Mark had begun fantasizing about suicide when he was 5. His initial attempt was at age 12, when he placed himself on the ties between nearby railroad tracks. He hoped to be crushed by an oncoming train, but he was so small that the train rode right over his body without causing any injuries.

*I'm only going to point out some details that I felt need attention, not to criticize or correct, but rather to discuss from the patient's point of view . . . You mention that I was attempting suicide by lying on railroad tracks to see if the train would crush me. At 12 I was not in tune enough to fully grasp death, nor was I interested in such a brutal or gruesome cause of death. At 12, violence was not as **tolerable**. I was not disciplined enough at that point to ignore pain. That amount of intense pain frightened me and was one of the reasons I looked to death for a place of peace and solitude.*

*At 12, I was not lying on tracks, contrary to what I might have said (if I did date the incident). I actually went back to some old letters I wrote [to his best friend] that are on my computer. It was at least a few years after that (though it seems in my memory like I was 10 when it happened) when I wrote him about my foolish acts. He was in college and he's two years older than I. That puts me **at least** a sophomore in high school.*

*I guess it's important to realize my ability to grasp suicide as an attention getter, a way out, and an obsession was not developed until there was an environment in which I could play it out successfully. In other words, I was not willing to attempt suicide until there **were eyes on me**, whether I lived or died. After thinking about this, I found it interesting to consider my reasoning and motives for choosing suicide when and where I did (in second period in high school).*

*The train tracks offered a **thrill** and a story to tell. Obviously, there are latent suicidal tendencies in such an act, but I really wanted to come off as a **bad-ass** rather than **dead,** at that point. I wanted the attention, but was not willing to die at that point, so I'd do one better — come damn close to dying. I found this worth thinking about, for myself.*

Through his suicide attempts Mark wanted attention, rather than to die. This is certainly an indication of how desperate he had become—that he felt this was the only way to get attention from the many *deaf* people who surrounded him. A few years ago, four adolescents tried the very same "bad-ass" stunt on the same railroad tracks in the same town. They died. So while Mark may think he was not interested in dying, he was certainly using lethal props.

Mark's second suicide attempt was ingesting the family dog's entire heartworm medication. This action did little more than make him sick. He then moved to wrist slashing, first rather superficially. Again in his room, he would cut his legs with a razor blade, watching the blood ooze from his body. Not long after this cutting behavior started, he made a near-lethal attempt. While his parents went out to celebrate their wedding anniversary, he hooked a hose to the exhaust pipe of the car, shut the garage door, and sat in the car with the motor running. It did not take long for him to pass out. He most certainly would have died except that his parents had a "premonition" that something was wrong and came home early. They found him lying unconscious on the garage floor. His father told me that he had never been so frightened in his whole life; to hold his son almost dead in his arms was a torturous, terrifying moment. Mark was rushed to a local county hospital where he spent the next two months in a locked, adult psychiatric ward. He pleaded with his parents to move him to another facility with other teenagers, but they did not. Mark has never forgiven them for leaving him in this unhelpful and scary place. His parents have told him that the hospital advised against moving him, but he always felt there was some way in which they could have taken him to another facility.

When he came home, he experienced yet another deaf moment. In a room surrounded by family and friends, his parents had invited the parish priest to perform an exorcism. This, despite the fact that Mark did not believe in either God or Satan. Again, he was the heretic, the evil son. The emotional forces that had impelled him toward death were again ignored, unacknowledged, untouched.

*On the next page you mention the **exorcism**. An incident I've done an excellent job of hiding from my conscious mind (**thanks for bringing*** *that up again). Ironically enough, I was lying on the railroad tracks a few years earlier only about one hundred yards from where they performed that very exorcism.*

After his failed suicide attempt, Mark became more of an isolated recluse at home. He was doing poorly in school, and it was not long before the school recommended, and his parents agreed, to send him to a private, alternative boarding school. I have always thought they sent him away because they really wanted him out of the house; having a suicidal, depressed adolescent at home was understandably overwhelming. As Mark said to me in a recent telephone conversation:

Well, I was always in their way, that I always knew. But also, I'm sure it was quite a trip to have me moping around the house. They were always alternating between ignoring me and hovering around me. You know the scene in the *Batman* movie when the Penguin is deserted by his parents? They found him too repulsive for words and just wanted to get rid of him. That's a pretty good description of how I felt.

At the boarding school, he discovered drugs—first marijuana and then LSD. He loved LSD because "*it made the room melt, it brought me into walls and into my friend's heads.*" He preferred this drug to all others because of the "weird" perceptual images he would see, which alleviated his anxieties that he was crazy. The drug also gave him a sense of tremendous closeness, a spiritual bonding, between himself and his friends. As Mark was quick to point out, LSD was not a drug to be taken alone. That friends were needed to "share the trip" made it all the more alluring to him because here, finally, he was in a world he could share with others. At least for a while, he felt he was in control and could determine just how much of the drug he would take and with whom. He could finally feel powerful while immersed in a union with others.

CONCENTRIC SYMMETRY OF THOUGHT AND RATIONAL EXPLORATION INTO THE INTELLECTUAL DESERT

I like the brief but important comments on Acid. Though you did forget one thing. LSD causes not only visual and audio distortions, it also causes a bend in reality. Mentally, LSD can be the most brutal of all drugs. In most peoples' opinions I've ever talked to who have used LSD the way that I did, they all said that LSD caused them the most **confusion** *of all drugs. I have not found this to be true for myself. Actually, for me LSD centered me mentally. I felt I was controlling the trip, and hence, whentripping with others, somehow controlling their trips. To a degree, that is very true.*

I was one of the only people I knew of who could, would and **cared to handle** *the amount of LSD I did put into my body. The LSD not only affected me physically, it also gave me a totally false sense of control. In other words, I took LSD to escape from reality to a drug-induced high which was total mental chaos – so I could control it.* **A false sense of control.**

I agree with the comments made by Bollas (1989) about LSD. Parents of users seem "psychically removed from their children" (p. 147); this clearly would pertain to Mark's experience. The LSD addict certainly is, to use Bollas's phrase, "deeply lonely and isolated" (p. 147) as a child. This perspective is similar to my own view that at the root of addiction is a pervasive, deeply felt sense of detachment and alienation. This feeling-state is in large part caused by unempathic parenting, even in the normative sense. The separations that are cut into the psyche are deep and wide; the indissoluble bond has been weakened.

Mark discovered early another way to feel connected with others. He became sexually active at age 16 and was proud of his ability to be an attentive and creative lover. Certainly, merging is a part of sexual intimacy and is in large measure why he so enjoyed this activity. Making an emotional connection through bodily interaction has its roots in all aspects of maternal care. Breast feeding, for example, allows the infant quite literally to ingest part of his mother's fluids. In this way a child learns to merge both emotionally and physically with this more powerful, protective other: he infuses himself with her substance. Mark never had had adequate merging experiences, as is clear from the history presented above. With sex, as with drugs, he finally found immersions that provided solace from the emotional alienation he otherwise felt. Having a girlfriend respond to his request for physical comfort, to respond with joy to his touch, melted his detachment and sparked his inner true self. That he sometimes chose women who had previously been sexually traumatized re-created his relationship with his mother, who essentially was frightened by his gesturing and frigid in his presence.

Side note: I became sexually active at 15 and I have always wished it was 12 or 13 but it is only 15, but dammit if I didn't get a lot in since then, but still, I wish it had been 12 or 13, even though I know I can never change the past like that or anything. I still wish it was earlier in life, maybe even 11, who knows, but it was **not 16. It was 15.**
Grin.

He remained at the boarding school for the next two years. He became drug addicted, was often suicidal, and was finally expelled. He returned home, where he continued to "drop acid" daily and began to sell drugs. What else he did during these two years is a mystery to him because he has absolutely no recollection of his activities, thoughts, or feelings.

TREATMENT: THE IMMERSIVE FRAME

At age 19, Mark decided to admit himself to the inpatient dual diagnosis psychiatric facility where, at that time, I was a clinician. He felt he could no longer control his impulses and was feeling dangerously suicidal. Three months before his hospitalization he had attempted suicide again, but this time had turned off the car before succumbing to the fumes. His parents' response to this suicidal gesture was to help him move out of the house (again) and get an apartment with a friend (also a drug addict). Once in this unstructured place, he increased his use of what was already an extreme amount of marijuana and LSD. On the morning he woke to find himself choking his roommate without provocation, he decided to seek hospitalization. As with many substance abusers, when he was able to admit that he could no longer control the fusion substance he craved so adamantly, he sought recovery.

I can still remember how he looked on the first day we met. He wore a blue and red striped poncho, widely ripped jeans, and sandals. He looked like a hippie from the sixties, with long hair and bloodshot eyes. It actually was not my turn to interview a new patient—I was doing a colleague a favor by handling this admission and had fully expected to turn the case over to this clinician after intake. Mark later told me that, from the first moment of our encounter, he felt understood. He said,

Some AA people think it was God who saved me, through my parents, that time when I was suffocating from the car fumes. But I know that was just my parents doing their thing. If there is a God, then the only time he has "appeared" on my behalf is when he made you the therapist for me and not the other clinician who had been initially scheduled for my intake. That's the only time I can believe God intervened."

*I find it interesting that you mentioned [something] I said about you. I still feel very strongly that it is true. That if there has ever been a **Divine Intervention** in my life it was when I got you. I've wondered since reading this initially what that must be like for you. To think someone who is so adamant that there is no consciously thinking deity has laid one huge monumental moment on you. I'd say you've handled it very well.*

*As I reread this thing, I want you to **understand** how much I **HATE** being called Mark.*

After our initial interview, I called my colleague and asked if he would mind very much if I took this case. There was something compelling about Mark, and I, too, had felt a genuine connection as we sat together. From the beginning, I trusted that he was sincere in his wish for recovery, and I therefore granted his request when he asked to leave the hospital after this initial interview so that he could return after the weekend. This was of course a highly unusual request, but I did not have the idea he was going to use drugs. I felt that he needed to feel the freedom of choice in his decision to enter this intensive level of care. That I allowed him to leave, even though his parents and the hospital were rather skeptical, convinced him that I would be able to tolerate all of his "zany" self.

*I've known you for four and a half years. I met you on a morning I was still coming down off of some really fucked up dope. But unlike the rest of the month, I remember it really well. I remember the relief of my parents as we pulled in. And the shock of everyone when I said I was gonna come back. Hell, I told all of you guys about all that Heroin I was doing. Ahhh, the concern someone might have thought **I was really okay,** just a little confused! Too bad I never really did try Heroin.*

Allowing Mark to be heard took various forms in our psychotherapy sessions and was one of the most crucial components of the treatment. For example, when Mark left the hospital to continue in outpatient (twice-weekly) treatment with me, I gave him my home telephone number to use whenever he felt it necessary. This therapeutic gesture was designed to help him hold on to me and to use me whenever he felt disconnected or detached. This is a crucial component of immersive treatment—the patient must have the feeling of accessibility to the therapist at all times. Especially in the treatment of drug addicts, this level of contact is imperative. Yet, never, in the years I have worked in this way, has a patient abused this aspect of our relationship. This is, of course, what therapists seem to fear: "Don't you worry they will call you all night long?" or "Don't you want some private space away from them?" My answer is quite simple: these patients need everything I can offer to help them feel connected, to shrink the wall of detachment that has surrounded them for so very long. It is my gesture of immersion that means the most here; patients have in fact never called me at 3:00 A.M. In fact they generally do not call at all, especially late at night. However, I do have an answering machine at home, and if a patient calls at an inconvenient time for me, a time when I cannot be devoted to his phone call, I will not answer, but will wait for a more opportune moment. The immersive approach requires the provision of as much connectedness as possible.

For Mark, it was crucial that he be able to reconnect emotionally with me whenever he needed to, not just in session hours. And indeed, he did make frequent use of the phone. Very often, he was able to reveal more about his inner self in these out-of-session phone contacts than in the sessions themselves. Perhaps this was because we were making contact when *he* wanted, rather than having to conform to my schedule. When an infant cries, he is demanding to be heard and to be attended to by his mother. When she hears him and responds to him both verbally and physically, she is indicating that she will enter into his world and take care of his need. In this way, the infant can begin to feel immersed with some of her power—he can inject into himself her love and devotion and can infuse himself with her presence. As he gives himself to her and she readily receives him, she begins to develop an empathic view of what her child wants and who he is. She enables herself to merge within her infant's self and to view the world from his perspective. The immersive moment is a two-way empathic process. The mother's ability to inject her child into herself is as crucial as his ability to take in her presence.

In Mark's case, his parents were totally unable to inject their son into themselves and to view the world from his perspective. They could not become one with him, to merge with his reality. Insisting he believe in Jesus and be exorcised, for example, indicates their inability to view the world as Mark experienced it. This impermeability of the parental couple was also due to their own enmeshed, fused relationship. The parents were always most attentive to each other rather than to their children. Both Mark and his sister agreed that their parents had *never* argued, not once in twenty-five years of marriage. In their concern for each other, however, they excluded their children. This is not an uncommon phenomenon in marriages that produce detached children; the same was true for James (see Chapter 1). The parents become such a formidable front and are so attuned to one another that neither feels free, for example, to argue against the spouse in favor of the child. Furthermore, the child has neither parent to validate his own perspective because the spousal loyalty is too great. We can view Mark's head banging metaphorically as his expression of frustration that the marital wall was impossible to permeate.

When I accepted Mark's phone calls and responded to his every verbal gesture, I was, like the mother of a young infant, answering his cries and coos. He required me to be a subjective object where he could place his emotional and intellectual being. Through these contacts, Mark began to feel that what he thought and felt were indeed important, that what he experienced daily did matter to an other. He felt heard, which made him feel that his life, his self, did indeed matter.

Early on, Mark seemed to expect that I would always be available to him. On the few occasions when I returned his call from out of town, he would display some irritability that he had not been "made aware of" my plans. He clearly needed me to remain inside his self-orbit, under his domain, and inside his transitional realm. My being out of town without his prior knowledge made him anxious about the state of our connectedness.

The immersive frame we established allowed him to break through the alienating, empty space that had surrounded him since infancy. He was able to feel a connective link between his inner world and the world around him.

> *An important, possibly the most important part is coming up. Oh, here it is. [In the passage above] you discuss the* **phone situation**. *The importance to me that you were available. It's important to point out here, much like I said at the beginning of this letter, that your presence was vital. The loving melting metaphor, and then again with my self-orbit and domain. I was (and still am) one hundred percent sure at that point you had no other person in your life as totally cool as me. I forgave [your husband], only because of the fact I wasn't looking to you as a girlfriend,*

a lover or a mate of any sort. He could gladly have that spot. My interests lay in looking to you as a **Mother, a shelter, a guide, a friend, and a verbal warmth.**

I knew, though I could not verbalize, what I needed. I'd never had what I wanted in a mother, and found you not only to be what I wanted, but you then went as far as to ask if it was helpful. Referring back to **Divine Intervention,** *I could not grasp (and still can't) the importance of the fact that I didn't end up with one of three things at [the hospital]: A Dad, A Shrink, or A Buddy.*

A father was not only **not** *what I wanted, but I believe* **not** *what would have* **helped** *me. I spent one hell of a lot of time working on being the things people say Dads are good for helping their sons develop. I wasn't interested in that at all. In fact, if you can remember (it was a long time ago now) when I first got into that shit hole . . . er . . . I mean, [the hospital], I was seriously questioning my own sexuality. Not a helpful thing to talk to a heterosexual male when you're feeling Gay. The thing I had always wanted was a Dad. The thing I always needed was a Mom.*

I had a Shrink once or twice before **(smile)** *and knew that one more of those* **Fucking Doctors** *would drive me* **nutso.** *You know something, those Doctors* **Seem To Have All The Answers?** *[My two other hospitalizations] taught me quickly that Doctors are scary people in some ways. They* **love** *that they can give out* **medications. Yikes!** *I had to see that guy when I was a kid, then that other guy when I got out of [the county hospital] and there was always that guy at [a third hospital] who told me I'd be* **DEAD** *unless I did exactly what he said. I've had enough of this male macho bullshit from these people. I had enough of that* **"the patient is a sick person who needs help and (s)he will never get out of this sickness unless (s)he does exactly what I say since I know everything because I can give out drugs."** *I hate that.*

Seriously, I know you're a doctor now and I'm not in any way trying to make a joke. Seriously. I mean it. I hate that shit.

I didn't need a Buddy either. It's like, **look, a friend is nice and all, but you're not helping me.** *Some of the* **doctors** *and some of the* **mental health workers** *were a* **pain in the ass** *through my life of hospitalizations. Every place I went, including [the last hospitalization], people would try to help by being a* **BUDDY.** *You know, like in school when you're 5. You go outside and* **every** *little 5-year-old* **must** *have a* *partner. A* **BUDDY. Augh.** *I* **hate** *that.* **Puke. Vomit. Yuk.** *That obviously was not and still isn't what I need.*

For me, not getting one of **those**, *but rather a young woman who was* **oddly sure of herself** *around me, the one person who most people were* **NOT** *sure of themselves with. By the way, my Dad reminds me to this day, that he believes the only reason I went to [this hospital] was because my therapist was* **cute. Can you believe that man? Unbelievable.** *To think I'd make a life-changing judgment on the* **look** *of a* **woman**, *rather than a* **God** *putting me in the right place at the right time and* **leading** *me through the decision.*

Frankly, I found any woman, at that point in my life, interesting. I obviously was looking for the touch of a woman, like you mentioned in that section, to comfort and soothe me. I'm still shocked at how fast I found [another patient] in [the hospital] to **actually give me head!** *Not* **really the thing I was looking for, but whatever.** *A good blow job is just that:* **a good blow job.**

I've always found it amazing how in touch you were with me. I tried so very hard to **piss you off**, *to shock you, to scare you, to basically make you* **blush** *in some way. I was convinced never to tell you about drugs since a* **stupid bitch** *who never tried* **Acid** *knew nothing about* **Acid.** *I knew you were sexually unaware since all people* **"That Age"** *were. I knew, in time, I'd have you switching with another doctor or therapist since you couldn't deal with this* **loony.** *Just looking for the obvious rejection soon to come.*

The sturdy, rigid Therapist **(who came off awful coy, I might add)** *I really wanted to spit on in that room* **EVERY** *time I saw her, was and still is, one of the only people who stands up to me. An important difference between* **You** *and* **everyone else.**

THE THERAPEUTIC RELATIONSHIP: IMMERSIONS AND OMNIPOTENCE

The content of Mark's sessions was as important as the contact itself. Much of what he discussed involved his intense desire to remain a nonconformist. Just as he needed to have time with me outside sessions, he also needed to discuss all his radical political and philosophical views. With friends and family, Mark enjoyed his argumentative politicizing and rarely accepted a popular view. He most enjoyed movies that were radical or free spirited, such as those starring Prince or Madonna.[2] As would be expected, he frequently had difficulty with rules and regulations, which at times cost him friendships and even jobs. For example, one job instituted a policy of mandatory drug testing. Mark adamantly refused to be tested and risked losing the position rather than submit to what he considered to be a totalitarian act. Of course the urine would have been clean, but he was firmly opposed to having his rights violated. (The company, interestingly enough, thought he was too valuable to let go, so they actually overlooked this policy in his case.) In the background of this conflict loom his parents and their insistence on utter conformity and agreement.

As I have emphasized in earlier chapters, infantile omnipotence is not a given. It occurs when mother meets her child's request with empathic attunement—which is often the exception rather than the rule. If she does not understand his request, chooses to ignore him, or refuses to acquiesce to his demands, he experiences infantile impotence. This, I propose, is the norm and not the exception. Opportunities for empowerment, too, often are ignored; opportunities for immersion are denied.

As is evident from Mark's history, he was never empowered by his family. Through the immersive nature of treatment, he began to embrace and empower his true, creative self. What he lacked most in his childhood was the opportunity to share his inner self with a protective and powerful other. I frequently encouraged him to show me his many creative endeavors. Mark brought me his imaginative writings, his film scripts, and his computer graphics. He frequently expressed his world views and, this time, found an appreciative audience. He brought me his true, creative self and found a receptive object. Metaphorically, I allowed myself to go wherever he wanted to go, to be under his control. Knowing what he was asking of me, I did not interpret his intellectual philosophizing as a defense or as resistance to the work. As far as I was concerned, this *was* the work, because, for the first time in his life, Mark was being listened to and even appreciated by a powerful other. He now had an active and involved participant in his every emotional thought. Through this experience, Mark began to feel powerful in himself. He was infused with the omnipo-

---

2. I must admit that Mark has criticized me for choosing two *mainstream* artists for my point about his radicalism. Please take this as a sign of my ignorance regarding current countercultural groups rather than as an indication that he might just be somewhat popularistic.

tence he felt in our sessions and was able to sustain this feeling throughout the week. In this way, Mark had successfully developed the omnipotent, immersive aspect of the transference that is so crucial to the treatment of the chemically dependent.

When I use the term *immersive therapy*, what I mean is that the more I can break through the detached wall between myself and the patient, the better. These patients need an active, involved other to re-ignite their spark that has long ago been trampled. Most patients, particularly addicts, have never been encouraged in any talent whatsoever. One patient brought in his humorous cartoons and shared his musical ambitions with me. As the treatment progressed, he joined a band, started music lessons, and awakened a part of himself that had been dormant since high school. Another, at the age of 60, returned to an earlier love of his—painting—and now spends weekends happily among his paints and drawings. He says that these moments, as well as his sessions, give him "a sense of serenity, a sense of spirituality" that he has found nowhere else. Like being a mother of a young child, it is part of my job as therapist of the deadened and detached to wake them up, to appreciate all of their creative endeavors, to encourage involvement and participation in life. Bollas (1989) puts the issue this way: "And we can see the problem that the therapist or analyst has in enabling this person to accept that ordinary transformational object that the analyst is, to discover in the ordinary work of analysis—in clarifications, interpretations, and silences—the value of object relating" (p. 152).

The way out of this difficulty is to view oneself as a crucial transformational object. We must be interested enough, caring enough, involved enough, to help the addict feel past his separated self and put away the drugs. For although we cannot compete with the drug (we are certainly less powerful), we must do what we can to be a close enough substitution.

THE AUGMENTATION OF SELF WITH A PROPORTIONAL EXPLORATION OF CEREBRAL CONSCIOUSNESS

Well, moving on. You mention working with me was becoming engaged in "intellectual" conversations rather than emotional situations. You said you let me run the directions I chose, and you felt this was okay and helpful . . . . I agree. Certainly at that point, I was confused about most everything. Having someone listening to things that I wasn't sure of and not doing what others before had done, helped a lot. Hell, it still does.

Mark, of course, saw me first through the transferential lenses of his earlier experiences, but as the relationship developed, he was able to separate me from these early introjects. Certainly, my ability to listen to his every thought and feeling, to involve myself with his intellectual processes, was part of this process. As well, my genuine enjoyment of his caustic humor and unique political perspective was of therapeutic benefit to him. No longer alone, Mark began experiencing me as being connected to him internally as well as externally. Bringing me his creative work and his intellectual ideas built a connective bridge between us, an area of immersion. It is crucial to note that this intermediate world was not of my making, but of his. My part was to be receptive to his offerings and to take in his developing self. Providing a period of omnipotent immersions within the treatment allowed Mark to feel empowered within himself and no longer controlled by an unloving, rigid other.

Mark's atheistic views bear further analysis in this regard. As I mentioned earlier, he had never believed in God and scorned his parents' religious devotion. How could he believe in a powerful and protective other when his parents were never protective of him? How could he turn to God for assistance when he could not turn to his parents? Indeed, his atheism can be viewed as a manifestation of a parental introject that was both abandoning and neglectful. It is interesting to note that the only time Mark postulated the existence of God involved the idea that divine intervention had enabled him to have me as his therapist. In this regard, God was connected with the more soothing and protective introject he had incorporated from our relationship.

ALCOHOLICS ANONYMOUS: DISHARMONY AND DISCONTINUATION

Allowing Mark to develop his creative self in my presence was only the first step in treatment. Once he felt that his entire self was welcomed by an other, he could entirely give up the attachment to drugs. During the first year of outpatient treatment, he continued to attend AA meetings, work the Twelve Steps, and be involved with a sponsor. He experienced this approach, however, as a repetition of his parents' rigidity. In fact, Mark began to hate the meetings. He saw the "old-timers" as rigid individuals who answered all his concerns with the pat slogan, "Don't drink, and go to meetings." He found the AA insistence on lifelong attendance, adherence to their doctrine, and belief in God (or Higher Power) too reminiscent of his family. He discussed these concerns with me many times, and I at first suggested he remain in the program, while pushing himself to express his individuality in the meetings. He did comply with this suggestion for a while and became more comfortable expressing his own point of view. But after a year and a half, and after switching to several different meetings and testing various group atmospheres, he became convinced that no one was hearing him, that the rigidity in the rooms was universal. He wanted to stop attending meetings. My experience as an addictions specialist told me that this was indeed a dangerous sign because it might signify the beginnings of a relapse. Although I voiced my concerns to him, I also agreed that he could not remain in a relationship that he experienced as so binding, controlling, and domineering. My agreement with Mark left him feeling "eternally grateful." Rather than responding as had his parents, I had listened to the intensity of his conviction that he could recover in his own way. Mark has told me many times that this acceptance of his wishes made him feel even more "emotionally connected to me." This acknowledgment of his true self, of his own style of thinking and feeling, enabled him to feel loved and to love. He found himself feeling free, feeling that he could indeed be powerful enough in his life to handle his own self. In this regard, he has said that I gave him his recovery: "My sobriety is because of you, not AA. AA was about dominance—they were controlling and rigid. You taught me how to have an emotional connection to others—and that's what it's all about." In fact, it was in this session that I disclosed that I was writing a dissertation about this topic. I did so because I was simply amazed at his mention of the emotional connection between us. I was surprised that he, too, felt it had been our relationship, our melting of his detached self, that had been the core of his recovery. Since then, I have made a mental note of other patients who have offered ideas about their sense of spirituality, how much "oneness" they feel in the therapy itself, and the like. I find these comments quite helpful because, in a sense, it helps me track how I'm doing in the immersive aspect of the therapy.

Further on, you go into the "breaking from AA." I'd like to mention an important point either I missed or you didn't mention (for reasons I'm sure

I'd understand.) AA not only pissed me off directly because of the pat answers, the rigid atmosphere, and the totalitarian bullshit, but also because not one person was **ALLOWED TO LEAVE**. It's important to note, that not only did I want to be different and not conform, but I simply could not live in AA and not conform at the same time.

AA states quite simply that you're a drunk for life. Sober or not. **Fuck that, Karen.** I'm not a drunk for life. I do not **feel** like a drunk sober or not. I **feel** much more than that. I cannot and will not surrender to anything again—well, not on such a foolish level. I believe by "turning your life over" and "bravely surrendering to the fact that you can not drink or do whatever it is you do" is one hell of a way to **totally ruin** a person's identity and self-esteem. Pot and alcohol are **NOT** that big of a deal.

Surrendering is fine, I guess. But so far, I see nothing in life I should surrender to. AA is such a passive-aggressive attitude. The thing they try so hard to fight. It's like, okay, quit this by saying you have no power. What? That's horseshit. Power is exactly what people need. As an individual. Not as a group. I needed to be told that I **DID** have power to stop drinking. Shit, it wasn't even the drinking. Just get with the reality of your life, pal. C'mon. Pull it together, and here's how.

What I've discussed about our relationship and what you've written is 100 percent more useful to developing an identity as an individual than AA teaches.

Let me put it to you like this. If an AA "Me" and a current "Me" were dropped into a situation that consisted of needing someone who could make decisions, be in control, and supportive of others at the same time and all by Himself, the current me would do much better. The AA me would need to ask his sponsor, get help from the group, and pray to whatever to get him through it. The AA me would wander back to the "rooms" looking for approval of his actions to make sure he made the **right choices**. Looking to you for approval is one thing, but having it required to feel good about myself from a group of people, that's not so good.

I hope that makes sense. Still, if the other me, the AA Me, has a name, I'm sure it's Mark.

ENCOURAGING THE POWER TO CREATE

During during the first year of outpatient treatment, Mark struggled with intermittent suicidal impulses. Each time, however, he called me before moving into action and discussed exactly what was generating the impulse. His wish to die was usually connected to shame and self-hatred at ongoing failures in establishing a "productive" career. Before we began working together, Mark had assumed he would die before reaching 21 and therefore had no need to formulate his own future. Once he decided to live, however, he had to grapple with choosing a career. He worked in numerous vocations, experimenting with various options such as child care, landscaping, and computer programming. He also started college several times, but found it too narcissistically injurious. Feeling directionless and identity-less stimulated again his childhood feelings of invisibility and enfeeblement, leading to suicidal impulses.

Mark's difficulties re-evoked his parents' frustration. They had long ago given up on him and had assumed he would remain a dependent child—an emotionally disturbed child—for the rest of their lives. They found his inability to succeed to be another example of his oppositional behavior and another example of his need to cause them pain. It was easy to imagine how Mark could internalize their anger and become self-hating. And yet in this area as in so many others, they had too quickly placed him on his own and demanded he find the world by himself. They expected him to find a career without providing him their guidance and support. When he was slow to find his niche, they saw him as a failure who would never be self-sufficient.

Mark and I picked up where his parents left off. We continued to analyze his struggles throughout all the many jobs he had tried and quit. We examined the difficulty he had with political networking and his impatience with bureaucratic formality. For the most part, Mark felt constricted and pressured by the atmosphere of conformity he found in all of these jobs, no matter how menial the work. Each time he quit, he was forced to ask his parents for daily living expenses, which would again stimulate self-hatred and shame. Each time he quit, he was thrust back into his parents' hopeless forecast of his chronicity.

At one of these junctures, during the third year of treatment, Mark came to session again feeling discouraged and depressed. He spoke of the impasse he was facing, that his life had become exactly as he had gloomily predicted years before—an infinity of nothingness. I pointed out that it was he who was creating this nothingness, giving himself a future so limited. He seemed surprised by this idea, that he actually had an impact on his life's course.

Mark, like so many other alcoholics, exemplified what Bollas (1989) calls the "fated" individual (p. 41). In the process of maternal provisions, the child begins orienting himself to a particular set of expectations. These expectations, whether fulfilled or unsatiated, of the external other become the frame for the individual's lifelong sense of hope or despair. With inadequate responses from mother, the child develops a fated view of life. He has very little sense of the future and believes life can provide no more than it has already (which of course has been minimal). This individual has no wish to imagine moments of his future because he is convinced it will replicate the present and the past. Thus, he lives in a state of despair because he can find no way to free himself from the shackles of fate. In contrast, the individual who can imagine many future moments has a "sense of destiny." That is, the person believes he can fulfill "some of the terms of his inner idiom . . . [it is the] natural course of the true self" (Bollas 1989, p. 34). This individual is able to project his true self into the object representation of his mother, where his future attains vision and validation. Bollas believes an individual so oriented will live his life with confidence that his world will supply him with objects and events that will confirm his true self potential.

Mark believed there was nothing he could do about the interminable hopelessness of his life. As we continued talking, I told him that he in fact *could* create his own destiny, that he no longer had to remain loyal to his parents' hopeless view.

I can still remember his face as I offered him this possibility. He lit up, in total amazement, at the idea that he could free himself from the chains of this tormented destiny. "You mean I could simply decide to have a different future? That I could create the kind of life I want for myself?" he asked in an incredulous voice. At this moment, Mark was transformed from a fated to a destined individual. He had discovered the essence of his own power: he could create his own existence and could do so with infusions from a supportive, protective other. What culminated in this poignant moment had been touched on throughout the years, because I had always been responsive to him and had demonstrated my faith in his being. Now, he realized that the struggle to find a career was part of the therapeutic process.

SPONTANEOUS KNOWLEDGE OF A LITANY OF PASSIONS AND FEARS THROUGH VERBAL EXPRESSION

Okay, so now at [the passage cited above], *we're talking about who? Bollas. Whoever this person was, has hit on something cool, so it's good you quoted him. The "fated" individual, as it were, was a terrible problem with AA also. AA teaches way way way way way way too much that you're born a drunk and will always be a drunk. Hence the fated part. By allowing me to be something else, say, a person who could control himself in ANY way, you helped me reach beyond the crippled life of an eternal drunk into an explorer of life. I felt safe with your support on that, and it helped to change my overall attitude.*

Mark was utterly transformed by this moment in the treatment, a moment in which he felt understood, trusted, and loved. He later would refer to this breakthrough as crucial to his newfound career success. Since this intervention, Mark settled on a career in computers while still writing his great American novel on the side.

Oh, I'm not writing the great American novel any more. If I were, that means A LOT of people would like it. That means I'd have somehow conformed. Yuk! No, I wanna write the arty and unknown books that make no money.

A year after this session, Mark moved to the Midwest, finally making the break from his parents. He stopped asking them for money and rarely involves them in his decisions. He and I, however, continued first in weekly, and then biweekly phone sessions during his first two years in the Midwest. At this point, he calls on average once a month so that he and I can maintain our connection. Recently I called him to discuss the material for this chapter. He had just been trying to call me, he said. And indeed, I have often found it to be so, with people I am close with in my life, whether family, friends, or patients. If I am thinking about them, they are thinking of me. It is as though there is another level of connection that stems from the immersive nature of our relationships together. Often termed moments of synchronicity, they are more than just coincidence. They are proof that the immersive relationship is a deep interconnection between two people, so deep that, even after months of separated living, the two remain intimately intertwined.

AFTERTHOUGHTS

Now that I'm done going through [all these many pages] and commenting on it, I'm gonna take a second to give some thoughts (yes, and feelings) on what it means to me.

First, the most noticeable thing from my view that you never mentioned (again, unless I missed it) is that I used to work with children. Maybe, that within itself was too much for the paper (book) but again, it's one significant time period that caused deep understanding in my own self. Just a note, that's all.

I've known you for four and a half years . . . . Today is August 16th, 1993. It's 2:00 A.M. I'm going to my "career" job tomorrow. There are two gentlemen sitting across the way talking over a smoke [his roommates]. It's silent, really, except for my typing and the sound of the fan. Once in a while I hear [my roommate] move around. And, after typing all of this in one sitting because my first attempts were simply not honest, I feel rather peaceful.

I've met a lot of people in this life, many of which have stayed with me. I'm finding, as I get older, I'm much more concerned with things that can change than things that can't. Constantly I hear of a boy and a young man who was so concerned about not being able to be understood or heard. And I've learned, from only you, that **I can be heard.**

I've learned so much, I'm not going to try and write it down, that'd be silly. Put simply, God or no God, AA or not, Dr. or Mrs. or whatever, it's the relationship that we've worked on that has made me into who I am. So few people I know have the balls to do what you did with me.

I feel a strong emotional connection with you, we've obviously established that. And it's odd, in a way, to have such feelings with someone who is (stuck??) entering your life to help you be different from who you are. Most people I meet, want to know me because of who I currently am. Not to help me be not who I am. I understand that there are some core things that don't change, but still . . . .

There are places I don't go often. I stay away from them for emotional reasons. I stay away from them for intellectual reasons. I feel awkward, still, years later telling you that I do love you. I feel it's a weird thing to say, in some ways. I'm used to saying that to people I hug. And, it has occurred to me, I've never hugged you.

After reading the section about me twice, I realized I had no interest in anything else in the paper. I realized, all I really wanted to find out was a little more about how you saw me and, most importantly, how you felt about me. I wanted to know how I had affected your life, since you have changed mine so much. It was a self-centered attitude, but I needed to know what you would tell the rest of humanity about me. **What would Karen say to everyone as to who I am?**

I'm rather pleased with what you did write. It was spooky to see myself in a detailed study like that, but then again, I'm used to it since we did it every day for six months at [the hospital]. I felt, as if there was a question, that you did understand, maybe too well, as to who I was. And most importantly, by portraying my person so well, you showed the world that you did understand who I was and who I am today. And that was the point of all of our work.

6

ALCOHOLICS ANONYMOUS AND TRANSCENDENCE

Maybe there are as many definitions of spiritual awakening as there are people who have had them. But certainly each genuine one has something in common with all the others. And these things which they have in common are not too hard to understand. When a man or woman has a spiritual awakening, the most important meaning of it is that he has now become able to do, feel, and believe that which he could not do before on his unaided strength and resources alone. He has been granted a gift which amounts to a new state of consciousness and being. He has been set on a path which tells him he is really going somewhere, that life is not a dead end, not something to be endured or mastered. In a very real sense he has been transformed, because he has laid hold of a source of strength which, in one way or another, he had hitherto denied himself.

Bill Wilson, *Twelve Steps and Twelve Traditions*

MARK, WHOSE CASE was presented in Chapter 5, gives a scalding review of the Twelve Step program of Alcoholics Anonymous. In his experience, the group was overpowering and his individuality threatened. He found the idea of being powerless particularly troubling and would not agree that he was powerless over *anything*. He was helped much more by Bollas's (1989) idea of creating his own destiny, of seeing that he was a free agent who could alter his present life course, than in viewing himself as a powerless victim. In his case, the use of AA was indeed problematic for the reasons he has mentioned. What is a clinician to do when faced with such a patient? Just about every inpatient rehabilitation program and outpatient day program stresses the importance of going to AA. In fact, standard treatment (both by these facilities and by the AA philosophy itself) calls for attendance at "ninety meetings in ninety days" upon initial abstinence. Recommending that his/her patient not attend AA meetings can indeed be a difficult decision for the clinician who does not want to support the patient's denial system and encourage him to recover "on his own"—which can be the tell-tale sign of impending relapse. How should the therapist respond?

I prefer to answer these questions by providing an overview of the AA program, its history, and the crucial psychodynamic issues that it addresses. As well, I offer the contradictory perspective of Stanton Peele (1989), who disagrees with the entire disease concept of alcoholism. There are valuable ideas to be learned from each perspective, and yet there are always reconciliations to be made between paradoxes. In between two opposing dialectics, there is a balance, a yin–yang waiting to be discovered.

HISTORICAL BACKGROUND

AA has its roots in the mystical, magical moment of immersion. Bill Wilson and the two men who influenced him before his achievement of sobriety had felt through their conversion experiences a sense of existential connectedness that they had never experienced before. And in a strange way, psychoanalysis and Carl Jung had everything to do with the inception of Alcoholics Anonymous. In 1931, an American alcoholic named Rowland H. traveled to Zurich for treatment under Jung's care. He worked with Jung for almost a year and left feeling confident and well. He soon relapsed, however, and reconsulted with Jung. Wilson (1968) wrote to Jung in 1961 regarding the significance of this return visit, noting

> the conversation between you [and Rowland] that was to become the first link in the chain of events that led to the founding of Alcoholics Anonymous . . . . First of all, you frankly told him of his hopelessness, so far as any further medical or psychiatric treatment might be concerned. [Second, Jung answered his question about other hopeful treatments with the idea of] a spiritual or religious experience—in short, a genuine conversion. [pp. 26–27]

Rowland took Jung's recommendation seriously. He joined the Oxford Group, an evangelical organization that was popular at the time,

and not only experienced a spiritual conversion but also did in fact stop drinking. He came back to New York, committed to circulating the principles of this group to other alcoholics. One of his friends, nicknamed Ebby, was on the verge of institutionalization when Rowland intervened and took him to meetings. Again, another spiritual experience, and again, a release from the alcoholic compulsion. Soon Ebby was visiting his good friend Wilson and urging him to "religion". Wilson was distressed by the idea that, for his friend, religion had replaced alcohol. He recalled that "it was an awful letdown. I had been educated at a wonderful engineering college where somehow I had gathered the impression that man was God" (1957, p. 58). However, he was intrigued by the transformation of Ebby through the Oxford Group and decided to investigate the organization for himself. He found himself battling yet again with sobriety while he sorted out the existential questions of religion, God, and his internal sense of alienation. He then chose to admit himself (for the fourth time) to the Towns Hospital because he felt he could sort out all of these answers better if he were totally detoxified. While in the hospital, Wilson experienced his own spiritual awakening, which he described in the same 1957 lecture cited above:

> My depression deepened unbearably and finally it seemed to me as though I were at the very bottom of the pit. I still gagged badly on the notion of a Power greater than myself, but finally, just for the moment, the last vestige of my proud obstinacy was crushed. All at once I found myself crying out, "If there is a God, let Him show Himself! I am ready to do anything, anything!"
>
> Suddenly the room lit up with a great white light. I was caught up into an ecstasy which there are no words to describe. It seemed to me, in the mind's eye, that I was on a mountain and that a wind not of air but of spirit was blowing. And then it burst upon me that I was a free man. Slowly the ecstasy subsided. I lay on the bed, but now for a time I was in another world, a new world of consciousness. All about me and through me there was a wonderful feeling of Presence, and I thought to myself, "So this is the God of the preachers!" A great peace stole over me, and I thought, "No matter how wrong things seem to be, they are all right. Things are all right with God and His world." [p. 63]

Wilson had experienced a moment of transcendence, a moment in which he felt transformed by a greater presence that had entered into him

and had made him feel powerful, connected, inspired. Echoing the oceanic feeling, it seems that he felt what Freud described as an existential connectedness, in which he "could not fall out of this world." Wilson was shaken by his experience—and rather skeptical. Either he was hallucinating and required an emergency psychiatric hospitalization, he thought, or he had just had a moment of sublime truth. He asked for an immediate consultation with his physician, Dr. Silkworth, to have him ascertain the exact nature of this experience. Thomsen (1975), in his biography of Wilson, described their meeting as follows:

> Silkworth had some questions first, probing questions, and Bill replied as best he could. When he was finished he watched the doctor sit back in his chair, his brow knitted. And as he did, as Bill waited, everything seemed to stop. Finally Bill could stand it no longer. "Tell me," he asked, "was it real? Am I still . . . sane?" And Silkworth answered, "Yes, my boy. You are sane. Perfectly sane, in my opinion." Then he went on to explain that Bill had probably undergone some tremendous psychic upheaval. He'd read about such things, and sometimes they had been known to produce remarkable results. But he was a simple man of science, he said, and he didn't begin to understand what some would call conversion, or a conversion experience. He knew that it could happen and something obviously had happened to Bill. "So . . ." he said, and he looked deeply into Bill's eyes when he said it, "whatever it is you've got now, hang on to it. Hang on to it, boy. It is so much better than what you had only a couple of hours ago." [p. 224]

I wonder how many clinicians today, after so many years of spiritual repression and so many years of mystical devaluation, would have answered as he did. Silkworth understood that Wilson's transcendent experience was indeed "so much better" than the painfulness of detachment. The doctor's answer was crucial because he helped the patient *believe in something greater than himself*, something that was not alcohol. This experience was crucial for Wilson, because he never drank again.

The next development in the foundation of AA also involved, primarily, immersive contact. A few months later, after some failed attempts by Wilson to inspire other alcoholic converts via the Oxford Group, he momentarily abandoned his newfound mission. Returning to his trade as a stockbroker, he traveled to Akron, Ohio, on business. There

he experienced a powerful urge to drink, but instead searched the phone book for Oxford Group members. He felt that he needed to talk with another alcoholic to help him stay sober. The alcoholic whom he finally was put in contact with was Dr. Bob Smith, a proctologist with a long history of alcoholism. This physician had recently become fascinated by the Oxford Group, and although he had not stopped drinking, he was considerably knowledgeable regarding the philosophies and tenets of the organization. The two met for what Dr. Bob, as he liked to be called, had planned as a very short meeting. Instead, their conversation lasted hours, and within days Wilson moved into the Smith's home for further extended discussions (something we might today call a retreat.) Kurtz (1979) has compiled a rendition of this meeting that gives Dr. Bob's subjective experience and demonstrates the impact of the immersive moment.

> Yes, here was somebody who really knew how it was! This stranger from New York had "been there." He had felt the obsession of craving, the terrors of withdrawal, the self-hatred over failure—all the things that he himself, Dr. Robert Smith, had experienced and was experiencing even as he listened.
>
> Something happened within Bob . . . . [He had never talked about himself, to anyone. An only child, he had always felt isolated. He had always felt a] lonely pain of the deep conviction that no one else would or could ever understand . . . .
>
> But here was someone who did understand, or perhaps at least could. This stranger from New York didn't ask questions and didn't preach; he offered no "you must's" or even "let us's." He had simply told the dreary, but fascinating facts about himself, about his own drinking. And now, as Wilson moved to stand up to end the conversation, he was actually thanking Dr. Smith for listening . . . . "I know now that I'm not going to take a drink, and I'm grateful to you." . . . . [Dr. Smith] had listened to Bill's story, and now, by God, this "rum hound from New York" was going to listen to his. For the first time in his life, Dr. Bob Smith *began to open his heart* (emphasis mine). [p. 29]

Although Dr. Bob did have one more binge during an out-of-town convention three weeks later, he returned to the caring arms of his wife and Wilson and never drank again. Wilson too had begun his lifelong sobriety with the hospitalization mentioned previously. The date was June 10, 1935, and the initial roots of the AA fellowship were firmly planted.

In addition to the relationship between Wilson and Smith, three other factors were important to the form and nature of AA. One was, of course, the tenets of the Oxford Group, a second was William James's perspective on religion and alcoholism, and the third was Dr. Silkworth's view that alcoholics are allergic to alcohol. From the Oxford Group, Wilson incorporated some of their basic concepts into the Twelve Steps; from James, he borrowed some of his ideas about spirituality and religious conversion; and from Silkworth, he adopted the idea that alcoholism was a disease, meaning "an obsession of the mind that condemns one to drink and an allergy of the body that condemns one to die" (Kurtz, 1979, p. 22). Of interest, the Oxford Group postulated The Four Absolutes: absolute honesty, unselfishness, purity, and love. Dr. Bob stated that the Oxford Group "members ought to achieve spiritual rejuvenation by making a surrender to God through rigorous self-examination, confessing their character defects to another human being, making restitution for harm done to others and giving without reward" (Buxton et al. 1987, p. 283). Along with these basic concepts was the belief that the alcoholic had to notice his horrendous condition and feel out of control; in the words of AA, he had to "hit bottom." A second important concept stressed that the alcoholic must push past his own self-absorption: humans are born to live with and do for others. And the third was the idea that the AA fellowship would work because, "in the kinship of common suffering, *one alcoholic had been talking to another*" (Wilson, 1957, p. 59).

The conversion process takes many forms, but the root is always the individual's realistic assessment of the predicament of his situation. He sees that his bills are unpaid, his house has been foreclosed, his employment prospects are minimal. And rather than drink to forget the miseries of his life, he becomes introspective. This is the moment of conversion, the moment when he realizes that he is in desperate shape and cannot continue living in the same way. Tiebout (1949), a psychiatrist prominent in the alcoholism field, wrote extensively about the necessity of conversion for the alcoholic's surrender. In fact, Wilson himself pursued psychotherapy with Tiebout in the mid-1940s. Tiebout notes that surrender occurs "when the unconscious defiance and grandiosity are for the time being rendered completely powerless" (p. 58). The act of surrender becomes the *state* of surrender, indicating the transformative aspect of the moment. If the surrender experience can be maintained, the individual shifts dramatically away from his former behavior. Every patient has faced his own confrontational moment with reality. For some, the moment occurs when they are alone and faced with their demons. Others have the reality forced onto them by spouses, jobs, or parents: an external other firmly stops the continued destruction of the self and others. Still others must endure further near-death experiences in order to be awakened from their denial.

What is important to remember here is the re-creation of the infantile experience. The baby knows he is separate, small, and powerless. He fights to get mother's attention and, it is hoped, is successful. He learns to seek help from a powerful and protective other; he accepts his limitations and enjoys the immersive experience as a mutual sharing between two selves. Other babies have not been so fortunate: in such instances, the baby knows he is small and helpless, but there is no external protection, no assistance. The wall of detachment is built, and inside, the child resolves to protect himself, to ask for nothing from anyone. This individual lives inside a protected, detached world. He drinks to "bolster" himself against the pains of everyday life. He has collapsed all of his needs into the one object of attachment: the drug. Finding this subjective object helps him feel independent, self-reliant, strong. And yet, the re-creation exists: he is still small and powerless. The drug, like mother, rules his life. He cannot get enough of her; he cannot get enough power in the momentary infusions of the substance to last throughout his daily life. And in moments of stark sobriety he sees the powerlessness of his being.

Tiebout (1954), drawing from Freud's view of the infant as "His Majesty the Baby," analyzes the alcoholic's character in relation to infantile narcissism. "He comes from the Nirvana of the womb, where he is usually the sole occupant, and he clings to that omnipotence with an innocence, yet determination, which baffles parent after parent" (p. 612). The baby, like a petulant monarch, is extremely impatient. Should these infantile characteristics persist into adulthood, the individual is seen as "immature" (p. 613). The alcoholic, according to Tiebout, is "possessed by an inner king" (p. 616) that must be reduced. Cutting the individual down to size is never completely possible, leaving the recovering alcoholic always in a somewhat risky position for relapse. Wilson, of interest, was uncomfortable with his therapist's portrayal of the alcoholic as "immature" and never seemed to fully resolve for himself this psychoanalytic perspective. Certainly, the perspective I am presenting here is that the predominant objective in the treatment of alcoholics is not to reduce their grandiose omnipotence but rather to lessen their feeling of infantile powerlessness.

Near-death experiences are frequent occurrences for the alcoholic and do not occur only at the point of conversion. The alcoholic seeks, indeed even welcomes, these moments as proof that his life is connected to a larger purpose, that his life holds significance. Here is the paradox: by testing his own mortality through risk-driven encounters with death, he has demonstrated that "he cannot fall out of this world"; by placing his life into the hands of fate and surviving, he is comforted that, despite his sense of existential alienation, there is some "force" that has actively intervened to keep him alive. Listen to the narratives of these three recovering alcoholics:

> *Gary:* I was constantly playing around with death. In fact I am totally amazed that I didn't die. I would mix heroin with all sorts of other drugs, and then shoot up, alone, in my tiny apartment. I swear there were more than a few times that I almost died—I can remember going in and out of consciousness, watching the room get smaller and smaller, as my body moved out of the room. What always saved me from dying was my dog. I'd look into his eyes and I would focus so hard on his little face and I felt like he was pulling me back to life. I stayed alive because that dog needed me.

> *Rick:* By all rights, I should be dead. Now that I sit here in recovery, I think it really was a miracle—there must indeed be a God. The time when my car flipped over backwards; the time I almost overdosed on that bad shit, the time the drug dealer got pissed off. It's too amazing for words. I am convinced that God has something else in mind for me—because by all rights, I really should have died.

> *Lynn:* I had missed all the signs of my alcoholic hepatitis. But I was so drunk all the time that I never felt a thing. I didn't even know what was happening when it acutely flared up. If a friend of mine hadn't been visiting, I would have died. She rushed me to the hospital, and by then I was in a coma. I was unconscious for six months, although I do remember hearing the doctor say that I only had a five percent chance of survival. And I knew then that I really did want to live. But still, once I was conscious and getting ready for

discharge, I drank some vodka that a friend brought for me on a hospital visit. That's when I knew I needed more help. After all I had been through, and I was at it again. I've often thought about that moment—that was my day of reckoning. And the last time I drank. Because it occurred to me that there must be some greater plan for me, because despite all the abuse I had put myself through, I hadn't succeeded in killing myself. If there had been no outside intervention, I would have died. But obviously there was—someone who had more power than me.

These addicts should not be viewed simply as people who are denying their own mortality, people filled with pathological, narcissistic omnipotence. Rather, their near deaths have served as affirmation, as confirmation in their minds that they were worthy of being saved. Only in these moments did they feel a transcendence, a sense that they were being held by a powerful, protective other. In the near-death experience, they were returned to their impotent baby-self; in the salvation, they were rescued, this time, from annihilation. The entire risk-taking adventure serves as a way to seek a transformational object, to find a new mother who will stretch her arms and protect, comfort, and soothe. In understanding this dynamic, it is also important to understand that the longer the individual has been addicted, the less likely that the drug itself will retain its original power and transformational properties. Since the high itself becomes more elusive, the search for other dangerous elements becomes greater. Salvation must then be sought at a greater personal cost and will be evoked through more perilous measures. These patients do not *start out* with such risky behavior (although drug use in itself is risky), but have instead escalated the risks because the drugs no longer provide the sensations of ongoing, miraculous salvation.

I am reminded of my daughter who, at the age of 2½, loved to play the game of "monster" with my husband and me. Daddy would be the pretend monster and chase after her as she would delightedly run to me calling, "Mommy, save my life! Save my life!" And off we would go, me holding her, running away from the monster whom we eventually always "killed" or "made him nice." I think the joy of this game came more from my saving her than from his chasing. She loved the idea that she could be held by me in a powerful, protective way—her little person was safe. The fears that are so common for a youngster always have this component. Mother and father are called upon to protect the child and to chase away the monsters, kill the spiders, and slay the dragons. In this enactment, the child is expressing his physical and psychic smallness. He is relieved to discover that he is worthy of salvation and rescue.

THE TWELVE STEPS OF ALCOHOLICS ANONYMOUS

1. We admitted we were powerless over alcohol – that our lives had become unmanageable.
2. Came to believe that a Power greater than ourselves could restore us to sanity.
3. Made a decision to turn our will and our lives over to the care of God *as we understood Him*.
4. Made a searching and fearless moral inventory of ourselves.
5. Admitted to God, ourselves, and to another human being the exact nature of our wrongs.
6. Were entirely ready to have God remove all these defects of character.
7. Humbly asked Him to remove our shortcomings.
8. Made a list of all persons we had harmed, and became willing to make amends to them all.
9. Made direct amends to such people wherever possible, except when to do so would injure them or others.
10. Continued to take personal inventory and when we were wrong promptly admitted it.
11. Sought through prayer and meditation to improve our conscious contact with God *as we understood Him*, praying only for knowledge of His will for us and the power to carry that out.
12. Having had a spiritual awakening as the result of these steps, we tried to carry this message to alcoholics, and to practice these principles in all our affairs.

Alcoholics Anonymous (1939), pp. 59–60

The moment of transcendence, then, is the first step to recovery because the alcoholic admits he is not alone in this world. The thrust of AA actually is to enhance this realization and to assist the alcoholic in a "spiritual journey" that continually increases his ability to attain moments of oneness in relation to other people, nature, or prayer rather than from any substance. Essentially the aim of the work is to shift the object of attachment away from the drug and back into the real world.

Wilson, who wrote much of the AA material, focused the recovery process around spirituality. Of interest, the word alcohol is used only in Step One. The rest of the eleven steps are concerned with developing immersive moments. Members are consistently encouraged to attend meetings, at which time a recovering member tells his individual life story in a candid and honest way. The group forms a fellowship in which members are urged to discuss their struggles with recovery and the cravings that may continue to plague them. AA strongly suggests that each newcomer obtain a sponsor, a member who has achieved at least one year of recovery, who will guide the new member through his beginning sobriety and lead him through the Twelve Steps. Books are offered for reading, and members often reach out to the newcomer with phone numbers, advice, and invitations for social outings after meetings. AA's basic text is known as The Big Book. It is, predominantly, a collection of stories from other recovering alcoholics – stories of their personal hell and the nature of their recovery. The emphasis is, as Wilson so emphatically believed, that "one alcoholic is talking to another." Here again, the program understands that to reach alcoholics it must engage them by immersion within relationships, not with substances.

In essence, the steps are a behavioral approach to attack the world-view of the alcoholic, who has dismissed any prospect of a powerful, protective object for immersion and attachment other than the substance. The program sets out to correct these transferential distortions so that the individual can begin to feel connected to a safe, soothing world. The first step is to return the alcoholic to his childhood sense of powerlessness and helplessness. Next, by admitting that a "Power greater than ourselves" exists and can help, the alcoholic begins the process of taking in a new transformational object while rejecting the power of alcohol. This power, clearly, was once mother. And for these individuals, she was either smothering in her presence or unavailable in her absence. The task for the alcoholic is to return once again to his infantile position and risk that, this time, his transformational object will indeed rescue, save, and metamorphose his being.

This process is no different from that of any patient entering psychotherapy, an idea also mentioned by Tiebout. The individual admits that his life is chaotic, or that his psychic pain is too great, or that his world is too difficult. Tiebout (1949) notes that "the phenomenon of release, which makes people realize that in losing their lives they are finding them" (p. 57), is a crucial aspect of the first interview. The patient agrees to try a new object, one different from his family and friends, and he has the hope that the therapist will be a worthwhile object of attachment. He hopes the therapist can help him change his life; he admits he cannot continue on his own. In the process, he projects onto the therapist images of his parents in what is called transference. Patient and therapist work together to resolve the transference impasses so that the patient can continue to see the therapist as a new, different, and, it is hoped, better object. Tiebout (1949) likens this to ongoing surrenderings: "I now believe that the abandonment of resistance during treatment is in reality an act of surrender which, typically, as in the conversion experience, is followed by a positive state of mind in which elements of resistance are no longer present" (pp. 57–58).

A young woman began therapy with hope and fear. She at first felt an immediate connection to me and believed that I was so very different from the rest of the people in her life. She was excited about the therapy and took in everything we discussed. But then, inevitably, came the session when she experienced me as exactly like her family: she felt I had been laughing at her while she was seriously discussing her pain. She wanted to leave the therapy immediately. As she said: "Why should I stay in yet another relationship in which I'm going to be hurt?" The task was to help her separate me from the transference distortions and to see this interaction as a repetition of her lonely, painful past. Indeed, as we explored her childhood more fully, she disclosed that her parents had often left her alone in the house for hours even when she was just a kindergartner. They would laugh at her fears and ignore her protests of despair. At times they would slap her, hoping this would teach her to stifle her cries. Instead, she resolved never to need anyone as much as she needed them, never to be laughed at by any other, never to love.

The third step is a difficult one because the task involves truly *believing in* the powerful, protective other. The language of this step interests me because it sounds like a step toward mother-love. To turn oneself over to the *care of God* is to indicate that God is caring, nurturant, loving. This phrase always reminds me of an infant who turns himself, smiling expectantly, when he sees mother coming to care for him. These first three steps, then, set the transcendent experience in motion. In a behavioral way, the alcoholic is pushed to experience himself as *belonging to* a greater and more protective world.

The fourth through tenth steps encourage the alcoholic to review his own character and reveal his true self to at least one other as well as to God. This is another aspect of the immersion process. The individual bares his soul; he tells his innermost thoughts, guilt-ridden feelings, and shameful actions to an other (most often his sponsor). The immersive experience is one in which the individual feels his true self shine through. He allows himself, because of the nature of this particular relationship, to push past his detached self and reveal that which he has defended so heavily against sharing. Secrets of the soul are barriers to immersion. This step, done in confidence with a willing partner who is empathically responsive, shatters the isolation chamber in which the alcoholic has lived for so very long. Typically, the sponsor shares some of his own shameful past so that the newly recovering individual feels less unique and less bad.

Certainly this action of revelation is well known to analysts and patients alike. Frequently, psychotherapy sessions become confessionals. The patient overcomes his resistance to disclosing his inner self and releases his most private secrets. The difference in the psychotherapy relationship, however, is that the confessional is not a behavioral edict and can come in tiny fragments throughout many years of treatment. As well, it is not particularly common for the therapist to self-disclose so as to help relieve the patient of his shame and guilt. Bollas (1989) does suggest, interestingly enough, that addicts may need more disclosure than other types of patients.

> I also think that the selective disclosure of certain details from one's life helps the tripper to feel that he is part of a collectively human experience, rather than a specimen of the freakish. Such persons really do lose their sense of perspective after a long period of drug abuse. They truly do not know what is freakish and what is human. Indeed they can develop a persecuting superego that adjudges all of their phantasies and dreams as para-criminal acts which must be kept under lock and key. [p. 156]

Chapter 7 presents a detailed case analysis of a drug addict who was painfully convinced that he was a "freak of nature." I would add to Bollas's comments that the drug addict very often has felt freakish before his drug attachment and that, furthermore, the root of this subjective state is the very detachment process that has been caused by unempathic parenting and traumatizing separation experiences.

A patient comes to mind who was struggling with rageful feelings toward her young son. She had been a neglected child, with a mother who rarely noticed her and a father who was always drunk. Her response to them was to become as nurturing and attentive as possible, ever hopeful that her loving behavior would reward her with their love. As a teenager and young adult, she turned to alcohol for comfort. Now in recovery five years, she sought treatment after her son's birth because she found herself easily overwhelmed by the demands of motherhood. She was, therefore, desperately frightened by moments in which her anger at her young child, whom she loved dearly, was extreme. We spoke openly about the difficult demands of mothering—we are not always able to be the mothers we had hoped to be. These self-disclosing moments between us always helped her in her relationship with me, as well as with her son. It was important to her that I was human too, that I was not always the "perfect therapist" who would always be calm, cool and collected with my own children. She would often say that these were her best sessions, because she was able to release herself from feeling shamed by her anger. She was relieved that she could disclose these moments to me.

I will add a caveat about AA's fifth step and God. The invoking of God in some of these steps, such as in Steps Five and Six, has alienated many recovering individuals and therapists alike. The use of God here can be seen as an evocation of the spiritual; admitting "defects of character" can feel holy and awesome. There is a similarity here with the confessional, priest, and God. Furthermore, the concept of the Higher Power, as I have attempted to demonstrate, can be any object that brings transformation: the sponsor, the therapist, the group, the moon, the vista on the horizon. One person's story in *Alcoholics Anonymous* (1939), for example, talks about his use of the radiator in his bedroom as his God because it was the only dependable thing in his life—he knew it would make a rattle every morning that would wake him like clockwork! The point is this: the recovering individual must become used to incorporating an other into his own being, developing trust with another object of attachment, and thereby releasing part of his true self.

Step Eleven continues the immersion process, although in a new way. The earlier steps offer the patient first an immersion into a powerful other and then a reflection back to the self as a separate being. As such, the separate self is taught to look again, in the relationships with others, for moments of connectedness by revealing "true self" feelings and thoughts. Step Eleven continues the immersive experience when the individual is actually alone. This concept is similar to Winnicott's idea of developing the capacity to be alone, an obvious difficulty for the alcoholic. Living in a separated state, the alcoholic is given tools to continue making contact. I call these techniques *immersion aids*, because they are helpful in strengthening and deepening the merger. Again, I do not like the term transitional objects because it denotes that these techniques are used in the service of separation, whereas I see them as being used in the deepening of connection. Prayer and meditation can be seen as a way to continue seeking the transformational object. The use of affirmations and creative visualization are two similar ways to internalize the immersive relationship and develop an internal power base. Affirmation literally means to make firm. The individual thinks positive thoughts about himself (i.e., "I am worthy of love"), and with enough practice, it is hoped that these thoughts will become incorporated into the self. How similar this is to the little engine who tells itself, "I think I can, I think I can, I think I can," all the way up the mountain and, having been successful, goes down the mountain rejoicing, "I thought I could, I thought I could, I thought I could." A somewhat more involved process is creative visualization, described by Shakti Gawain in her popular book of the same title (1978) as follows:

> Creative visualization is the technique of using your imagination to create what you want in your life. There is nothing at all new, strange, or unusual about creative visualization. You are already using it every day, every minute in fact. It is your natural power of imagination, the basic creative energy of the universe which you use constantly . . . . Imagination is the ability to create an idea or mental picture in your mind. In creative visualization you use your imagination to create a clear image of something you wish to manifest. Then you continue to focus on the idea or picture regularly, giving it positive energy until it becomes objective reality. [pp. 2–3]

For alcoholics especially, who were rarely as children given hope for their dreams or encouragement of their talents, the employment of these techniques can be thrilling. Just as Mark discovered he could release himself from the confines of being a fated individual, so can other recovering alcoholics, who were never offered dreams to touch or futures to love. Indeed, immersion can ignite a powerful spark in the relationship. Just as mother infuses her child with the nurturant milk that makes him grow and thrive, so can merger fill the adult with love and power. Let me add a caveat, however, to the use of these techniques. Individuals who are markedly depressed may find that these tools can have little effect. Trying to imagine a better life for oneself, when only darkness prevails, is often so frustrating that the individual actually feels worse. These techniques are often best utilized in conjunction with other therapies. If, for example, an individual finds he can only affirm the badness in him, therapy can help him uncover what has made him so stubbornly attached to this negative introject. These approaches can be intertwined and used together for best results.

Therapy itself is also a process of shifting internal thoughts and beliefs and of utilizing the therapeutic relationship to dislodge toxic introjects. The therapist may suggest to a patient that he find a way to "hold onto" the relationship outside the session, via reliving moments of the relationship or offering himself such thoughts as "What would my therapist think of me doing this now?" As Seinfeld (1991) has discussed, helping the patient keep the therapist as an internalized object is crucial to the success of the treatment. By internalizing the good object of the therapist, negative introjects can be lessened. The process of internalization and the success of using the immersion techniques listed in Step Eleven are crucial to building moments of oneness. Through these measures, the recovering alcoholic smashes through the wall of detachment and strengthens his indissoluble bond with the external world.

One of the major criticisms leveled against AA is that it promotes further dependency in the alcoholic. Instead of relying on the substance, these individuals become AA "zombies," as one of my patients puts it. Attending meetings, becoming involved with a sponsor, committing to the philosophy can be overwhelming to newcomers. As with my patient Mark, the idea of seeing oneself as powerless in the face of a more powerful other can be troubling indeed. But that is the very root of the alcoholic's problem. Kurtz (1979) states that the core of the AA philosophy is in conflict with the twentieth-century emphasis on self-reliance. "To the modern understanding, 'full maturity' means *absolute, total* independence; and for the modern understanding, of course, only *full* maturity is satisfactory. . . . [To the AA way of thinking] human dependence . . . is not to be denied. . . . To be human *is* to be dependent . . . Accepted ultimate dependence is the essence of the experience of bottom" (p. 216). Certainly this same criticism is raised about psychotherapy: the patient becomes so attached to the therapist that the patient no longer can rely on his own self. These views come from the societal norm that equates separateness with adulthood and attachment with infancy.

As I have stated previously, the levels of dependence shift with the needs of the individual. A newcomer to the program, for example, will most likely require attendance at more meetings, more contact with his sponsor, and more involvement from the group. Over time, his stability returns to him, and he quite naturally reduces the quantity of immersion. For example, one patient has been sober for fifteen years. Originally when he began, he was so fresh from his last drink that a few of the old-timers kept him up all night with coffee and got him through the first few days with almost round-the-clock care. He attended meetings daily at that time, and when his sponsor suggested he make the coffee for one of the meetings, he gladly agreed. (This is a responsibility of honor, often given to a new member to help him feel welcome, part of, and involved in the group.) Soon he was asked to make the coffee at a second meeting, and then at a third. He told his sponsor that he was now making coffee at four meetings—wasn't that enough? And his sponsor answered, "Well you're still sober, aren't you!" This patient readily agrees that AA got him sober and that making the coffee gave him something to do, a responsibility to follow up on, and a feeling of identity in the group. He is quite sure that, without the help of his sponsor and a few other members, he would never have made it past those first few days. And yet, as he gained sober time, he lessened his meeting time. Over the years, as he continued in sobriety, he lessened his attendance again and again. He still has fond, indeed loving and grateful, feelings for the program and its help to him, but he now rarely attends at all. Was he *dependent* on the program? Was he an AA "*zombie*"?

My feeling is that attachment is an ever-shifting, although ever-present, phenomenon. The infant requires mother to handle all aspects of his care because he can do so little for himself. As he grows, she does less of these basic functions. He is not dependent on her for breast milk, for example, or for mobility, or diapering. As he develops, their roles shift again, as she then helps with homework, transportation, and supportive advice. Is he still dependent and attached? Of course. Has the format and function of his attachment shifted? Of course.

This perspective answers the question of reliance on AA. Initially the newcomer (or the relapsed member) requires a great deal of assistance. As he internalizes the group, the philosophy, and his sponsor's suggestions, he shifts to a less externalized dependence. As to the AA philosophy on powerlessness, I would say this: the alcoholic is someone who has found it untenable to admit self-limitations. The philosophy of AA boldly points out this fact and suggests ways to cope with feelings of smallness and separateness. Certainly the newcomer can attain this same philosophy elsewhere—some patients would prefer to shift their object of attachment from the drug to the therapist alone (or vice versa). Such was the case with Mark, who was more comfortable tackling these feelings inside my office than inside AA. In either setting, these are among the most important dynamics that must be addressed with the recovering alcoholic. In fact, the setting is not as significant as the patient's ability to accept external attachments. Yet, AA is a welcome therapeutic partner because it offers many valuable services, including (1) a ready-made support system, complete with volunteers who are available 24 hours a day; (2) a ready-made group framework; and (3) a sound behavioral approach that complements the analytic frame.

One of my recovering patients has accused me of idealizing AA. My focus has centered on the theory of AA, not its actual practice. The program is made up of individuals, however, not theories, and it is important to tease out the philosophical tenets of the program from the realities of individual group dynamics. Some groups are inappropriate for some patients, and some members might offer possibly the worst suggestion for a particular individual. The idea, for example, that an individual can never leave the program or he is *absolutely* going to drink is an unfortunate message to emphasize. For Mark, this concept was one of AA's most stifling ideas. I view the issue differently—the alcoholic can always choose to come back, to come "home" to the program if he wishes. That is the point. Returning is not a sign of weakness and not a triumph for the group who cautioned against leaving. Just as some patients return to psychotherapy, the work can always be continued because we are all simply living works in progress. Thomas Wolfe felt one can never go home again. In the immersive process, however, there is always the possibility of connection, return, and recontact. The indissoluble bond exists forever.

In *Diseasing of America: Addiction Treatment Out of Control*, Peele (1989) has written about America's emphasis on disease. Everything these days, he writes, is called a disease—premenstrual syndrome, adoption syndrome, uncontrollable rage disorder, battered women syndrome, and the like. Furthermore, he completely disagrees with the idea that addiction is a disease. This idea he feels "does more than excuse addicts and alcoholics for their past, present, and future irresponsibility. It actually sets them up for relapse and retards personal growth" (quotation from the book jacket). He believes it is the psychoactive effects of the drug that addict people, rather than the psychobiology of one's genetic inheritance. It is the *experience itself* that is addicting. The narcotic's ability to reduce pain, the cocaine's ability to produce euphoria, is powerfully addicting. There is no "supposed chemical bondings or inbred biological deficiencies" (p. 151) required to form addictions, argues Peele. He makes the point that, in fact, most people cure their addictions alone rather than in treatment facilities. For example, smoking is considered, even by addictionologists, to be the most difficult addiction to stop. How is it possible, then, that 40 million Americans have stopped smoking and 95 percent have done so without any treatment! The common denominator seems to be determination, a belief that the cigarettes have become more damaging than enjoyable to the smoker. In conclusion, Peele offers therapeutic recommendations for stemming the addiction problem in America. First and foremost we need to correct the isolation present in our society, to improve a sense of community and connectedness, because addiction is so often caused by a sense of alienation. Furthermore, child-rearing approaches have not provided individuals with what he terms positive values nor helped them develop positive senses of self.

What is of the greatest interest to me is Peele's prescription for curing addiction. Without using the term immersion, Peele believes that our society must increase the level of immersion in our lives, in our child-raising techniques, and in our societal goals. I am simply surprised that he cannot extend these ideas to the program of AA, which, despite his dislike of the religious conversion aspect of the program, does indeed focus on developing personal responsibility, seeing one's behavior as having consequences for others, and developing a spiritual, or transcendent, connection to others. He criticizes AA for its disease-model approach. In actuality, however, the program stresses that alcoholism is not only a biological illness, but a "physical, mental, and spiritual" disease.[1] Looked at in that light, the alcoholic's belief that he has a disease means that he must take responsibility for all aspects of that disease. He must accept that

---

1. This view of the pathological roots that cause alcoholism is well known to AA members. The written source of this phrase, however, is more obscure. Kurtz (1979) traces its origin to Dr. Clarence P., who delivered a paper in 1949 at the First National and International Meeting of Physicians in Alcoholics Anonymous.

he is harming his body, that he is emotionally vulnerable, and that he is spiritually lacking. The emphasis on the disease model that prevails so thoroughly in this country today has everything to do with treatment costs. As long as alcoholism is viewed as a medical illness, individuals are eligible for treatment at hospitals and in outpatient settings. Should alcoholism no longer be categorized as a disease, then insurance companies may no longer feel an obligation to pay for treatment, and therefore, most individuals would be unable to pay for the exorbitant costs of treatment.

In conclusion, Peele offers therapeutic recommendations for stemming the addiction problem in America. Because addiction is so often rooted in a pervasive feeling of alienation, he feels that there must be a societal shift from the isolation presently found in our culture. A sense of community and connectedness must be built into our neighborhoods and cities. Child-rearing practices must facilitate the development of positive values, which include taking responsibility for one's own actions; developing a sense of achievement, self-awareness, and self-respect; and deepening intimacy. "Addiction is an endless effort to overcome the inability to transcend oneself through real engagement with other people. To achieve this kind of genuine intimacy requires all of the values listed here, including even competence in dealing with the world . . . . More than anything, we need to increase in our society and in our personal lives our opportunities for real contact with others" (p. 286).

Peele's point is well taken. What actually makes the addict put the substance down? In part it is the fact that, from the user's perspective, the drug has been shifted from a positive transformational object to a poisonous one, and in part it is the fact that the addict, through a conversion experience, has committed himself to life over death. One of the techniques I use with this population involves helping these individuals continue to view alcohol as poison and cigarettes as death. I tell them to "imagine your death every time you inhale. And then tell me every thought and feeling you have while you are smoking, so that we can understand your intense wish to tempt fate." AA also focuses on debunking the joy of drinking. One emphasis in A. A. is to "keep it green," meaning to provide members ongoing and accurate remembrances of the effects of alcohol so that they can maintain their shift from viewing alcohol as God to seeing the substance as the devil. The impact can be great, and both newcomer and old–timer are further persuaded to keep all temptation at bay.

Peele stresses community as curative. Indeed, this philosophy is the overall emphasis of the fellowship and its overriding message. I would add that the cumulative emphasis of AA, and of psychotherapy for the addicted individual, is to evoke, sustain, and encourage moments of oneness. When the transformative object is shifted to the AA group, the sponsor, and/or the therapist, the results can be powerful. The indissoluble bond is again invoked and strengthened, only this time it is held between humans rather than dissolved into substances.

A young woman told her story at the AA meeting in front of fifty members. She spoke of the desperation she had felt before recovery, of her sense of isolation and loneliness. When she came to her first meeting three years ago, she was surprised by the intensity of what she called the "bond" she felt with the people in the room. "I liked what I saw, and I've stayed ever since." She went on to talk about her recovery, about her loving relationship with her sponsor, and about her developing relationship with God. She ended her story by saying, "The biggest thing I've gotten out of the program is my spirituality, my connection with God, because," (her voice trailing off as she continued), "Because, you know, people disappoint. . . ."

7

THE POWER OF IMMERSION

Amazing grace! How sweet the sound
That saved a wretch like me!
I once was lost, but now am found,
Was blind, but now I see.

John Newton

THIS CHAPTER PROVIDES a detailed case illustration that demonstrates the full extent of the immersive transference and the use of
immersion aids. One of the suggestions I had made to this patient, Tony,
early on in our work (October 1987) was that he start a journal. I felt the
writing would help him, quite literally, collect his thoughts. I also felt it
might be one way of evoking my presence when I was not physically with
him, helping him remain involved in self-analysis despite our separations.
What a fortuitous suggestion this has been. Now, eight years later, he still
writes fairly frequently. As well, he has graciously allowed me full access to
this *independent* account of his therapy. It is rare to have access to such
records from a patient. I feel indebted to him for this gift. Selections from
his diaries, printed in italics, are interspersed in chronological order within
my narrative.

Tony is tall, tanned, and thin and in his eighth year of treatment.
Thirty-six years old, recently remarried, and expecting his first child soon,
he wears several crosses and Catholic medals as necklaces and rings. His
presentation in my office gives no hint of the emotional pain and suffering
he has been through and no indication of the distress he was in when he
and I first met.

Tony presented himself for admission to the dual-diagnosis unit
where I then worked because he was feeling totally out of control with

drugs, alcohol, and food, and as well was acutely suicidal. He was clearly agitated and anxious, attempting throughout the interview to stress the importance of his need for hospitalization. Tony indeed was desperate— his job was in jeopardy, his wife was suing for divorce, and his debt stood at $10,000. He was a giant mound of flesh—200 pounds overweight and unable to breathe without wheezing or walk without stumbling. Tony had no other clothes than the torn black shirt and jeans he was wearing because his mother and brother had evicted him from his apartment.

Tony had been addicted to crack cocaine for the last three months, following an inpatient program at another psychiatric hospital for marijuana addiction and compulsive overeating. While in the hospital he did well, losing 100 pounds and maintaining his sobriety. He was treated pharmacologically with antipsychotic medication and had seemingly good results. The hospital diagnosed him as a schizophrenic with a dependent personality disorder. Once he left the hospital, however, he was unable to sustain his abstinence from either excessive eating or drugs, and he discontinued all medication. He began experimenting with crack cocaine because he had continuously heard from other inpatients that this drug was the "ultimate high" and was not to be missed.

HISTORY

Tony was born the second of four children. He was sandwiched between a brother twenty months older and a sister thirteen months younger. His younger brother was separated from the older three by eight years. Perhaps in part due to birth order, Tony was always neglected and forgotten in the family. His older brother, also his father's namesake, was the favored child. His sister was special because of gender, and his younger brother was showered with attention because he was the "baby."

Tony's mother worked in her family's real estate business during much of his early childhood. She was a nervous woman whose beauty hid her extreme anxiety and low self-worth. In part because of her work schedule, Tony remembers spending more of his early years with his father. Mr. B. had been raised in an orphanage and had been subjected to physical abuse by the staff. He joined the military at 17 and became a police officer after his honorable discharge. The abusive style in which he was raised greatly affected the way he raised his children. An active alcoholic, he was physically and emotionally cruel to all of them, in particular to Tony because he was of slighter build and more timid. In a moving passage written in his seventh year of recovery, Tony described an early memory of his childhood, his father, and food.

May 27, 1993: I remember my first clear picture of my compulsive, obsessive behavior when I was in, I guess, second grade, or it could have been first, or even third or fourth, but I remember distinctly being in the cafeteria of my Catholic school and my friend John—[an] alcoholic now and drug addict, who had come in [to the AA program] for a few years, now left it, is active—but he would go around to each table and take everyone['s] bread and . . . he would almost eat a whole loaf. I would go back for seconds and I think thirds if I could get more food the third time around; but I remember eating very fast and compulsively, like the food would run out. And then . . . [there would be] several children, maybe two or three sitting together and even others, and they would point out how fast I was eating and the way I would gulp my food down, and when I was aware of them laughing or talking about me I couldn't seem to slow down or stop going back for more. That was school.

I think at home I remember being so fearful all the time because of my father's anger and mood swings back and forth of rage and sometimes love. But at the table I sort of remember the way I would eat fast and would want a lot and even though to this day I hear my Mom say eat slow and my father saying chew your food, I think it was that I was so afraid of my father's explosive anger and rage sometimes, just in his eyes it was like eat fast to get away from table before [the] shit hits the fan. The family . . . [at] that time didn't and still don't do well with eating together with love and intimacy.

Mr. B. was also a "ladies' man," continuously flirting with every woman he met. Tony had many memories of sitting in his father's patrol car and watching the sergeant beep at all the pretty girls on the street, stopping his car to flirt with those who came toward him.

By the age of 8, Tony had become preoccupied with the idea that his penis was too small. This worry became a fixation when, at age 10, his father took him to the pediatrician for what Tony says was an examination to confirm his deformity. He felt humiliated and shamed as he watched the doctor and his father talking in private about his physical condition. For the next twenty years Tony lived with the absolute conviction that his penis was malformed and that he had no chance of being loved as a "real man."

When Tony was 13, his father was severely injured during a police shoot-out, leaving him bedridden. His wife devoted herself to his care, and in two years he was almost fully recuperated. To her surprise and that of her children, soon after his recovery Mr. B. announced he was going to divorce her and start a new life out West. Despite her desperate pleadings, they separated six months later and divorced six years after that. This precipitated her first "nervous breakdown" and Tony's first experimental use of marijuana. He moved into the caretaking role for his mother and simultaneously began using marijuana daily. Throughout high school Tony became more and more engrossed in the use and sale of marijuana. He enjoyed being a "big man" on campus, which helped relieve the stress and burden of his mother's neediness at home. Two years later she became deeply devoted to another man, who seemed to love her dearly.

With his mother reinvolved in a romantic relationship and with high school behind him, Tony moved out West to be with his father. Mr. B.'s drinking had gotten worse, however, as had his verbal abusiveness. Tony became depressed and despondent and in one instance held his father's police gun inside his mouth while fantasizing suicide. He instead decided to move back East and live with his mother and younger brother. At 25, Tony married a woman four years younger who was desperate to get away from her abusive family. She suffered from depression herself, and frequently the two would sit silently in their apartment, attempting to smoke away their hopelessness and anhedonia. Three years later Tony's mother had another "nervous breakdown" following the unexpected and untimely fatal heart attack of her fiance. She became increasingly needy and hysterical, constantly demanding that her children help her and care for her. Tony became increasingly involved in her difficulties, and, over time, she was able to convince him that some of her cousins were trying to kill her over an inheritance. Tony began carrying a gun in his mother's house and keeping an all-night vigil to protect her. As part of this role as protector, Tony went to the offices of one of her alleged enemies and created a confrontation so intense that the police were called in to mediate. On his return to these offices a few days later, he was arrested and imprisoned.

Tony strongly believes that his arrest was part of a plan to harm his mother and family. He believes he was drugged and tormented for several days by the police. In one instance, for example, he says that he was wrapped in a blanket with his face smothered by a pillow while the police punched him. They said to him, "How's it feel to know you're gonna die?" He is convinced that the only reason he was not killed was because he had purposely caused himself physical injury by head banging and body banging so that his body would alert the medical examiner to foul play. No doubt because of his bizarre behavior, he was taken in handcuffs and shackles to the state psychiatric hospital for observation. Tony spent ten weeks incarcerated in this facility and was diagnosed as having an atypical psychosis. It was assumed that he was a burgeoning schizophrenic who had just experienced his first break. Tony was released with a recommendation for ongoing outpatient treatment and given a prescription for continued antipsychotic medication, which he promptly trashed.

Soon after his release, Tony began to eat huge quantities of food in an effort to forget his recent experience of humiliation and to contain his rage at being rendered so helpless. In a single year he gained 200 pounds. He continued to live with his wife and returned to his job as an electrician, until a year later, at 440 pounds, he entered the first of two private psychiatric hospitals of his own volition. At the conclusion of this stay, Tony started his use of crack cocaine and was admitted, three months later, to the dual-diagnosis unit where I worked.

DEVELOPMENT OF ALTERNATIVE FUSION OBJECTS

In reviewing Tony's history from the standpoint of merging phenomena, it is clear that he had infrequent immersions with others and learned to rely on substances, such as food and drugs, instead. Tony first began to use food as a merging substitute at about 8 years of age, coinciding with the time he began to feel sexually malformed. The symbolism of his belief that his manliness had been damaged indicates his underlying self-belief that he was an inadequate and powerless child.

August 4, 1993: What is fear? Fear is love's absence. Growing up as a child, love's absence was a constant, so what did I do? Fear was in the form of being afraid of my abnormality and being afraid I will be alone forever.

His belief that he was sexually malformed certainly can be interpreted as castration anxiety, and it does indeed indicate his fear and hatred of his punitive, powerful father. However, his sense of impotence began as an infant and young child, predating oedipal issues. He was continually demeaned in the family. For example, one Christmas while his brothers and sister were unwrapping their presents, his mother suddenly remembered that she had bought him only one gift. She scurried to write him a check for an amount equal to the presents she had given his siblings. From this incident and the many others like it, Tony felt unloved; thus the symptom as symbol of his physical malformation. He assumed he was a freak and would always be unworthy of love. He had an overwhelming sense of doom in his future, expecting little in life to be offered to him. Tony believed he was forsaken by God and that he was fated to a life of minimal pleasure.

In addition to this sense of isolation and unlovableness, Tony was highly sensitized to abandonments. He recalls as early as age 2½ being pulled away from his mother by his father while screaming for an "extra hug." Tony remembers his mother as inconsistent in her attentiveness. She would ignore him for days and then, out of the blue, lunge toward him in what Tony terms "swooping love." Indeed, the moments of fusion with this soothing other were too few and too intense. Tony learned to crave these moments, but he also expected each one to be "the last one" he might ever get. This worry continues to preoccupy him at times and has caused him to cling tightly to any fusion experiences while resisting all separations. He has had great trouble denying himself some of his favorite foods, for example, because he fears it might be the last time he would ever eat them.

This enfeebled self-representation also alternated with a grandiose self-concept. To cope with his extreme alienation, Tony grew to believe that, like Jesus, his life was created for a greater purpose. He believed, in fact, that God had made him the family savior by giving him the affliction of penile malformation. This belief certainly soothed his weakened ego, although he always felt alienated from God. He accepted a greater purpose, although it entailed enormous self-suffering and a lifetime of deprivation that he did not want. In fact, this omnipotent perspective was the only way Tony could conceptualize the lack of love he received and his own sense of unlovability. That he had been caused to suffer for the greater good of his family made his pain all the more noble and worthy.

Tony's use of food as momentary mergings also coincided with the birth of his youngest brother. His mother's unavailability after her youngest son's birth was even greater than before. For instance, Tony remembers being scolded by her first because he asked to hold the baby, which she refused to allow, and then to hug the baby, which she also refused. He began to focus on his "smallness," a perfect and unconscious symbolization of his insecurity, unlovability, and alienation. Similarly, Tony's use of marijuana in adolescence began as a way to soothe himself during his parents' divorce. He felt whole, protected, and sheltered by using the drug. With marijuana inside him, he could face the separation from his father and tolerate his mother's weakened emotional state. As they were preoccupied with their own issues, Tony sought moments of fusion, moments of love, from marijuana. Just before his last hospitalization, it is interesting to note, he found comfort in a combination of marijuana and cocaine because, with the marijuana as a fusion base, he could experience once again the momentary exhilaration from the "swooping love" action of the cocaine.

This extended discussion of Tony's history has demonstrated that the stark circumstances of his childhood lay the foundation for his dependence on food and other substances. The discussion of Tony's treatment will focus on how his ability to experience and to create positive merging moments has enabled him to maintain recovery for the last eight years.

TREATMENT

Tony's hospitalization provided the foundation for his metamorphosis. In the twenty-four-hour intensive facility, all aspects of maternal care were provided. Indeed, the hospital served as an external protective covering that surrounded him at all times. He saw me as the overriding protector, almost as though the rest of the staff were simply extensions of my self. In a meeting with the nursing and clinical staff, for example, Tony once told everyone that "God may be my pilot but Karen is my co-pilot."

Tony's dates in his earliest diary entries are inaccurate, no doubt reflecting his overall difficulties in reality orientation. Neither Tony nor I can be sure about when these entries were written, but it is safe to assume they represent a three-week period beginning October, 1987. As his mental status improved, the dates become accurate and have been included here.

[First entry in diary]: She's [K.B.W.] the best! I thought that she made mistakes but I found out differently today. My Jesus has sent me the right person into my life. The person that will and is flying me through the lightning and thundering black clouds. I love her in a different, special way. She's number one in my book. Jesus says I am the way, the truth and the life, she's showing me the way and the truth, and she's doing a damn good job in the life department. She's the kind of person that I would love to meet and marry. Wouldn't that be great? Yea, right, that's what they all say. If I could just meet someone like her or 1/2 or 1/16 of her, I could stay sober for ever!

[Next entry]: She makes me feel good about myself . . . . She never puts me down or talks down to me. I love her for that. She makes me feel good about myself and not too many people have ever done that for me except two other people that come to mind [a nurse on the unit and his mother]. If any three needed anything I think I'd go to any extreme to complete it. I'm feeling good this morning; that's not too usual for me so I'm going to enjoy it.

Over time, he began to infuse some of this external caring. He started to lose weight, sometimes up to ten pounds a week, and battled his drug urges. He attended both Narcotics Anonymous and AA meetings on the hospital grounds, soon obtained a sponsor, and began working on the Twelve Steps. By Tony's fifth month of inpatient treatment, he had lost 100 pounds while maintaining his sobriety. Clearly, the hospitalization had provided him an omnipotent other to merge with, to feel safe in, and to become empowered by. A rekindling of his core self had been stimulated by the staff's caring attention.

[Next entry]: [A nurse] has a way of getting on my shit case. She says she's not talking down but it makes me feel like shit and like a little kid being scolded, like when my father put me down and made me feel like shit, and like that little person . . . . The more I think about it there are a lot more people out there that make me feel pretty good about myself [i.e., other staff and patients.]

The next step of his transformation was for Tony to find ways to re-experience the protective immersion even when outside the hospital setting. As discharge loomed before him, Tony began to have increasing difficulties. In fact, he experienced a brief psychotic episode after I had to inform him that he would not be able to continue in private outpatient treatment with me upon discharge, because the day hospital he had agreed to attend wanted him to be free to form new attachments with their staff. Tony was so traumatized by this news that he almost collapsed in my office. He recalls thinking that he wanted to run away and use drugs immediately. Once back on the unit, even with the assistance of one-to-one nursing staff and antipsychotic medication (as necessary), to help him calm down, Tony remained grief-stricken. He kept saying, over and over again, "I want my pipe [for smoking crack], I want my pipe, I want my pipe." This sounded to me as though he were saying, "I want my Mommy! I want my Mommy! I want my Mommy!" (Had I understood at the time the importance of the immersion process in the treatment, I would not have agreed to this disruption in the therapeutic process.) Tony wrote in his diary throughout this period and provides a full account of his psychic suffering. Simultaneous to losing me, his wife of three years filed for divorce, and the termination of his marriage was almost complete.

October 16, 1987 (in quiet room): Well here I am in the quiet room on Agnes' [his wife's] birthday. I'm crying now a little just thinking about it. I thought that I would never be up here but I am. Karen told me yesterday that she may not be able to see me after a transition period. That floored me and devastated me. I've been feeling alone a lot knowing Agnes is leaving me and then when the lady in my life [i.e., the therapist] tells me that she may not be in my life, says she's going to possibly not be there for me, says that, that scares and frightens the living shit out of me. So much so that I told Karen that I feel I could get high just thinking of that, and I'll jump out of the window to prove it to you. Then I said I can't die but maybe I can break a leg or maybe I could break my neck. Talk like that caused her to be concerned about me . . . .

[Next entry]: I wish there was a pill for this . . . . I'm feeling hopeless because of thinking of being alone so much, and there is no one around me but myself and since I don't like me that makes it easier for me to want to give up and not deal with myself.

Tony and I both believe that, had he been out of the hospital setting at the time of this incident, he surely would have returned to drugs. I mention this to underscore the depth of loneliness such individuals as Tony feel when in their own detached, alienated self and when separated from their object of attachment.

[The next several days record Tony's continued anguish]: I don't know what to do with myself. I don't know if I'm coming or going. My therapist

still has me freaking out. I want off of this status [he was put on one-to-one status] *but I still feel I am tense. I don't like this medication and the tense feeling I get but I feel that I'm thinking clearer.* . . . .

Yesterday was a little better but I still am depressed about Karen. It feels worse than my divorce . . . .

[Next entry]: *I found myself pleading and begging* [the nurse] *and Karen to get high* . . . . *I'm depressed still. I want her—period.* [The nurse] *told me to believe in me. I don't want to shave or shower, exercise. I'm mad at God when I shouldn't be.* [The nurse] *said that God's saying, What right do I have to be doing this to myself? I love Karen. I don't want to lose the only person that has ever understood everything about me. I'm scared and lonely.*

[Next entry]: *Today or tonight I'm feeling almost a lot better. The medication Navane is making me feel less tense. I start Lithium tonight* . . . . *Karen is on the unit now* . . . . *I don't want to lose her. My session with her went okay. I told her how much she meant to me, and I was crying again telling or asking her how much I need her, to stay clean.*

[Next entry]: *I don't know what I would do without her. I feel that I just can't make it and that I would like to get high over it instead of dealing with it. I have to be more powerful and ask Jesus for help and support through this. I equate it like losing Jesus, not exactly that much weight, but similar* . . . . *Karen said . . . that she would find me a good therapist but it just won't be the same* . . . .

[Next entry]: *It feels worse than my divorce or being left alone without my father. I feel sad and depressed, alone and abandoned like I won't have love ever again.*

[Next entry]: *I talked with* [a mental health worker] *this morning and she was saying that I should use the first three Steps and the eleventh Step. She was saying how I'm powerless over getting Karen or keeping her as a therapist.* [The mental health worker] *was also saying to use two and three Steps to accept that God will help me find another therapist and how it's not good to depend too much on Karen.*

[Two entries later]: Karen and I had another good session. I went in telling her I was cured which meant that I felt like I was [not] stuck in treatment. I started crying and I told her how alone I feel without being with her, my wife, and my father and she was all I had. She understood the aloneness that I'm going through, a lot of losses in my life. She said [that's a] big reason for acting the way I [did]. She said the next time I look in the mirror, say 277 pounds.

Tony's anguish and his psychotic, suicidal episode were in response to the loss of his newfound object of attachment. I am reminded of Bowlby's stages of separation trauma, the first two being protest and despair. Tony was desperate not to lose the one person with whom he had formed an empathic, immersive connection. In fact, he disorganized because of the impending loss of this attachment, and he required an increase in his medication regimen to deal with the onslaught of this blow. Staff members clearly were helpful in trying to shift Tony's object of attachment away from me. In fact the suggestions that he utilize the AA Steps, to place his faith in God and not in his therapist, were quite helpful. (This is what later caused him to say "God is my pilot but Karen is my co-pilot.") In retrospect, now, I feel we were in error and could have ameliorated his pain and anguish: I might have insisted with the day hospital, for example, that I remain involved, although distantly, so that he would not have to feel lost without me. I remember that the staff seemed to think the depth of his attachment to me was rather odd. Staff members would make a few jokes or roll their eyes in staff meetings when his continued longing for me was discussed. This attitude was certainly uncomfortable for me, and I wondered what I had done so very wrong to have this patient cling so deeply to me. Despite my self-doubt, the thought had occurred to me that he was simply trying to keep a loved object, for once, because he had spent so many years alone and alienated. He was trying to prevent what had happened to him throughout his life from occurring again—he was desperately trying to avoid more abandonment, loneliness, despair.

In viewing the therapist as the transformational other who is powerful enough to shift the drug addict away from his drug and into human relationships, it is to be expected that the patient idealizes, loves, and clings. He responds to this powerful other as he has responded to the drug: he needs it, he wants it, he can't live without it. Tony had felt the immersive connection in his therapy and, understandably, did not want to lose it. He fought long and hard to get me to change my mind, but at the time, my view of the immersive transference had not yet fully crystallized. Placed in this situation today, I would have intervened in other ways.

It is to Tony's credit, indeed his will to survive, that he did emotionally reorganize after this tremendous blow. He did, however, resume his compulsive eating. Even in the controlled hospital setting, Tony nevertheless gained back thirty pounds in just two months: if he could not keep the immersive connectedness to the hospital staff and myself, he could internalize us by ingesting our food. At the time of his discharge, few staff members would have given Tony even a twenty percent chance of making it. For example, in a clinical conference, the evaluating physician described him as quite manipulative and, based on his demanding neediness and his past psychiatric failures, predicted that Tony was going to need a lifetime of external care that would be provided by either the mental health or legal system.

Once discharged into a halfway house and attending the day hospital, Tony continued to gain weight, but he did not resort to drugs. The day hospital requested a meeting with me to consult on his aftercare treatment. When I visited him at the day hospital, it was clear that he was on the way to relapse and was forestalling it by eating—he had already gained back about sixty pounds of the original 100 he had lost. He asked if I would see him when he was discharged from the day hospital, and this time, I agreed. Tony was so infused with hope after our contact that his progress was quickened. He was tapered off all psychotropic medication, but continued to gain back the rest of the 100 pounds he had originally lost while in the hospital. It was because of his tremendous weight gain, I think, that the day hospital agreed to his insistent wish to see me before his discharge from their program.

May 22, 1988: I can't believe it yet, even though I talked with her today. Karen has let me come back to work with her. It proves to me that Jesus answers prayers . . . .

July 5, 1988: Well, it's July 5th and Jesus has given Karen back to me. I've been seeing her for about five weeks now and she has helped me get back into the groove of dealing with my eating disorder. I've lost 20 pounds since 17 days ago. I can't say how grateful I am to Jesus for Karen. I wish I could put it in to words. All I want to say is thank you Jesus, I LOVE YOU JESUS. I can't explain it. I feel so secure and happy inside, she is so important to my life and sobriety and

abstinence . . . and she told me I don't have to worry, and she will be there for me
till she's old and gray.

Within six months of the resumption of our outpatient treatment,
Tony had lost 125 pounds. Part of this, no doubt, was due to his enormous
relief at regaining the transformational relationship. I had made the
interpretation that he had gained all that weight back as a way, like a
hamster, to store me inside of him while he was separated for the winter.
Now that we had begun working together again, he no longer needed to
replenish his food supplies.

He wanted to know about love in psychotherapy. I explained to him
that psychotherapy is a very special kind of relationship and that it evokes
all kinds of strong feelings, including love. I spoke to him about empathic
connectedness, about moments of oneness. And I told him that there are
many kinds of ways to love, this being one. Tony was really asking me if he
were lovable, if I loved him. He had always felt like a freak of nature,
meaning that he had never felt loved by anyone. Since he shared
"everything" with me, he needed to know if I thought that his core self was
indeed lovable or if it were inalienably bizarre, untouchable, unlovable.

July 13, 1988: I can't wait to see Karen tomorrow. I miss her. I think of her
and talk about her on and off during the day . . . . I asked her how she feels
about me, and she said how do I think she feels about me and I said I feel she is
concerned about me and cares and has a lot of understanding toward me, and she
said that's love and that's how she feels about me.

One of the crucial components of Tony's outpatient treatment was
helping him build an internal feeling of being held and soothed by a
protective other who could merge with him whenever he felt alienated,
alone, or abandoned. Similar to Winnicott's theory of the capacity to be
alone, Tony needed to feel that he was always in my presence even when
we were separated physically. The foundation of this process began with
the frequency of our sessions—three times per week for five years, tapering
to two sessions weekly and then to one, with additional marital sessions.
And, as with other patients, he had my home telephone number should
he need to reach me after hours. Interestingly, Tony has rarely called me
outside sessions, because the fantasy of always being able to reach me has
been comfort enough.

Although this frame offered him a foundation for further immersions, I knew that I needed to actively encourage and even to aid him in creating a soothing and protective immersive area. I spoke with Tony quite frequently about the importance of "taking me with him." I told him:

> After all, you have never had someone available to you to help ease your loneliness. You have had a "swooping love" mother, who gave to you so inconsistently, that you have been very much alone. If you could create an image of me, and call it up when you are about to eat or even eating, you could take me inside of you rather than the food. If you could imagine what I might say to you when you are about to binge, then you could help me stop you from continuing this destructive behavior.

One of the first symbolizations that Tony created to internalize me occurred in the first 6 months of our outpatient treatment. He was trying to lose the weight he had regained so destructively, but was unable to refrain from any impulse he had to eat. I asked him why he allowed himself to be so burdened, why, with his weight, he was carrying a cross even heavier than the one Jesus had carried. I suggested that he might find some other way to carry his burdens, some other way to suffer. Tony seized this suggestion and decided to buy himself a beautiful, fourteen-carat gold crucifix with the engraving on the back "Jesus Saves" vertically and "Karen" horizontally. Ironically, the engraver misunderstood and wrote instead "Jesus—Karen" horizontally and "saves" vertically. Tony debated taking the cross back, but he liked the powerful positioning of the words. Throughout the rest of treatment, he always wore the cross to remind him of his urges to suffer. After this symbolization, Tony lost another fifty pounds by May 1989, making a total of 220 pounds lost in the one year of our outpatient treatment. In all the years that have passed since, Tony has never gained this weight back. Yes, he struggles at times with food, but the struggles are always within a ten-pound range. Tony calls this a miracle.

This patient came to therapy with a strong, Catholic belief system. He had tried to see Jesus as always loving, but his own experience taught him differently. As he felt that it had been God who had given him his freak body, he had a great deal of fear toward this powerful object. He was continually angry with God for creating his malformation and could not understand why he had been so cruelly gifted. And yet, his belief in this powerful other was pervasive: he would pray several times a day and constantly would seek advice from various priests. This anxious attachment required analysis especially because of his need to rely on the comfort that these merging moments of prayer could give to him. Therefore, we needed to have his God come into our sessions, to transform Him from an object of fear to an object of comfort, love, and security. In essence, doing so would help correct the split between the all-good world of the therapy sessions and the sometimes-bad world of his daily life. Bringing God to the office would encourage the God of his outside world to be more soothing as well.

Tony has always had a very creative imagination and has taken many of the moments that we have discussed and symbolized them in his own special way. Although I do not recall the exact way in which God joined our sessions, I do recall Tony's delight in having God be invited. He actually designated a chair for Jesus—a way of making Him as real as possible. And I know that this particular patient actually desired to achieve that kind of contact with his God, a God who would sit next to him at all times. Winnicott (1935) writes about the religious patient:

> There is a practical point here, for in the analysis of the most satisfactory type of religious patient it is helpful to work with the patient as if *on an agreed basis of recognition of internal reality* [emphasis mine] . . . . It is necessarily dangerous for the analyst to have it in his mind that the patient's God is a "fantasy object." The use of that word would make the patient feel as if the analyst were undervaluing the good object, which he is not really doing. I think something similar would apply to the analysis of an artist in regard to the source of his inspiration, and also the analysis of the inner people and imaginary companions to whom our patients are able to introduce us. [p. 133]

October 6, 1988: When I feel like I'm in trouble or hurting bad I can call upon Jesus and ask him to be there with me and I know he will not abandon or leave me when I need him most. When I talk to [Karen] I feel that whatever I say I won't be punished or judged and because I have some fear that Christ will still do that to me if I am evil or do the wrong thing, I feel somewhat safer, more secure with her than I do with Christ in some ways. It's not that I don't feel God will help me but by seeing her there right in front of me in the flesh it just seems . . . safer [than] Jesus . . . . As I'm thinking, I was taught and believe that Jesus is in all of us male and female and is part of us, and as I see more of Karen and try to

*understand why I have been so gifted and fortunate to have had a person like her,
being put in my life . . . . Thanks, Jesus. Goodnight.*

*October 10, 1988: My session with Karen on Friday was the most
Jesus-like presence since I've been with her. We had a great or the best session
ever. I shared how I feel Jesus in her and how he works through her and how I feel
great inside about myself and moral in the way I feel and think about her. I said,
"He's in the chair right next to us and I felt His presence." When I shared I feel
him working in and through her, I saw her excited about it . . . and she said, "I
love it," and when I said, "Excuse me, what did you say?," she said "I like it, that's
great." . . . I felt euphoric and high like I was on drugs (crack), and I said to her
I had to put the brakes on because the only time I've ever felt that high I was on
cocaine, and it freaked me out how I could feel that euphorically high without a
substance. She's the best, thank you Jesus!*

*October 20, 1988: I did it! I lost 100 pounds through the grace of Jesus
Christ and Karen Walant. I'm going to take some credit also . . . . Karen was so
proud of me. She was savoring and that was her word . . . . She had a smile and
clapped for me . . . . I love her as I love Christ, and male and female didn't come
into play . . . . She told me in Tuesday's session that when I had binged on
Chinese food, pizza cheese, and spit out the dough, and two cookies and one
brownie that I'm hurting her and other people that care about me when I do that
and not just myself . . . .*

For Tony, my asking him to bring his God into the session was
extraordinarily important. To this day, he will find a few minutes to pray
before session and will often talk about his religious ideas. And at this
point he has found a way to be comforted by a loving God; he has been
plagued, however, with fears of Satan. Although God and his therapist are
objects of transformation and love, he has shifted his concentration of
fears and torments to a secondary object, that of Satan. The task at hand
is to help him view his own self, in conjunction with the powers of his
positive immersive objects, as mightier than the devil. For the most part
this effort has been successful. The world of his fears, however, has not
died and will probably remain a contender for many years to come.

Tony actively involved himself in the immersive process and would
sometimes even suggest ideas that he thought would help him. For
example, he asked me to write down several of the key phrases that I often

would say to him, such as "Put your thoughts and feelings into words, not into food." He then laminated these sheets and would pull them out frequently when by himself so that he could evoke my presence and be soothed. In a similar manner, Tony asked for a picture of me so that, again, he could have a way to evoke my presence when he felt abandoned and alone. Yet, I was certainly not the only object in his life. He was still living in the halfway house at this time, was attending an AA or Overeaters Anonymous meeting every day, had a sponsor in each program, and was going to church to pray at least once a day. But despite all of these avenues for comfort, he was frequently devastated when alone. It took an enormous amount of work and dedication on the part of this patient to utilize all of these objects and to make me real to him when I was not with him. He was determined, and still is, to improve his life; he was convinced that he would die if he returned to any kind of substance abuse.

All of these immersion aids were helpful, and yet Tony continued to feel too alone and too far away from my range of power. Soon after his second anniversary of sobriety, he spoke in session about his frustration that he could not have more of me. He said: "If only you were a genie, then I really could have you whenever I needed you. I could just pick up my genie bottle and ask for you to come out, and there you would be, ready to help."

I seized upon this idea and encouraged him to find a genie bottle, a bottle big enough to hold me and small enough for him to carry. The very next session Tony came in, quite excitedly, telling me

I found the genie bottle, and I bought two!! They are kaleidoscopes, really, and I like that because I can see millions of Karens as I look at you through the lens. You multiply, just what I need so that you can stay with me all the time. Here—you keep them both in your office for the next week so that your presence can get into the bottle, and then I'll take one home with me. And if you'd keep the other one in the office, I'll switch them when you go on vacations.

Tony had created his very own immersion object to help him remain connected to me even during our separations. For the next three years he carried the bottle everywhere: to work, to meetings, and even into the operating room when he had surgery. He would sometimes put different objects inside the bottle, such as a pebble he particularly liked or a particular passage from the Bible. The genie bottle withstood his aggression, surviving crashes or bumps. It perfectly fit Winnicott's criteria for a transitional object, because its durability outlasted destruction and resurrection. By using the genie bottle, Tony could completely dominate his representation of me. Indeed, the genie bottle was a marvelous symbol for the kind of relationship he needed: as a subjective object, but also an omnipotent object that he could command. He still keeps the genie bottle but more for sentimental value, like an adolescent who keeps his teddy bear just because it was so meaningful at one time in his life.

Kernberg (1975) discusses a patient who, similarly, had viewed the analyst as a genie. He writes that the patient had built the analyst up as a "powerful slave, totally at the patient's service" (p. 259). In between sessions, this patient realized that he had the feeling that the analyst "disappeared into an only potential existence, as if the analyst were confined in a bottle that the patient could put away." Upon coming to this realization, the patient felt apologetic that he had not seen the analyst as a separate being and expressed gratitude that "the analyst had been willing to 'stick with him' in spite of his chronically derogatory behavior." How different our perspectives are. Tony's genie is viewed as an aid to the attachment process so that he could cope more adequately with our frequent separations. His use of me as a "powerful slave" was, in essence, a description of the subjective object that I think is so critical to the treatment process of a powerless individual. In contrast, Kernberg viewed his patient as severely disturbed *because* of his need for a therapeutic genie, because of an inability to view the therapist as a separated object.

December 22, 1988: Jesus is going to be born in three days and I feel like I'm being born all over again . . . . I see beautiful places when I drive all over, and between the beautiful ocean and sunsetting skies and lakes, and nothing comes close to the beauty I see in her. Christ is working through her. She is filling up so much of that loneliness that has always been in me. My insecurities . . . for 20 years [disappear in] her presence. I get outside of myself and . . . I can feel love for the first time 'cause the substances aren't distorting my thoughts and I'm trying to learn to give love a little at a time.

Tony is another patient who relies on the spiritual connection he has with nature. He has always looked to nature for immersion and will spend his lunch hour, for example, watching the waves at the beach or walking through wooded acreage. Again, these kinds of merging moments are important to emphasize for the detached patient.

*December 25, 1988. A DREAM: I went over your parents' house [and I]
was with a girl. You said to me when we were talking about doing things for
people, family, that you do a lot and I asked, can you tell me what that is and you
said that you shop for your parents, and I said, all of the shopping? And you said
not all, but most. I had visited once before and this was the second time. You
bought a lot of groceries, and I said are you expected to be snowed in? It seems like
I was alone with you at times in the dream and at times I was with a girl and you
were with your husband, and at other times it was just you and I. And once there
was a person who I think was your sister who would smoke a cigarette and
sometimes although it didn't look like you, or she was you. You wanted to make
a fire, and I remember you going in the fireplace and was going to start it and then
it was you who was the person smoking and it didn't look like you. The person I
was with and your husband didn't seem to be around.*

We did discuss his dream in session, and I recall making an interpretation something like this:

> You have so frequently viewed me as unattainable and unreachable,
> as though I were a God. And yet here in the dream, you are visiting
> my house, meeting my parents and husband. I've become a regular
> person. That you have brought a girlfriend with you, and I am with
> my husband, says to me that you are beginning to see that you, too,
> can have a wife and family; you are no longer the freak of years past.
> You notice all the food I buy, indicating that you see me as a
> nurturer even outside the office. But you also see that I am
> smoking—do I have an addiction? And so this makes me even more
> human. I'm building a fire, so that everyone will be warm—again, a
> sign that I caretake for others. But I think the overriding feature of
> this dream is that I'm not so god-like here; I'm becoming a human
> being, which is definitely something we've been discussing in session
> recently.

It is my point of view, similar to Kohut's, that a patient's idealization
of his analyst is often necessary. To Tony, I represented so many things he
was not, so many things he felt he never could be: married (which meant
to him that I was loved); not obsessed by food, drugs or alcohol; and
educated (he had barely received his high school diploma.) These *were*
things to idealize! Over time, as he remained in sobriety, as he continued
to lose and to maintain a 200-pound weight loss, he could begin to wish

these things for himself. I wanted to show to him that he was indeed transforming his being and that he could ask for and get more in his life. The significance of the dream was that Tony was beginning to lessen his idealization of me not because of empathic failures on my part, but because of his own growth, maturity, and achievements. In this regard, I find myself in disagreement with Kohut because I do not think it necessary for the therapist to fail in order for the patient to lessen his idealizing attachment. Searles (1961), too has commented that the resolution of the transference symbiosis is due to the patient's disillusionment with the therapist. In order for the patient to feel separate, Searles feels he must render the therapist helpless; no one, patient or child, would otherwise willingly give up a perfect, all-powerful other. In contrast, Tony demonstrates the point that patients, as well as children, will lessen their idealized attachment as their own growth and development matures.

Up until this point in Tony's treatment, he would discuss his wish to have sexual fantasies about me, but would refuse to allow himself even this imaginary pleasure. He had made no attempts to date either, feeling he was too sexually unattractive, even repulsive. He was proud of his ability to deny any sexual ideas about me; it seemed that he wanted to see me as pure and virgin-like as possible, perhaps to place me in a similar virgin-like position as himself. He liked seeing me as his personal Virgin Mary. The oedipal overtones here, too, are clear. He was frightened to view his mother in a sexual way either, as though afraid his father might discover his wishes and punish him. I did attempt an oedipal interpretation once, but Tony felt incredibly misunderstood—he told me he *never* had had sexual feelings toward his mother! So I kept the issue between him and me, understanding that resolving it through the transference was as important as altering any historical dynamics. I felt that, if he could feel loved especially by the idealized woman that I was to him, then he could begin the task of finding a loving woman in his life outside sessions. He had to stop excluding himself from being fully human. Interestingly enough, in adolescence Tony had surrounded himself with very attractive girls, none of whom, however, he ever dated. They liked him because they knew there was no threat of sexuality from him, and he enjoyed being in their beautiful presence.

In theoretical terms, the immersive transference had been complete except in the arena of sexuality. Until he could allow himself to be one with me in fantasied sexual union, he would continue feeling freakish and impotent. These kinds of fantasies are not necessary, of course, in every patient's treatment, but for this patient who had such intense feelings of separateness, such a core belief in his own alienated being, they were crucial.

January 15, 1989: I still look at her during every session and still go through a mesmerizing feeling. I think of the picture of Jesus in the Garden of Gethsemane and Jesus looks so beautiful in this picture and he looks very serious and I see her face when I think [of] this picture and I take that picture with me throughout the day and it gets me through it . . . . Her petiteness is what I like a lot, which I also never talk about. I wish I could meet a woman like her and have a close sexual relationship with but I can't get everything I want . . . .

May 18, 1989: Things going well lately. I love Karen so much I can't believe I can love someone this much and it's the most beautiful feeling I ever felt, it makes crack look like nothing (yuck.) I had a dream I was a priest after a session where Karen said I was like a priest. In the dream I was naked except . . . my underwear was on. When I was giving host, Karen said it's the way I felt my whole life—like I was a freak and meant to be a priest [and never marry or have sex] *because of my problem* [meaning his penile deformation].

June 8, 1989: . . . I don't want to lose you, Jesus, and Karen, and I know with the help you've given me this is going to be okay and it's a good and comfortable scariness I have because you and Karen have taught me that it's okay to have other people in my life working through and in you. I see a beautiful, unconditional loving, kind and caring person in Cynthia [the first woman he has let himself become interested in since his divorce], *and she reminds me of Karen.*

In his June 9, 1989, entry he writes of his first dream in which he makes love to me and we *both* "loved it." From this point on, Tony began dating women, making love to several of those he dated. From this point on, he continued to maintain his dramatic weight loss.

In his first two years of treatment, Tony built an immersive area in which he sought magical mergings and continuous soothing. With Jesus and me incorporated into a fused object, his relationship with his God became less alienated and distanced. He even began to feel loved by God. Indeed, now when he overate, he knew that he was ignoring both me and

God. He had developed an elaborate system to keep me, and all other important objects, with him at all times. He had successfully abstained from drugs and alcohol and had lost 220 pounds. His inner world was becoming filled with good, soothing objects, and he was less preoccupied with feelings of smallness, powerlessness, and freakishness.

In our third year of treatment I became less idealized, because Tony had begun to experience himself as more powerful and significant. He also became more involved in other friendships, became a sponsor of several newcomers, and even worked for a while as a mental health counselor at the halfway house in which he had once resided. Of primary importance, he frenetically began to date women.

At first Tony could hardly believe that even one woman would accept his invitation for a date. It was difficult for him to change his childhood self-concept of freak or to forget the "elephant man" he had become as an adult. Tony was like an adolescent experiencing the hormonal thrill of sexuality for the first time. He began to keep a little black book with all the phone numbers of the women he met, and he kept track of which one-liners got positive responses. In this regard, Tony felt the power and exhilaration he had observed in his father as Mr. B. had patrolled the streets, stopping to flirt with every pretty girl. Tony was certainly in competition with his father, feeling at times that he, the son, was the more successful. He began dating as many women as he could simultaneously until the complications of this lifestyle became overwhelming. Like his addiction, he had to work hard at limiting his impulses. Once he did, he found himself fixated on the "millions" of pretty women he would see surrounding him every day—each woman more beautiful than the next. He began feeling his childhood sense of deprivation again because he realized the impossibility of dating every woman he saw.

In a fit of desperation, he attached himself to a first girlfriend, a cold narcissist who demanded a constant showering of attention and money. Her three children lived overseas, but nevertheless Tony became concerned about them and would send them money. Because he could not meet her demands, this relationship actually re-stimulated his sense of alienation and freakishness. The two remained involved for about six months, during which time Tony would say to me, "I have to stay with her. She's the only woman who will ever love me. It's the only chance I have." When I would question his sense of doom, he would insist that this was his fate. Even the striking similarities between the neglectful relation-

ship with his girlfriend and with his mother only fortified his commitment
to her. He was convinced he could do no better.

When I took a vacation that fall, Tony was still struggling in this
relationship. As usual, he had great fears of my being away. For some
reason, he thought that on this particular vacation he was not allowed to
call me—a factor significant to what transpired next. Tony became
desperate during my perceived disappearance. He was frantic in his sense
of loss and began to feel suicidal. One evening, in less than one hour, he
fantasized first about killing himself and then had a fleeting thought about
killing me. These thoughts so frightened him that he was jolted right out
of his depression and right past his urges for drugs or alcohol. He called a
recovering alcoholic who worked at the hospital and with whom he still
kept in touch and was able to calm down. The next morning I received a
solemn phone call from the hospital unit advising me to call Tony at
once—it was imperative! We then talked, and Tony was much relieved by
making the contact. He has said this was one of the scariest moments of his
life because his desperation took him to a fantasy he had never thought
possible. And it actually convinced him how powerful our relationship
really was, because the thought of my death was enough to make him
choose life. I can understand his wish to kill me and himself: because he
did not know he could reach me, he had experienced my leaving as though
I had killed off our relationship. It was as though I had already died by
going on vacation and leaving him disconnected from his source of
attachment. Tony details in his diary the events of this traumatic evening.

*September, 1990: When I was falling asleep, I got up [from] bed and went
to the kitchen to get a banana and had some cherry syrup with it. After having
this I said fuck it. I think I was angry at Elizabeth [his girlfriend] for not calling
me so I ate three pancakes. Everything was quiet, so I started thinking as I cooked
the pancakes, and the pancakes somehow made me think of suicide (maybe
because from bingeing on food or pancakes, or more because they are flat like
when you kill yourself by jumping off a building and you are flatter? not sure!)
Then thought of how I associated the process of cooking crack while cooking the
pancakes, and I said how I learned to cook food but not crack. I ate the three
pancakes. It was like a ten-minute high, looking back at it now. I was in another
world, not thinking of no person or thing, just a ten-minute high. Then I grabbed
the syrup bottle right after I finished the food and threw it toward the sink. It
broke violently and the syrup went all over the walls and pipes, and glass*

shattered everywhere. I then was just sitting at [the] kitchen table and look[ed] down at my body. I was naked and I saw what I've seen for 28 years, a freakish dick + fat ugly stupid human being. Then I said how did I get this way? Then [I] thought of my father, and felt rage and extreme anger toward him. I felt as though I could kill him if I was to see him. In the middle of this anger I felt like calling him and telling him how I felt like disowning him. I just wanted him to feel his worst through my words of talking to him. Then [I] just sat there and was numb again. Then grabbed the knife I was using to eat the pancakes. I just held it. Then I was feeling suicidal. As I held it I thought of what it would be like to stick myself with it. It was a small blade, the most three inches. Then for a split second ran it along my incision of my operation I had had a few months back when my loose skin was removed. This made me feel squirmful and felt real uncomfortable. Then [I] thought of how it would be real painful. Then I think I thought and saw my penis, and it felt so small I felt I don't have to cut if off because it was cut off already. Then thought of my wrist and thought of my veins as I ran my eyes along the length of my arms. Then my eye caught hold of the Equal sugar substitute packages that I abuse like food and the drugs in the past. As my eye caught hold also of the letters on the knife, it said pearing [sic] knife. There happened to be a pear on the table and I began to stab the pear violently so I associated the sound of me slicing the pear [with] . . . how it would sound if I would stab myself. Then I saw the Equal on the table and started stabbing the package of Equal, kept stabbing it. My next thought was how Karen knows that Equal is a killer and I feel cane sugar is a killer. When I ate the pancakes I mixed sugar in with the syrup. I thought of how it would be nice to think about getting high, before that thought I was remembering a video from a movie where a musician was spending all his time on the road and cheating on his wife. When he was in town she would come home and he was playing his piano and she was trying to get his attention but couldn't because he was so wrapped up in his music and drugs. I was thinking at this time of one particular scene where he was sitting at a kitchen table like me and he was looking at the pot and hashish on the table and was rolling a joint. Then I replayed that exact scene in my mind and sat the same way and was reliving this scene.

Then I opened more Equal sugar packages and poured some milk on the Equal and began to mix the Equal and milk together to form crack. It reminded me of how crack is processed. Then I started entertaining [the thought of] the crack high. Then I was remembering what I say to patients at the hospital when I tell them not to entertain the thought of getting high. Then thought to write to Karen or call her up, then went back to dwelling on getting high. Then I was remembering the first time I tried crack about two years before my three months

*run with it . . . . Then I had such extreme anger toward my mother and father
that I wanted to kill I felt so homicidal. Then I seen the genie bottle on the table
and I was saying how the fuck come that I didn't see that earlier tonight. Think
I grabbed the genie bottle and had an impulse to sit on the third-floor balcony of
my apartment to look at the stars, it was a clear night. I gazed at the stars for a
few moments. I was completely naked at the time. No one could really see me but
I could see the crack drug dealers selling the drugs on the street, which was when
I started dwelling intensively on getting high on crack, and then thought of the
two hundred dollars I had in my apartment and was thinking that I would need
at least five crack vials all combined in a pipe, because I would want that intense
blast. I knew I should call the hospital and hope that [the mental health worker]
would be there but something told me I could handle this and do it alone. It was
about 2 o'clock in the morning. So I'm preaching at the hospital about calling
there any time and I could not do it. Then from the third-floor balcony I said to
myself if I jumped how I would die or just be crippled for the rest of my life, with
my luck, and how I would continue to see Karen in a wheelchair and how that
would suck . . . . Then I thought if I die by jumping I would want to leave an
impression—my thinking was if I die how it would have to be the most intense
dramatic death, so if I killed someone I wanted to be well known like when John
Lennon of the Beatles was killed. Then out of nowhere in my mind, like a
thought of how did I, could I, ever think that thought, which will be the hardest
thought to share with you, Karen, ever that I shared, and I hope it doesn't change
anything of how you think of me, but anyway it was the thought of killing you,
Karen, and [your husband]. When this thought happened, instantaneous after I
was like stunned of where this, or how could I think this, and I gave a quick smile
to myself and shook my head in a snapping out of that trance motion, and literally
leaped through my kitchen window as if by holding the genie bottle. And having
the thought about hurting you, Karen, brought me back to reality, and I called
the hospital and my friend was there and he talked to me and walked me through
the urge to get high and made me promise to call you, Karen, which I said I would
if I had any urge to hurt myself in any way. Then I received a call from you,
Karen, the next day because he had called you to let you know what happen[ed].*

Several months later, Elizabeth broke up with him. He was despondent and spent the next six months in a depressive fog. He tried desperately to woo her back, without success. I was on vacation overseas at one
point during his period of grief, and he called me in Hawaii to be assured
of our indissoluble bond. (This time I made sure that he knew he could call
me!) Finding that our connection still held transcontinentally, he was

greatly relieved. Of great significance, he did not become psychotic or suicidal or use drugs in response to this loss. He did periodically binge, but never gained more than ten pounds before controlling and rectifying his behavior.

January 1, 1991: Karen, I can't take the pain and noise of Elizabeth in my mind. I don't know where to turn, my avenues seem exhausted, the positive and negative ones. Jesus doesn't seem to be doing it, you being gone seems to shatter my hopes and I feel quite alone. AA seems extremely distant on helping me get through this and [my sponsor] has been probably my best support. I love Elizabeth, Karen, and today Wednesday seems to be the first day that I don't care or feel as much for her, and I feel empty, lost, lonely, isolated and numb. I wish I could not be here—you seem so far away and yes, you are but I pulled what I could of you back today, and I still feel empty, lost, somewhat confused, somewhat desperate. I hate feeling my feelings. I am in touch with my feelings I feel today, as be[st] that I can. I feel that my future is hopeless somewhat like my past . . . . I'm noticing my stomach growing and seem to be looking forward or wanting it to grow. I think so I can be one with myself again and as I see it growing, give myself the attention and warmth that I can't [get from] Elizabeth or possibly you Karen. I've been noticing that change of my stomach in the last ten or whatever days, and it seems to be my companion, and my therapist, my lover, my hater, my teacher, my pet? my friend, my everything . . . . I'm not sure if I don't or do want it to grow more . . . .

Knowing I see you in six days and seeing the ring on my finger wants to rekindle Christ but just don't seem to know how. Karen, even though the feeling seems to be dull or numbed over, I know deep in my heart I love you more than life itself and wish that I could have with you, or I mean with Elizabeth, the relationship I have with you. My 45 minutes is one minute over and the phone just rang. [Perhaps this was my return phone call to him.]

Tony wrote in his journal of a dream that he had had as soon as I came back from vacation. What is interesting to me is that he also described his associations that make the dream clear from his perspective, a sign that he has understood the process of dream analysis.

January 13, 1991: Karen, welcome back! In a dream you and I were getting on a elevator to go down and there was a fire in the building. So many were going to get in, so me and you were first when the elevator door opened and we went to the back. But I was the protector again and was putting you in the corner (controlling, also) and my body was like a shield so others wouldn't press against you (part of my eating and gaining weight paid off because of my size— it protected you more). The elevator went up instead of down and stopped at the floor below the fire, I think the 17th floor. A pretty Hawaii motel (was praying for your safety [in] helicopter and planes). Then the door wouldn't open but somehow I got out and through the top of the elevator. I got through with someone and when we or I pulled people out you weren't on it, you were on the other side of the elevator adjacent. So time was short (feeling desperate) and I was ripping through the top quickly (like ripping [my] stomach? I don't know) . . . and when I got it open I said, "Karen Walant first to come up because she is pregnant with child," even though you weren't, but I wanted you up first (protector/controller) and they didn't listen. But I pulled you up finally and I think last, and you went downstairs ahead of me and I couldn't catch up to you or maybe you took a different staircase . . . .

Clearly, this was a traumatizing separation dream in which even the world was going to end because he and I were separated. I am interested that the tables were turned, and he was my protector—actually a good sign, demonstrating the change in the analytic situation. Tony no longer felt he had to have my protection at all times but that he, too, could protect me. I am reminded of Seinfeld's (1991) comment:

Taking precedes giving in developmental chronology. The individual must be given and must take in enough love, he must know how to take care of himself, how to say no when necessary, to secure and to enjoy his own intake. Then there is a natural inclination to give or to give back . . . . It is this generativity, this giving and taking with love that enables us to overcome the absurdity and nihilism that is also a pervasive, inherent part of human existence. [p. 139]

Tony was experiencing himself as able to give something to me, an important development in his sense of self. Drug use can be seen as an individual's attempt to keep taking, because he was given so little in childhood and feels that there is nothing for him to give to others. The drugs represent the hopelessness and insignificance of his own being: the nihilistic view that he is nothing and can never provide anything for anyone else. This is a reason why the AA program can be helpful to newly recovering individuals. Just by their very newness they are helping another recovering member keep his sobriety for the day. Remaining ever mindful of one's past (i.e., "keeping it green," an AA phrase) encourages the recovering member to hold onto his hard-earned sobriety.

As Tony tried to cope with his grief and loss at Elizabeth leaving him, he became angry again with God for taking away the only woman, he felt, who would ever love him. He also became angry with me because I did not share the feeling that this was the only time—nor the last time—he would ever find love. I was unwilling to agree with his gloomy forecast. I asked Tony to explain how it was that God would want him to "settle for" a lifetime of deprivation after all he had been through: "Why would God only present you this one woman, after all the work you've done? Why is she your only choice? It seems to me that you are assuming that your fate still has not changed—that you are still destined to suffer."

Tony began to examine his view of God and realized that he still viewed Him as capable of being punishing. Although he experienced some moments of God's swooping love, he primarily felt neglected and abandoned. In my challenge of Tony's assumptions, he was forced to examine his view of the world: "What if there really is a different future for me? I am a child of God too, and maybe He doesn't see only deprivation in front of me. Maybe it's me who is seeking this kind of suffering. You're right, Karen, Jesus already did take on the sins of the world, and I guess I don't have to."

February 1991: Dear Jesus, thank you for what you've given me, and I can say thank you for taking Elizabeth away. But thank you for taking away a lot of pain—physical, spiritual, and emotional pain, thank you for taking away 220 lbs of a physical nightmare, thank you for the friends[hip] of people on their journey in AA, such love that I couldn't ever imagine as a child [being] so alone every hour. They give me the hope to go on although I only admit that Karen gives me the only hope. Help me see life now, the hope they give me. Thank you for taking away a drink and [keeping me] dry for **44 months***. I had only 30 days to go before I would have been bones in a casket—my heart could not take massive amounts of cocaine, food and alcohol, and deep depression. Thank you for taking away, thank you for the three guys I sponsor in AA and all the support I have there, and thanks so much for Karen who has been the core person that I have shed my core innermost soul and heart with and told her every thought no matter how twisted and she still loves me unconditionally. Thank you, Jesus, for giving me your love beyond what I sometimes feel worthy of, but yet today I read something in a meditation book that true humility is when I can give up that* *not-worthy-of attitude, and also it said better [to have] that attitude toward life. So help me, God, to feel worthy of what you have given me and taken away from me. I feel I would like to be humble in your eyes.*

With this shift, Tony was free to enjoy more fully his prayers and his spirituality. He began attending *The Course in Miracles* meetings with Marianne Williamson and reading the manual for this spiritual program. One of the suggested exercises was to "get the Devil (or badness) out of yourself." Tony came to his next session anxious to perform his own exorcism. And he did. He sat with his eyes closed, feet in yoga position, and started imagining the freak in him being removed from his body. He imagined his impulsiveness being taken away and his self-doubting thoughts disappearing. He was almost screaming at himself to get rid of these self-hating feelings. He could have waited to perform this in his own home or at a *Course in Miracles* meeting. He chose, however, to exorcise these demons in session so that I could absorb the "badness" from him. He felt protected by my presence as he performed the ritual. When he had finished, he felt he finally understood the dangerousness of his ingrained need to suffer. He realized that he was in effect trying to control God to keep himself in the neglected position of his childhood. He said,

> When I would ask God to keep my girlfriend with me, I was being extremely controlling of Him. I was expecting that I knew what was best for me, and in this way, I was really being co-dependent with God. I didn't look at the fact that staying with her was only a way to avoid my fear of loneliness and abandonment. I was sure that God wanted to keep me suffering. Now I see that it's *me*, that I have a much greater effect on how my future can be. It's not God who is trying to hold me back, it's me. That's what you've been trying to tell me—and now I hope you can keep all this stuff that I've poured out of my body. Keep it and don't let me have it back, and remind me whenever I start to go back into the "suffering savior" position.

Indeed, Tony had experienced God as a powerful, punitive object. He had spent his life praying to and merging with an object who granted him little happiness. As stated earlier, Tony had to turn this neglect into a grandiose experience of being chosen by God for suffering. He had so internalized the idea that his life had been created to suffer that he was convinced God wanted it this way. When God did not answer his prayers to keep this girlfriend in his life, Tony had to examine his belief that he could control his fate and his God: he had to give up being the noble sacrificer.

As he felt more loved in his relationship with his God, he discovered a whole new world of possibilities for himself—he became more selective in the women he dated as well as more optimistic about his overall future possibilities. Furthermore, his relationship with me changed. As he no longer needed me to be so powerful and omniscient in providing for him, he could ask for things he needed from me. He made my office environment more his own during the time of our sessions by lowering the temperature of the room, shutting off a light, or rearranging the sofa pillows. He would reset these objects before the end of session, but his self-assertiveness to ask for what he needed was an important shift in his level of self-esteem. I encouraged Tony to assert himself in these ways so that he could experience a greater sense of self-empowerment. He would angrily tell me that I had started late or that I hadn't given him his "full" forty-five minutes. In this way I was no longer the all-powerful or all-protective object because he could take care of himself.

[Undated entry, made sometime after February 21, 1991 and before September 14, 1991]. Do my assets out[weigh] my liabilities? I can say quite clearly my assets outweigh my liabilities because I get to live my life to a richness or blissness [sic]. Then I still to this day can't comprehend the joy and peace, happiness, laughter and love that come from not overeating and bingeing because I've always lived in the liabilities or the pain and misery or the morbid hell of the disease. So I can't comprehend all this good stuff because simply it's never been in my life because I willed differently because I didn't know better. Food was what I knew best . . . .

September 14, 1991: [I can't] beat myself up for the past any longer because it was a survival mechanism to literally stay alive. But today I can't say it's a survival mechanism that literally keeps me alive because of the awareness of this program, so my assets again when I [am] not in the food are deep peace, happiness and laughter and love and when I don't let all that good stuff come in my life it's my own choice but the asset of when my emotions I'm feeling can't feel all the good stuff, I'm blessed with dealing with it and going through it if I don't choose to pick up the food. Show forth the life of Christ, share the life of Christ.

I have come to a realization and I am beginning to accept that I cannot eat like other human beings. It's a tough one to accept, and it's coming in a processing *way so I will accept it for today. My will can be taken back if I choose, and I can have hell returned and pain and misery. It sounds torturous and sadistic and it is, it's powerful and incestuous to come to a realization that I can take that first bite and actually die in many forms and somewhat scary of how close it is in my reach but so is crack 100 yards from here and beer 30 yards from here just like the food.*

September 29, 1991, 3:20 in the morning: I've been on my knees for about forty minutes just out of gratitude. Don't know where to begin but putting the writing off for almost four months now startles me and amazes me of what it takes to get myself moving. To think now that, OK [only] four months [to do] this writing but about four years and four months ago I was smelling like an animal from not bathing for five or six weeks and telling people to cut my brother's throat because he was telling the drug dealers not to sell me the crack also startles me and amazes me. I have so much today and 95 percent of it seems to be from or on the inside. My God has been good to me in a very unconditional unlimited and unchangeable loving way. My Lord is very forgiving and has taught me to forgive myself to an extremely large extent. So I want to move on with these fucking steps [completing his Eighth Step] that seems to be a limiting factor here. I limit my life by not having a more peaceful and serene feeling.

Soon after this entry, he did complete the rest of the Steps because he finally felt comfortable enough with his new AA sponsor. Tony also found a new girlfriend who was devoted and desirous of him. His ability to take in this loving person indicated again the enormous shift in his object relations: he no longer needed to surround himself with food or drugs to achieve moments of fusion. Not only did he now have powerful immersions with me and with God but also with another loving object.

Coinciding with this shift, Tony noticed that I was pregnant with my first child. He was ecstatic about my pregnancy, glad to have the opportunity to share me with a younger brother or sister. He felt that this time, unlike in his family of origin, he would still receive enough love even though a new baby was joining the family. He allowed himself to re-experience the intensity of the merging phenomenon in our early sessions by imagining that he was inside me along with my baby. For example, he told me that one day while he was swimming, he curled up in a fetal position under the water because he wanted to know what it might feel like inside my belly. As he lay in this position, however, he began to miss the unconstricted freedom of stretching out his arms and legs. He realized that being in the womb might be restrictive because a baby cannot exert his own will. With this knowledge, Tony pulled himself out of the water and decided that, although it was a nice feeling to be so totally surrounded by a warm and soothing other, he no longer wanted this quite so literally. He realized he wanted to regulate the immersion experience so that he could still have his own individuated self. *"So if it's okay with you,"* he told me, *"I'll let the baby stay inside of you and I'll stay out here."* This moment heralded the shift he had made through the treatment. He no longer wanted to be a baby because his grown-up life was so much better. He also did not need to worry about my baby being a threat to him because he had internalized enough of me. Having said this, however, the *reality* of the baby's birth (and my six-week maternity leave) did cause him some second thoughts. In this next journal entry, he imagines being a child again and how it had felt to have a new sibling. For him, this experience had been quite painful: he was only 13 months old when his younger sister was born, and so his primacy as baby in the family was quite short-lived. He starts this passage wishing to be my only baby and ends up wanting me to mother all the family members he loves so dearly!

[After my daughter's birth in October, 1991]: *Thy will be done. I had a sense in the bathroom that I'm growing up and I love it and hate it also. Like a feeling of losing my only loving mother. For some reason you [Karen] seem lost or I'm losing or lost you. I feel like a 5-year-old going to first grade or school for the first time and would much prefer to stay home with you and my new sister and let [your husband] go to work or going out and away but not me or the baby. And don't take Mom away from our home. Does Mom want me more away from her because that's what she thinks is best for me or that's the way it's supposed to be. When I went to school my first day I don't think I cried or was too scared, well maybe scared but detaching from my natural mother wasn't all that bad or hard, but from my adopted Mom it seems scary but it doesn't feel good at all, some ways scary being more alone to the world and more independent, but I'll feel more safe or secure on your lap Mommy like last week with my baby sister on your lap.* [He means that he saw me with the baby on my lap before session.] *I don't know if I want this new life because the safety I've felt with your Mom is like the nectar fruit of heaven, why would I want that when I've had what baby sister had? I want that growing up can't be more beautiful and comforting and safe, secured, loved for, or embraced with love like baby sister has. Mommy can I have that instead of this new life with a woman that I'm not sure can promise me that.* [He imagines my baby saying to me] *"Do you have to work so much Mommy, I need you now and I need you more than [other] people that . . . come into my house and whoever they are at your office. Please Mommy I want to maybe go to school if that's what's best for me but I want to see you the second I come home. I will understand that the baby sister needs your love and attention and you can even give Daddy to me but that's all . . . ."* [He then goes through a list of numerous other friends and family who he wishes I would help.] *When I grow up and become an adult and it's time to get married, maybe I will marry Mary* [his current girlfriend] *if you think it's okay, Mommy. My real Mommy is also afraid and fearful that I never feel happy inside next to her the way me and baby sister was next to you. I just want to say I love you Mommy this much and don't ever leave me, I don't think I want to live if that happens.*

My pregnancy helped Tony cement his increased individuation and his ability to utilize his internal representation of me. He still looked for and received immersive moments in the treatment—these always remained at the core of treatment—but the intensity of his need for these points of contact had lessened. My pregnancy helped him see that I was also a separate individual, with my own thoughts, wishes, and ideas. My physical transformation (i.e., the enlargement of my belly), made it clear that I was not always under his control, and yet, he was still able to rearrange my office. Tony accepted my separateness because he had become more empowered in himself and because he could still seek therapeutic infusions whenever he desired.

Tony's choice of girlfriend this time was a loving, intelligent woman who was the child of an alcoholic. She did not have a weight problem, but understood Tony's obsession with food. She intuitively knew that he needed to feel her love and that he would turn to food if he felt abandoned by her. She would say to him, "Why are you choosing food over me? I want you to be with me, not with the doughnuts!" Tony had found a woman who spoke his language, a woman who understood his abandonment anxiety and was willing to immerse herself in his world.

For several months, Tony had difficulty allowing himself to believe that his destiny had changed so dramatically. How was it possible, he wondered, that he could have such love from a beautiful woman—he, the greatest freak of all time! He spoke of his incredulity at God's plan. He was amazed that, once he stopped expecting to have pain and suffering, he had found love and happiness instead. Indeed, when he was able to let powerful others have their own separate initiative, he no longer felt he had to be in control. His God had provided him with something he never could have imagined, and indeed, God had acted on His own powers, not on Tony's wishes.

Over the next year, Tony became more comfortable with his newfound love and with being loved. He became more confident in himself and in his abilities. He continued *taking in* his girlfriend's love and attentiveness and began finding other areas to feel loved in as well. Over time, he was finally comfortable enough with the change in his fate to ask her to marry him. She immediately accepted, a response that gave Tony a moment's pause to reflect on the changes in his fate.

July 14, 1992: I decided I want it all, Mary in marriage. Your will, God, not mine. You guide me, life begins again.

August 10, 1992: I feel weak as far as my wanting to eat but I just read I can do all things through Christ who strengthens me. Last night I asked Mary to marry me . . . . I felt in my heart to ask her last night. I knew it was time in my heart so I asked her to sit and read the letter [a letter he wrote to her mother, asking for her daughter's hand in marriage]. *She was crying. She was very afraid if the mother ever got the letter and that I would back out of it that she couldn't make the mother suffer to that extent, it would just be too much for the mother to bear. So when she got to the part of where I asked the mother for permission to marry her, that's when . . . I said I love you Mary and I want you to marry me and will you, she just continued to cry and so I got on my knees to pray and she joined me. And I said to Jesus with her by my side that I ask you Jesus to be present with God the father and the Holy Spirit and that I asked for communication with her father in Heaven and that I ask you for your daughter's hand in marriage and I grabbed her hand and said I love your daughter and will be faithful and love her always and I asked her again will you marry me and she started to pray to Jesus like I never heard her pray before, the words were the most beautiful prayer about us being together forever and for about eight to ten minutes she talked to Jesus and the beautiful words she spoke I can't remember but they were from the heart. . . . She will love me always and our children will have so much love from both of us and then she turned toward me as I was still on my knees with her and she said I love you and I will marry you . . . .*

August 15, 1992: Last night I bought the [engagement] ring at 5:30 P.M. and gave it to Mary at a party with her friends.

It is so fitting that the two surrounded themselves with God and prayer as they joined together in body, mind, and soul. Two years after their marriage, they are expecting a child—due on Christmas Day! In yet another miraculous moment, Tony applied for a federal housing grant that was awarded by lottery. He prayed and prayed for months to be the first chosen. Out of several hundred applicants, Tony and Mary were indeed the first to be picked. In being first, they were able to pick the townhouse of their choice before all others. Ironically, the townhouses are on property once owned by a local church, and some of the artifacts and architecture of the church will be incorporated into the townhouse design. Simultaneous with the birth of their child, they will be moving into their very own home.

Although the therapy continues, primarily in the area of his food struggles, he has come such a very long way from the depths of despair. He has made the shift from pathological infusions of drugs and food to healthy objects and, in the process, has discovered his own power and strength. The immersive approach has been extraordinarily helpful to him, in part because it tapped into his already developed sense of prayer, transcendence, and fate.

It is fitting to end this chapter with a passage from the Bible that Tony loves:

I waited patiently for the Lord;
And He inclined to me,
And heard my cry.

He also brought me up out of a horrible pit,
Out of the miry clay,
And set my feet upon a rock,
And established my steps.

He has put a new song in my mouth—
Praise to our God;
Many will see it and fear,
And will trust in the Lord.

Psalm 40: 1–3

8

POINT–COUNTERPOINT AND OTHER TREATMENT ISSUES

I shall light a candle of understanding in thy heart, which shall
not be put out. . . .

Apocrypha, II *Esdras* 14:25

TONY'S CASE DRAMATIZES the intensity of the idealization process
that is often integral to the immersive transference. One must remember
that his addiction was all encompassing, involving not merely one substance but four alternative fusion objects. In fact, it is not uncommon for
an addict, having put down his drug, to reattach to another transformative object. The therapist must allow himself to be used as a powerful
object by the patient until he has sufficiently infused and internalized this
object relationship. The patient had originally idealized drugs too, being
able to forget and deny the dangers inherent in the high. The therapist is
not under the same illusion as the patient and knows his own strengths
and weaknesses. He simply chooses not to disclose his human foibles,
knowing that the patient will learn of the therapist's character as the
therapeutic relationship continues. By analogy, the mother is the world to
her young child, but her simultaneous struggles in the larger world are
inconsequential to his needs. Originally, the baby seeks the mother as his
primary object of attachment; in the treatment, the patient is helped to
use the therapist, AA, and other transformative objects as new primary
objects of attachment.

In my conceptualizations, any object can be an object of attachment: some individuals attach to food, or money, or television, or
computers. Many people never attach as strongly to other human beings
as they do to inanimate objects and are therefore detached from the

interpersonal realm. In the therapy, it is crucial to uncover the objects of attachment used by the patients we treat and to understand the symbolism, the importance, and the function of these attachment objects. As Bowlby (1969) notes, "A child in disgrace sucks his thumb; a child separated from his mother overeats. In such situations it is possible to think of the thumb and food as being symbolic of mother as a whole or at least of nipple and milk" (p. 219). In many cases, the therapist must be inserted as a new object of attachment so as to help the individual shift from his mode of primarily relating to inanimate objects. The work, then, involves constantly analyzing both the internal and external objects of attachment, helping shift the patient from loyalties to internal toxic objects, and helping him to find sustaining and fulfilling external attachments as well.

The capacity to be alone develops out of the baby's ability to hold onto the internalization of his mother, even during her absences. It is not just an image of mother that he retains but also her loving devotion to him. Thus, when alone, he can feel confident and secure as he continues to infuse himself with her love. The addict has had so few loving attachments in his life that when alone he is returned to his detached, alienated self. This feeling-state can be compared to a young child's fear of monsters—without a powerful other to help him, the monsters continue to live somewhere within the child or his environment. It is not uncommon for patients to be found on either side of an attachment pendulum. On the one hand, many patients immediately latch onto the therapist, as in the case of Tony, whereas others return to an external object–less state, such as Kristin, who is presented later in this chapter. It is invariably easier to handle patients for whom the transference erupts in the idealizing attachment phase than those who view the therapist as a powerful and distrusted intruder. In either case, the assistance of adjunct therapies such as AA can be quite helpful.

Some patients struggle so painfully with the therapeutic separations that outpatient group therapies, or even hospitalization, may need to be considered. In these days of managed care, however, the immersive approach can be used to help prevent a possible hospitalization. This is an important consideration. In years past, when hospitalization was more fully available as a means of relapse prevention or to assist a patient whose therapy had moved him into a more regressed state, some of these techniques would have been circumvented. The hospital became the primary idealized object of attachment. Indeed, Kernberg (1975) suggests that hospitalization should be considered even in patients without psychosis "who . . . would most likely continue to be able to function outside a hospital" (p. 99). That is not likely today.

Let me give an example of what I have in mind. Sarah began treatment just days before she stopped abusing alcohol. She was certainly motivated to end her addiction, but even so, she struggled greatly in the weeks and months that followed. She began attending AA, although she was frequently uncomfortable in meetings. In her initial consultation with me, she had told me her primary fear was of separations. She had never lived away from home despite being in her early thirties and had not been involved in a serious romantic relationship for many years. The end of sessions, particularly early on, were difficult. She would say, "So now what? I leave here and do what? Feel what? Talk to whom?" There were no supportive others in her life. All of her friends were addicts, and her family, including her parents and siblings, were also active alcoholics. Sarah had no place to hide and no place to develop her own sense of self. Furthermore, she was frightened by the uncovering process of therapy — she knew that she had so defended herself that all of her emotions were carefully guarded within her internal prison.

The only way to reach Sarah was through the therapeutic relationship, which she clearly wanted. She seemed to want continuous contact with me. We moved to twice-a-week treatment because she could not tolerate longer intervals between sessions and because I felt that she required a more intensive immersive experience to begin her sobriety. (Even in this era of managed care, this patient's twice-weekly treatment was approved because the argument that this kind of treatment was most cost effective was indeed persuasive.) Despite the increased contact, she at first found the time-limited nature of therapy sessions more of a tease than a help. I suggested she call me, as needed, between her biweekly appointments. She did call, only to tell me that she felt as though she were "falling apart." And in a sense she was, because the more she exposed herself, the more pain and the more memories she experienced. She described this sensation of disintegration as a feeling of her own self "unraveling": she could no longer anticipate or control what she was thinking, saying, or feeling. She mentioned the idea of hospitalization, saying that she might be more able, in that setting, to shed her defenses completely and uncover her inner self. It was difficult for her to dissolve the layering of false self structure while continuing her daily activities, socializing with friends and family, and maintaining a business facade at her job. As we discussed hospitalization further, she also discussed her fears and worries of being separated from all that was familiar and comforting to her. I told Sarah that although hospitalization would provide her with a twenty-four-hour support system, it would also mean that she and I would have more limited contact. And, although she would have other competent clinicians involved with her care, she would have to allow herself primarily to attach to them and not to me. This she did not want.

And so, instead, she finally agreed at my insistence that she find a sponsor and began to speak more frequently in the meetings. I encouraged her to call some of the recovering women who had reached out to her so that she could create a new family, a new home. To this suggestion she retorted, "That's not so easy when you don't trust anyone." But as she did trust me to a limited extent, I asked her to begin the building of her new family with me. I suggested she keep a journal, write me letters between sessions should she wish for more contact, or leave messages on my office answering machine should she only want to touch base. We arranged a mid-week phone contact that she utilized for several weeks so that she could build a continuous, internalized image of me, of her therapy, and of the new self she was creating. Sarah added to these ideas. She sent me poetry and recorded a tape for me of her favorite songs.

Very often, when patients are given the opportunity to utilize the therapy relationship in an immersive manner, they can become very creative in their attempts to maintain and deepen the connection. When Rebecca, a patient mentioned in Chapters 1 and 3, was at this same early stage of internalization, she asked if she could take home with her something from my office in order to keep me close to her. When I asked what she would like, she pointed to a little plastic toy on my desk. This particular toy was an interesting choice. It was a wind-up marching bear holding musical cymbals that, when wound, would crash together. She loved the idea of pretending that I was clapping for her and that whenever she needed a hug she could "wind me up." These days, with fax machines, car phones, and beepers, psychotherapists have an even wider range of ways to enable patients to keep in close contact.

Yet, the building of the therapeutic contact is primarily an internal process. The amount of actual contact these patients require has been, in reality, quite minimal. It is the offer, the fantasy that they have unlimited twenty-four-hour availability, that is most helpful. A useful image is to view the therapeutic relationship as a protective umbrella that surrounds the patient at all times. In Sarah's case, she was able to contain her contact with me to the biweekly sessions after less than three months of therapy, except during periodic moments of increased distress. She learned to rely on her sponsor and on other group members for most of her soothing needs.

When a patient is in crisis and has not contacted the therapist, the question of "Why didn't you call me?" becomes an important therapeutic matter. Often, patients state that they did not want me to feel they were too burdensome or needy. This issue is crucial in their treatment, because patients deserve to be "bothers," just as children deserve attention and responses to their requests. An infant does not have the physical means to care for himself, just as a patient does not have the psychological ability to cope in times of crisis, drug urges, or suicidal ideation. I often tell patients, especially drug and alcohol patients, that I expect, as part of their treatment, that they will contact me even outside the therapeutic hour should they be in more distress or in an acute crisis. For many, this therapeutic gesture is welcomed and is indeed relieving. Like an umbrella, the therapeutic relationship can be pulled out and opened during stormy days.

Of course, for those patients who do not want to involve the therapist in their actions, this kind of approach is experienced as frustrating and claustrophobic. Very often, these are the patients who will return to drugs or alcohol—they cannot relinquish the substance. It is especially true that, with these individuals, the lack of therapeutic involvement must be continually confronted. For example, one patient was an overeater who frequently binged on doughnuts and candy during moments of stress. Despite his seemingly close connection to me during his sessions, he stubbornly refused to internalize the therapeutic relationship outside our actual contact. In his fourth year of treatment, he only recently has realized the intensity of his belief that food is his only rescuer. Over and over again, I have pointed out that he chooses food as a soother rather than searching for human contact. This man, and the many others who similarly remain entrenched with their secondary attachments, has remained in deeper contact with substitute attachment objects than with anyone else. He must be encouraged to examine the roots of his detachment, the multiple experiences that taught him to rely on no one. He must also be shown that his illusion of self-reliance is just that—an illusion. By offering a therapeutic relationship in which immersion is the expectation, he can begin to make strides toward human contact and comfort. Seinfeld (1991) makes the observation that psychoanalysis has its roots in techniques that are inherently distancing: the use of the couch prevents eye contact, the therapist is trained to conceal his own feelings, and very often there is an emphasis on intellectualization. Indeed, this may be one of the reasons why alcoholics have traditionally done so poorly in psychoanalytic psychotherapy: the treatment they require involves intense emotional contact.

Kernberg's (1984) treatment strategies are in direct contrast to the immersive approaches that I am suggesting. He gives an example of an alcoholic young woman in her twenties who came to therapy seeking crisis-oriented relief. She was situationally depressed, with suicidal ideation, weight loss, and reduced academic functioning. From the beginning, Kernberg established a restrictive frame of treatment, contracting with the patient that, should she not be able to meet these requirements, she would be hospitalized. Not surprisingly, the patient committed to the therapist that she would change her behavior—she would stop drinking, refrain from any suicidal means, and gain weight. Soon after this verbal commitment, however, she resumed drinking. Kernberg candidly writes of his feelings in the session in which he suspected her return to alcohol. His thoughts include "moments of concern and strong urges to express this concern. . . . [and] to confront her" as to whether she had been equivocating about drinking, and to point out that she perceived him as an authority figure (p. 125). He goes on to say that he had "a growing sense of *impatience* in myself, a combination of *worry* for the patient and *irritation* that the treatment program as set up was falling apart and *inordinate demands* were being made on the psychiatric social worker and me to change the treatment arrangements" (p. 126, emphasis mine). Finally, he realizes that "the predominant human relationship enacted at that moment was of a frightened little girl who wanted a powerful parental figure (whose particular sexual identity was irrelevant) to take over and protect her from pain, fear and suffering in general" (p. 126). I agree with him; this probably is what she wanted and, had he offered her this thought, as well as his genuine concern for her drinking, he would have been working in an immersive way. Instead he comes to the conclusion that if he told her of his anxiety for her, she would hate this parental figure because the anxiety would be generated out of her "suffering" and not out of "natural concern, love, and dedication to her" (p. 126). He tells her none of these supportive thoughts, but instead tells her that she is offering him "contradictory wishes: she wanted to reassure me that she was still in control of her life, and at the same time she was conveying quite dramatically that things were falling apart" (p. 126).

But is this conclusion correct? The patient comes to session notice-ably impaired. Is she saying she is in control? Or is she just frightened of the punishment that he, like a parent, might inflict on her for not being able, on her own, to correct her alcoholism, suicidal ideation, and depression? The patient answered him that she felt "completely hopeless about herself" and was angry that her parents were late in sending her the money to pay for her sessions. Kernberg replies with the interpretation that she is, essentially, not concerned "so much about whether the psychotherapy would help her as about whether I was genuinely interested in her or just concerned about getting paid for the sessions." He feels that she is presenting herself as weak and incompetent as a way to try and "extract" his help. He additionally says to her that "any help from me would be like the irritated, angry reaction of a parent who would prefer not to be bothered but had no alternative but to take care of an unwanted child" (p. 127).

With this, the patient began to cry. Her boyfriend was ending their relationship, and she felt she had "no right" to ask for any help. She explained that she had only been given this psychotherapy because her parents were able to afford it. She asked, "Why should [I] be treated when there [is] so much suffering in the world?" She felt hopeless, unable to be helped. Kernberg believes that this passage indicates a shift because she was now analyzing her "masochistic character pattern" (p. 127) as well as becoming concerned for herself. He feels "that the pressure on me to take over was decreasing, and that she was beginning to feel guilty for having failed to keep her part of our agreement while also beginning to under-stand that this failure was an expression of her feeling that she did not deserve to be helped"(p. 127). In sum, Kernberg believes this case demon-strates the importance of utilizing "technical neutrality" (p. 127), so that the patient could, and did, temporarily strengthen her own ego.

Let me review this case from an immersive perspective. The patient has said that she feels undeserving of therapy and of help. She feels there is nothing special about herself and that if she did not have access to her parents' money, she would mean nothing to the therapist. She feels unworthy, unloved. Her boyfriend is leaving her, and she wonders if the therapist will too. She is concerned that she cannot meet the requirements of his treatment frame and that, as with her boyfriend and probably her parents as well, she will be abandoned. The therapist never discloses what are his genuine, concerned feelings for her, which certainly would have helped her feel valued in at least this important relationship. He does not comment on how she must feel to be so dependent on unreliable parents for money, nor does he offer her any support about the reality of their late payment. Perhaps therapist and patient could have discussed the need for her to pay for her own sessions, thereby encouraging her separation from her undependable parents. Perhaps he could have wondered with her why she feels so very unlovable and unworthy, and, rather than simply point out how she has attempted to recreate this dynamic in the therapy, offer his feeling that he disagrees with her self-assessment: he *did* in fact feel concerned at seeing her condition in session, and he had wanted to know how to help.

In Kernberg's overt attempt to be neutral, he actually responds to her with countertransferential feelings. He tells her that she would not accept any help from him because it would be like the "irritated, angry" (p. 127) response of parents who are obligated to care for an "unwanted child" (p. 127). It is he who is feeling irritated and angry that she will now make "inordinate demands" on him and on the psychiatric social worker. She indeed needs more care, and like a child who is suffering in anxious attachment, she is both protesting and despairing the inaccessibility of her protective others. Mitchell (1988), remarking on therapeutic neutrality, states that "if one is invited to a dance, one either attends in some fashion or does not attend in some fashion. Remaining silent and refusing to respond constitute powerful responses and are experienced by the analysand as responses" (p. 207). Indeed, neutrality is another word for detachment.

Every child deserves to feel special, valued, and worthy of attention and love; every patient deserves to experience in the therapy his own true self and to find a mutuality of respect, admiration, and deeply felt interest from the therapist. And yet, Kernberg (1980) views it as a mistake "to gratify the patient's transference demands by indicating that [the patient] was indeed 'special' to the therapist by shifting from a position of technical neutrality into that of an orally giving parent" (p. 207). He feels that therapists who do express positive regard are likely to act on their feelings by providing extra session time, expressing their feelings, or even holding the patient's hand. It is an unnecessarily exaggerated and pejorative view to suggest that therapists who feel comfortable eliciting human warmth in their work are going to act out by hand-holding!

Kernberg details the following case (1980) to demonstrate the importance of technical neutrality. A female patient, who had been working with him intensely for over four years, tells him that she continues to view him as distanced and personally uninvolved. She has previously told him that she feels he is "just tolerating her," and she goes on to say that the process of psychotherapy has neither alleviated her sense of loneliness nor her sadness in not finding a fulfilling relationship. Despite her comments, Kernberg continues to push her to examine her feelings without mention of the contributions that his particular treatment philosophy may have had to do with her isolation. In his commentary, he notes that, in this particular session, he had "sensed considerable emotional warmth . . . [and] that the patient felt reassured by my interest and dedication without having to explore this issue *verbally* at the moment" (p. 206, emphasis mine). He assumes that she could, despite her transferential view of him as just "tolerating her," determine his unspoken interest and dedication (p. 202). If only because she felt so detached and alienated, he might have shown her, *in words,* the kind of attachment and interest he actually felt for her. She might have thrived with the knowledge that, at least in her psychotherapy, her unique, inner self had value and worth. She might have then been able to take this newfound confidence and apply it to the many other relationships in her life.

Kernberg (1975) sees behind every idealization a devaluation just waiting to happen. Like Klein, he views the child as having an inborn aggressive capacity that is exhibited in oral rage and envy. "What regularly emerges is that behind the consciously remembered or rediscovered 'disappointments' from the parents are the devaluations of parental images and the real parental figures" (p. 287). Similarly, in the transference, he feels the patients' "devaluation of the transference object for the slightest reason" (p. 287). That is indeed an easy way out of handling the negative therapeutic reaction. In examining another case that Kernberg presents, however, it is clear that the patient had in fact very good reasons for her responses. In this case, the patient had spent the first two weeks of her hospitalization "yell[ing]" (p. 86) at the therapist, but was observed as always being calm with other patients and staff members. The therapist's response was to limit (behaviorally) her aggressive outbursts. The patient, it should be noted, had "engaged in bitter fights with her parents for many years" (p. 86), a sign to Kernberg of her abnormally high innate aggression. Could it not be that her parents had engaged *her* in bitter battles, that they had been particularly unempathic, and that this patient had been raised in, at the least, a family filled with normative abuse? Perhaps her yelling at the therapist was because of his authoritarian stance, or because she did not feel her hospitalization was necessary, or for any number of other reasons. Stolorow and Lachmann (1980) argue that Kernberg's confrontational approach actually induces a negative transference and aggressive acting out. Druck (1989) believes the patient experiences the therapist's confrontation as an "invitation to battle" (p. 256), causing hostility and creating a paranoid flavor to the treatment. The self psychologists, as Mitchell (1988) notes, view Kernberg as "continually creating the monster he is perpetually slaying" (p. 191).

I further disagree with Kernberg's opinion that idealization and the patient's need to have omnipotent control over the therapist must be analyzed systematically. Like Seinfeld (1991), I feel this process can strengthen the patient's resistance to analyzing his dependency issues, as well as actually push the patient into a position of extreme frustration and anger. Telling a patient that his idealization of the therapist is pathological is similar to telling a young child that his parents are just adults without any special protective powers. The child knows differently; the patient too often feels the therapist as a powerful other who is indeed helping him transform his life. Druck argues similarly that narcissistic and borderline patients may indeed need the therapist to serve as a protective container for some time in the therapy, and that this is not necessarily an unrealistic request.

Kernberg looks at the patient's need to control the therapist as a way of devaluing and depreciating the therapist's individuated self. Quite the contrary: the therapist's ability to suspend his self-needs to care for the patient as he would like indicates the strength of his separate self. The patient is aware of the differences, the separateness, of the therapist. When the patient is able to have the therapist "do his bidding," the patient, like a young child, becomes reassured of his value and his ability to be loved. The patient's wish for a subjective object is viewed by Kernberg as pathological grandiosity and is seen as defending against intense and infantile envy and fear of the hated object. I prefer to view these wishes as attempts by the patient to try yet another object, a different object, for human connection, warmth, and immersion. The only reason for an aggressive reaction is when the object responds as mother originally did, with a narcissistic and ungratifying "no." Kernberg's view is an example of a quite common countertransferential reaction to the immersive transference. The therapist can feel put upon, drained, and angry from the demands of his patient. Frequently therapists call these patients manipulative and needy. In so doing, they fail to see the powerlessness behind these requests, the fearful belief that lies underneath: the patient feels unlovable, his requests are overdemanding, he has tired the other out.

One final case example of Kernberg's (1975), also involving an alcoholic and drug addict, furthers the point. A single woman in her late thirties was hospitalized to stem her addiction. She came into outpatient treatment after her discharge and developed a "friendly" transference (p. 94). She maintained her sobriety at first, but quickly went through boyfriend after boyfriend. She soon relapsed, became suicidal, and admitted herself back into the hospital without consulting her therapist. After two more similar episodes the patient revealed an early abandonment trauma of her childhood. She had been left alone at home, sick, in what turned out to be a dangerous and severe illness, because her mother did not want to cancel her own social plans. The analysis showed that the patient had not wanted to reveal "how much she needed [her therapist] and loved him" because she was afraid "she would destroy him with the intensity of her anger" (p. 95) over childhood abandonments. She was viewed as splitting her aggression into her drinking, her friendships, and her lovers, instead of her therapy. When the therapist tried to bring all these pieces together into the therapy, she became anxious, angry, and distrustful. She began to drink again, and he rehospitalized her.

Again, the underlying issues are fairly straightforward. Here was someone who had gotten so little care, nurturance, and protection from her mother that she felt she had to take care of herself. She did not believe anyone else could care for her—and what would tell her otherwise? The first time she sought rehospitalization she did so without informing the therapist. How self-protective she was being: her mother did not know when she needed assistance as a child, and so she believed the therapist would not either. Rather than aggressive splitting, she was seeking friends and lovers to reassure herself that she was indeed loved, and she drank to protect and soothe herself. She may also have been identifying herself with her socialite mother, who had placed her relationship with friends over the needs of her daughter. Although it may indeed have been empathically correct to rehospitalize her when she became angry and anxious (or perhaps it is simply that she was revealing her inner, detached self), it might have been more helpful to have offered her immersive techniques instead. The rehospitalization again pulled the patient *away from* her struggle to attach deeply to the therapist; it might have been more useful instead to intensify the therapeutic relationship.

Certainly, patients project their childhoods into the therapeutic relationship. And there is no denying that analyzing the transference is crucial to the release of these toxic introjects. One way of reaching transferential issues, however, is to help the patient experience the therapist as a separate and different kind of person from his family of origin. If this is not made clear to the patient, then how is he to know when the therapist is simply resembling his parent in transference only? How is the patient to know that he has not, yet again, been experienced by an important other as overly demanding, unlovable, or unworthy of attention? As with the patient who was constantly told by her mother that she was "Rebecca-ed" out, it was important for me to tell Rebecca when her expectations of me were unreasonable. In her five years of treatment, she only once asked more than I could supply. After her fourth year, she decided to "take a break" from therapy. She sought to return to therapy a year later and called me for an appointment during my vacation. I responded to her call, but told her I could not see her until after the vacation, offering her a referral should she be in more desperate need before I was again available. Rebecca was furious that I "hadn't cared" enough to respond to her emergency, despite my own vacation plans. As we later analyzed her feelings in our first session after my vacation, she told me that she had realized her anger was not only misplaced but totally uncalled for. As she said, "I realize now that you are a separate person from me, and that I was expecting you to drop your entire life just for me. It was very important for me to see how unrealistic I was being, and that sometimes I really do demand from others things that they have no ability to give." Rebecca, it was apparent, had little ability to determine when her demands were actually reasonable, because she had always been told by her mother that every request she made was too burdensome. Her mother, who had been overwhelmed by having three small children in five years and had her own medical problems, simply had no reserves left to attend to her. This was a crucial understanding—with this knowledge, the patient was freed from her internal sense of guilt and self-hatred.

The examples above illustrate some of the common countertransferential feelings elicited by work with these patients, such as the discomfort in being relegated to the status of a subjective object, an object with no self-needs. When Tony, for example, wanted to turn out the office lamp or move a pillow, there is no question that I found myself irritated with him because he was, momentarily, taking over my "space." I have found it particularly important in such moments to remind myself of the under-lying neediness and sense of enfeeblement that have caused the patient to become so controlling. I remind myself that, just as a mother does toward her young child, I must allow the patient to use me in his own way—to fashion me into his own particular object. Furthermore, by becoming an object under his control, I am essentially feeling what he felt as a child. It was he who was a subjective object, demanded upon by his mother to do *her* bidding. Spotnitz (1976) calls this the "induced feeling" (p. 49), which regularly occurs in countertransferential feelings. From my vantage point, these induced feelings are golden moments of immersion, moments in which the therapist can evocatively experience the patient's affective state.

Spotnitz (1976) has written that one of the most difficult aspects of training new analysts is their fear of feelings: "Many students are afraid to have feelings for a patient. They are averse to having them and using them. In their attempts to get rid of the feelings, they tend to operate in such a way as to get rid of the patient. They have to be helped to recognize that the issue is not one of having or not having feelings for the patient but of using their feelings to help him improve (p. 362)."

Spotnitz is of the opinion that the emotions of one individual can greatly influence the feeling-state of another individual, just as infants can easily detect and resonate the feelings of their parents. This being so, a patient's emotional state can induce similar feelings in the therapist. The induced countertransferential feeling is readily noticeable because it is not a feeling that the therapist usually experiences in the course of his day or with other patients. It is a feeling directly coming from the patient and being absorbed by the therapist. In this moment, the therapist feels exactly the way the patient himself is feeling; it can be a powerful example of immersion. "Mutual contagion [of feelings] emerged as a basic factor: The analyst has to experience the patient's feelings in order to 'return' them to him; the patient, through experiencing them from the analyst, is helped to discharge the feelings in language" (Spotnitz 1976, p. 53). Very often in the work with detached patients, the induced countertransferential feeling is one of a sense of failure, inadequacy, and frustration in being unable to find a way to reach the patient. Indeed, in these moments the analyst has become a mirror to the patient: he feels as detached and removed as the patient himself.

For example, one patient continually rejected any comment,

thought, or idea I offered her. Soon, even a simple "uh-huh" by me began to be critically evaluated by her, and I had the feeling that I was fumbling in my ability to speak even the most mundane dialogue. She had previously told me that she had never felt valued, loved, or special and that she had never been able to trust anyone with her true self. The feeling induced in me had provided me with a deeply felt understanding of her that was more powerful than words: I too was feeling inadequate, inept, and unworthy of the title "psychotherapist." Her induced feeling provided me with the visceral understanding of her isolation and alienation.

Other countertransference reactions include feelings of tiredness in the session, worrying in off hours about a particular patient, and hesitancy in canceling a particular patient's therapy hour even when necessary. In the last case, this hesitancy no doubt comes from the therapist's reluctance *in any way* to resemble the patient's family of origin; the therapist is well aware of the excruciating frequency with which the patient has been disappointed by others. These feelings are all understandable and expectable aspects of the immersive relationship and indicate the intensity of the work with these patients, particularly in a private practice setting. It is certainly understandable that the therapist would like to have some worry-free evenings without wondering if any patient will be in distress. As it can be difficult always to feel on-call, it is probably best to avoid an entire caseload of recovering alcoholics and addicts. Feelings of disappointment and anger, should patients relapse and return to alcohol or drugs, are also common, as is a feeling that the therapist is responsible and has somehow failed in helping the patient. Again, the therapist's feelings are similar to those of the patient, who no doubt feels in this moment a sense of failure in his behavior. Should the patient eventually return to the therapy, it would be important to analyze his ability to seek comfort and contact only from the substance and not from the therapeutic relationship.

With patients who resist so heavily the process of attachment, feelings of frustration are common. The therapist has been thwarted in his ability to penetrate the wall of detachment that has been fortified for so many years. Frustration is often accompanied by feelings of anger at being left out of the patient's inner self, as well as a sense of futility that the therapy is really a waste of time. In this case, the therapist has experienced an induced feeling of the deep, detached encasement that surrounds the patient and is finding himself feeling as separated from the patient as the patient feels from the therapist. It can take many, many months of limited emotional contact for a patient to move to a deeper level of intimacy, all the while testing the therapist's endurance, reliability, and interest. One patient would begin every session with seemingly trivial information. Just about halfway into the session, when I would begin wondering how much longer I could endure this lack of contact, she would shift into the painful, introspective issues of her life. It was as though she wanted to know that I would accept her entire self by first testing my interest in the false self, a self that she so easily presented to the rest of the world. Only then—and perhaps only after she detected that I was fighting to stay connected—would she reveal her inner feelings. It is important, with patients like these, to continually remind oneself that the patient is making as much contact as is possible and that, when he wants more, the therapist will be ready.

One therapist whom I supervised discussed a case in which her patient was silent for more than half of every session. And yet this woman had continued coming to therapy for over a year, never missing a single session. The therapist was, understandably, feeling uncomfortable with the silence and kept thinking she had to do something to engage the patient. She would sometimes ask questions or offer topics, and thoroughly pursue any avenue the patient had opened. In discussing the case with me, we decided it would be best to shift away from seeking any overt contact. The patient had had a history of severe sexual abuse, and so we felt that her wish for silence was actually a wish to be involved with an other who would ask for nothing, who would wait patiently for the "incommunicado element" of the self to seek revelation. As the therapist refrained from seeking contact, the patient became more comfortable in offering her thoughts and feelings. So many of our patients are detached due to sexual trauma that it is necessary to learn ways to feel immersed in the therapy with the patient while not pushing or demanding contact.

Of course, other feelings are stimulated in the immersive moment. I do not consider them to be countertransference in the way it is usually understood, because this term usually denotes pathological or dangerous emotions that the therapist must analyze for himself lest he act out in some manner toward the patient. Feelings of love, admiration, and closeness are not at all uncommon, especially with patients who have recently awakened their previously unreachable attachment needs. For example, I am often awed by the dramatic recoveries of the substance abusers whom I treat: Tony, for one, or Mark, or Dan. These people and the many others like them have been able to sustain a dramatic shift away from a powerful albeit dangerous object. That is indeed something to admire, respect, and love. Weinstein (1988) comments, "In my own experience the more powerful the feelings I have toward a particular patient, the greater his or her involvement is in the treatment process and the greater the likelihood of therapeutic success. I am speaking now about the inner awareness, not the overt expression, of such feelings" (p. 194).

I wholeheartedly agree although I do feel that there are often appropriate moments to give voice to the feelings of love that are stimulated in the therapist. Usually, the more powerful the feelings, the deeper the work. The immersive experience, for this reason alone, should be encouraged, applauded, and cultivated. In time, the internal walls of alienation crumble.

However, the waiting can be long and hard. For example, with James, described in Chapter 1, the waiting took a few years. With Mark, there were intermittent glimpses of his inner self but much seemingly extraneous discourse. With Kristin, presented below, the road to her inner self was blocked by frequent detours.

KRISTIN

In this case, the patient's overwhelming fear of merging became the central focus of treatment. Her fear of domination and abandonment by those to whom she attached made the therapeutic relationship difficult to sustain. Further, this case demonstrates that there are some instances in which the therapist's desire to provide immersive moments may be unwelcome and unaccepted by the patient.

Kristin sought treatment because she was plagued by an agonizing relationship with a young man who was ambivalent in his feelings for her, alternately craving and rejecting her. She would respond to his rejections with depressions and self-hatred, coupled with suicidal thoughts. When he sought her love, she became animated and exuberant. She found herself tied to his whims and wishes, which infuriated her because it so pointedly attacked her own self-image of being an independent, self-reliant individual.

Kristin came to her first session during one of his alienations. She was dressed totally in black, from her jet black, dyed hair to her fingernails. The blackness that surrounded her seemed in contrast to her fair complexion and pale blue eyes. She assured me, however, that this black armor was purposeful and well thought out. When in this mood, she hoped that her outfit would be so off-putting that no one around her would seek to make contact. Kristin was also a regular AA member, and here, too, she was successful in keeping the group from penetrating her inner self. This was a more difficult realm in which to remain unnoticed, but Kristin worked hard at it. She rarely spoke at meetings except to offer a sardonic or critical comment and talked with her sponsor only about superficial matters. Kristin had three years of sobriety and was proud of her abstinence from alcohol, her drug of choice. She was motivated to become sober after realizing the self-destructive wastefulness of her binge-ing. She did not utilize the relational or the spiritual aspects of AA because these were too connected with interpersonal involvement. She essentially maintained recovery because relapse would be too narcissistically injuri-ous.

Kristin was able to tolerate the intensity of sessions only on a biweekly basis. Unlike many patients, she was comforted by having to pay because doing so provided a business frame around the treatment rela-tionship. Since she was buying my expertise, she could deny any emo-tional attachment. It felt as though she wanted me to be a computer, spitting out assessments of her character structure without factoring in any emotional data. She insisted that she had no feelings whatsoever toward me, although she mentioned there were times when she would think about my comments outside session or would mention me to her boyfriend. She was curious to know about my life, why I chose the therapeutic profession, where I was raised, and what my personal beliefs were. If I did not answer her and instead tried to analyze the feelings behind her questions, she would become defensive and immediately return to the businesslike arrangement of our relationship.

History: Development of the "Burden of Badness"

Transferentially, Kristin needed to see me as a cold, narcissistic figure like her mother. Kristin was so acclimated to a non-loving relationship that she rarely allowed me to move out of this frame. She remembered very little emotional contact with her mother, who seemed to have avoided any intimacy with her. She knew that her mother regretted being pregnant with her and would have preferred to have had no children. Kristin told me,

My mother says girl babies rob the mother of her beauty. When she was pregnant with me, she was tired all the time and couldn't do anything she had hoped to do. She felt weak and sickly. She refused to eat good foods to help me grow because she was hoping I wouldn't survive. Then, when she realized she was in labor, she locked herself in the bathroom and sobbed. She refused to go to the hospital and had to be dragged out of the bathroom by my father. She didn't want to deal with me inside of her, let alone outside of her.

Indeed, Kristin had always felt like a burden. She was a classic example of Fairbairn's (1943) "burden of badness" (p. 65), because she continually felt, in her words, that she had "ruined" the lives of those around her, that she was "too difficult" for people to care about. She felt that I could tolerate her because she was paying me to do so, but that most people, such as her on-again, off-again boyfriend, could not.

Kristin assumed she had been sexually abused as a very young child because of some early but hazy memories. She also believed this because of her long-standing fascination with sadomasochistic bondage. She believed this fascination was pathological, that no 4-year-old would fantasize about being tied down and raped by older men. She could not gain access to more memories regarding this suspected abuse and said she really did not want to know more because she did not want to confront those responsible. The veracity of her memories was not as significant as her belief that she had always been treated in an abusive, tormenting manner. Kristin also recalled being sent to bed alone at a very young age and crying for hours in her room without being attended to by either parent. She knew she was frequently separated from her parents because they traveled a great deal, leaving her with other relatives. She sensed that she was unwelcome, unwanted, and unloved, but felt it was she who created this reaction in others.

We can assume that during her formative years Kristin was frequently misattuned and unprotected. Just as she was able to survive in the hostile environment of her mother's womb, however, she had learned to live in an unloving household. Protective of those around her, she believed it was her doing that made her parents ignore and even mistreat her: she was so unlovable that it was understandable for others to abuse her emotionally, physically, and even sexually. Interestingly, by viewing her alienation as self-willed, she could feel an immersion of power with each individual whom she successfully pushed away. She was the master of her fate; she controlled the human world around her.

Fear of Immersive Contact

Kristin's relationship with her boyfriend mirrored this internal sense of unlovability. Although she craved his love, she was also convinced she was unworthy of more. Indeed, he had recently told her he no longer wanted to have sex with her—that he would "save" this for the other women he was dating. Although angry, she felt he was "entitled" to find a better sexual companion. In therapy, she dictated the cold way in which she expected to be treated and did not allow herself to take in any warmth or nurturance from me. She denied the importance of our relationship and was clearly uncomfortable whenever I accurately understood her inner feeling state. In fact, one of the most difficult aspects of this case was that, the more accurate my empathic attunements, the more uncomfortable she became. To her, these moments of union were terrifying. Mergings meant abuse and domination; fusion equaled annihilation. The other was expected to be powerful, sadistic, and unrelenting. Should I be able to understand her, I would be in control of her. She would have no self because I would become the owner of her being. In this regard, Kristin had not been able to develop an immersive area surrounding herself, in which she felt protected and comforted. Her worry, that I could read her mind, was based on the powerlessness and vulnerability she experienced when involved with others. Only in the silence of her self, surrounded by no one, could she feel safe. Kristin's black garb was part of a protective armor that she could not build internally, and her sarcastic, alienating, hostile humor was her main defense.

Despite her protests against developing intimate relationships, Kristin seemed to crave attachment and involvement. For example, she once described the kind of relationship she had always dreamed of, a relationship where fusion was not synonymous with annihilation.

There was this scene on *Paper Chase* [a Corporation for Public Broadcasting series about a Harvard Law School professor and his students] in which the professor asks the class, "What does it mean to have a meeting of the minds?" Most of the students answered that it is when two or more people agree on a particular thought or idea. The professor said, "No, a meeting of the minds occurs when two or more people can understand and accept many different opinions, because there is nothing to agree upon if there is only the same, universal opinion. With two or more ideas, the entire world is allowed to coexist." That's what I want: a world in which my opinion is allowed to coexist side by side with everyone else's.

What Kristin was looking for was a place for her self to emerge as a powerful entity within the context of other powerful entities. She was able to tell me that she longed for the time when she could take off her black coat, but that she never expected this ever to happen. We were beginning to move into her underlying discord with her self-imposed alienation, when the therapeutic process was derailed.

Pregnancy, Merging, and Flight

In her tenth month of treatment, Kristin noticed that I was pregnant. (At that point, I was seven months pregnant.) She retreated back to her sardonic, no-need-for-relationships frame. The steps we had made in lessening her fear were erased. Rather than express her hurt directly, she spoke in generalities about parenthood and pregnancy. "No woman wants to get pregnant. Either it's a mistake or the guy has forced himself on her." She herself felt, after all, that she had been a mistake and that she had burdened her mother even in the womb. She asked me many questions about how I was feeling, and she could not understand why I would go through the pain and suffering involved in having a child. She most certainly would never want to be put through this, she told me, just to get "a little me" out of herself. And furthermore, she would never "let herself" be convinced by a man to carry his child. She was "surprised" that I had "let myself get taken over" by a man; she had thought I was stronger than that. In her comments, it was clear just how identified she felt with the "weaker sex," with the fact that women are "forced to succumb" to their husband's power. Kristin spoke of her concern that she was "draining me," that I must be too tired to continue the therapy. This, of course, was a transferential statement that could easily be traced to her mother. But what was most significant was that Kristin really believed she could be that much of a burden to me, and that her being caused others to be sucked dry of their power. Similarly, she subjectively felt that others could drain her of her essence, furthering her fear of interpersonal relationships.

After a six-week maternity leave, I called Kristin to reschedule an appointment. She told me she had decided to stop treatment because "you want to show me how to have relationships and I don't want any." She agreed to one final session "out of respect." She came to session in her all-black outfit, signifying her underlying vulnerability. Kristin discussed her decision to leave treatment, stating that she wanted to break free of all relationships and that even therapy meant involvement with an other. She did not want contact with anyone—she had decided instead to strengthen her armor, to strengthen her resolve to avoid others. I suggested that perhaps she might use therapy to further build this coat of armor, meaning that she might be able to build an internal covering of self-protection. However, she did not want to spend any time that would mean involvement with others, including the therapeutic relationship. She was adamant, and in leaving treatment she thanked me for helping her see that "the only choice I have is to harden my resolve to stay away from others."

I am sure that, underneath this resolve, Kristin had found my pregnancy and maternity leave too painful. In her mind, I had abandoned her, just as had those others who had succeeded in penetrating some of her narcissistic armor. I had also demonstrated a weakness that made me too similar to her own flaws—she believed I had succumbed to the power of my husband's self in agreeing to have a baby. As well, perhaps she was envious of the baby and of the merging she saw in my growing belly, and perhaps she was envious of the relationship she knew I would build with my child, one that she had never had with her mother.

Postscript

About eight months later, I saw Kristin at a local mall. She had gained what appeared to be about fifty pounds and was walking by herself amid the crowd of shoppers. Food had become her new nurturant immersion, her mother substitute, one that was devoid of human interaction.

The development of the detached, false self can take many paths. What follows below is a description of this development in two preadoles cent girls who exhibit detached styles of relating but present in contrasting images, and have had quite dissimilar childhoods.

Laura, at 10 years old, was shy, awkward, and withdrawn. In my office she often sat curled in a ball, with her eyes distantly reflecting her inner world. Sometimes I could draw her out by asking questions about her day. She had been traumatized in early childhood by her father, who was an abusive alcoholic. He had not wanted a child and had certainly not wanted a girl. He was verbally cruel to her, frequently teasing her about her small size and shy manner. He was also dangerously abusive to her physically and even used a belt on at least one occasion to whip her small body when she was no more than 2 years old. This whipping was in response to her crying; he was particularly angered by any sounds she made (at birth she had been colicky and frequently unsoothable), as though they reminded him that she was indeed alive. Her speech, not surprisingly, was delayed and her language acquisition slow. When she was 3, her father deserted the family and never returned. Laura barely remembers him, but for the fear she experienced in his presence. She was a quiet child, rarely asking for anything from her mother and rarely offering anything from herself. Her mother had told me that by the age of 2, Laura had become markedly silent.

Very often, in session she would sit without comment. We began discussing these silent moments, these moments when the walls between us were so very high. She told me that it was difficult to let her internal thoughts out, to speak of them outside her self. Her solitude was protective, her silence a camouflage. I used this as a metaphor and discussed the needs of animals and insects to be disguised so that predators would be unable to discover their whereabouts. She immediately identified with this image: she had done her best to hide from her abusive father and her concerned but enfeebled mother. Her mother had also been frightened by those years of her husband's abuse. Herself a child victim of physical abuse, she was hardly skilled in protecting her young daughter. In the years since her husband's disappearance, she had attempted to penetrate Laura's detachment but the damage was already severe. This fact is crucial to mention. That early physical abuse had created an almost impermeable wall; she lived her young life as though, apologetically and fearfully, she felt she should not speak, should not take up space, should not exist.

Having no protective external other, Laura camouflaged herself instead behind an almost invisible psychic cloak. Interestingly, the only time she ever took off this protective armor was when she wrote her poetry. She often expressed her inner world on paper and sometimes shared her poems with me. At times she would write poems to me that I greatly treasured; some I even framed and, with her permission, put in the office (to her delight). The content was always the same—her walls, her retreat from others, her fear of the world. Over time, she began to notice the pervasive barrier that she had placed between herself and the rest of the world. And every now and then, she would push her way through this wall and reveal something from the heart of her existence. On these rare occasions, she showed herself to be a remarkably perceptive and sensitive young girl. But these glimpses were rare, and the best I often could do was simply to tell her that I knew the wall between us had returned. The cumulative effect of our work was to lessen, albeit only by degrees, her camouflage. I mention her case to illustrate the effect of such early, traumatizing damage and to comment on the incremental steps she took to inch her way out of her walled-off self.

Jessica, on the other hand, was an outgoing, exuberant 13-year-old. She felt, however, continuously submerged by her mother's overly intrusive manner and yet felt compelled to share too much of herself. Often, if she shared something personal of her self, her mother would divulge this information to her husband, to her own mother, and to various other close individuals. The result was that Jessica never felt comfortable within this maternal relationship and, by extension, never completely trusted anyone. She told me that she "always kept a *little piece of myself* separate, secret" from everyone around her. It might look as though she had close friends, but she was always aware of a high boundary between herself and them—a protective barrier against intrusions. In sessions I sometimes became aware of the illusion she had created: here was a charming, bright 13-year-old who seemed so self-assured, who seemed to be so honest in her self–revelations, and yet I had the feeling that I was being fooled, that something was missing between us. She spoke, over time, of her fear that I would reveal her inner self to her parents; I assured her that I had no reason to divulge her self with anyone. She talked of her deep desire to "finally trust someone with my whole self," but discussed her fear of engulfment. She mentioned that she kept a diary, but as can be imagined, she never fully disclosed herself in her writings for fear that the book would be read by other family members. In fact, at one point she had even forgotten where she had last hidden the diary, a circumstance that prevented her from writing down her thoughts for quite some time. As the sessions passed, Jessica would alternate between moments of being the charming child and the insecure, mistrustful inner self in my office. Her attachment to the therapy was hallmarked by her decision to bring me her diary "for safe-keeping" so that I could lock it in my file cabinet, away from any prying eyes. She would bring me new entries and place them into the cabinet, taking them home when she wanted to review her previous feelings. Over time, she became less protective of her "secret self," but core remnants of her detached self certainly remained intact. Again, the beginnings of detachment had occurred at an earlier point in time, and again, despite the very different outward presentation, this young patient felt an inner isolation, which had been created, not out of sexual or physical trauma but out of normative abuse.

Releasing a patient from his use of secondary, addictive attachments requires a strong, therapeutic intensity. To build the bond of immersion, the therapist must match the power and strength of the substance with his words, his warmth, and his attunement. He must continually confront the patient's wish to withdraw into isolation while simultaneously encouraging the patient's growth as a separate, yet connected, individual. Creating an area of immersion is similar to building a bridge between two distant shores: the oceanic feeling runs between both beaches, while the same waves, the same water, reaches both sands. Freud understood how different he was from his friend Rolland, who was able to touch the mystical. He wrote to Rolland in 1931, expressing the kind of bridge that immersion can bring, noting that "I have rarely experienced that mysterious attraction of one human being for another as vividly as I have with you; it is somehow bound up, perhaps, with the awareness of our being so different" (Parsons 1993, p. 386).

9

WORKING IN THE IMMERSIVE TRANSFERENCE

Always be drunk. That's it—that's all that matters. So you won't feel the horrible burden of Time which breaks your shoulders and bends you to the ground, you need to get drunk without end.

But with what? With wine, poetry, or virtue—it's your choice. But get drunk.

And if sometime—on the steps of a palace, on the green grass of a gulley, in the somber solitude of your room—you wake up, the drunkenness already diminished or gone; then ask the wind, the wave, the star, the bird, the clock, all that runs away, all that groans, all that rolls, all that sings, all that talks—ask them what time it is; and the wind, the wave, the star, the bird, the clock, will answer you: "It's time to get drunk! So you won't be martyred slaves of Time: get drunk; get drunk without end. With wine, poetry or virtue—it's your choice."

Charles Baudelaire, "Enivrez-vous" ("Get Drunk") from
Le Spleen de Paris

THE CASES PRESENTED in this chapter have all elicited the immersive transference and have incorporated the use of various immersive aids. The first two cases illustrate some of the difficulties in attempting to sustain a therapeutic relationship with a newly recovering addict, and the third demonstrates some of the struggles that a patient actively immersed in the therapeutic process can experience. A discussion of Eugene O'Neill's play *Long Day's Journey into Night* follows, to detail more completely the immersive experience of alcohol and the longing for continuous moments of the oceanic feeling.

SUSAN

Like many of the addicts I have worked with, Susan would only tolerate momentary infusions of a relationship with me. Like the drug, she wanted only to get a "quick fix" from me so that she could continue the illusion of self-reliance and independence from all interpersonal relationships.

History

Susan was hospitalized for detoxification of her methadone addiction at age 29, soon after her wedding and her inability to complete medical school. She struggled throughout her two-month hospitalization with fears regarding the staff's ability to care for her. She worried that we would not be "gentle" enough with her and would push her too fast to give up her ten-year relationship with the soothing methadone. This feeling was a direct consequence of her relationship with her mother, who had had four children in as many years and had hurried Susan in reaching all developmental milestones. When Susan was 5 her mother, who was white, and her father, who was African American, divorced primarily because of a clash in cultural values. Mrs. D. soon returned to work as a nurse, working long hours and overtime. Although Susan did not see much of her father, a heroin addict, she had heard many stories about his "badness" from her mother. Despite these stories, she longed to know the father she never really had. Her attempts to reach him angered her mother and alienated her from her siblings. At 15, she learned that he had been sent to prison several years before for drug trafficking, and she began corresponding with him. Unfortunately, soon after their reconnection occurred, he died unexpectedly.

Susan went into a tailspin after this loss. She began experimenting with drugs and found that, like her father, the greatest attraction for her was heroin. She was somehow able to complete high school and, being quite bright, was accepted into a good Ivy League college. She faltered in the winter of her freshman year because her heroin abuse was out of control. She entered outpatient drug treatment and dropped out of school briefly. After numerous failed attempts at abstinence, she was advised to begin a methadone maintenance program. She remained in this program for ten years while completing her college degree and four years of medical school. Complications occurred when she met and quickly married her

African American husband. Susan did not tell him of her methadone use because she felt he would then reject her. Holding onto the secret, however, made her feel "bad" and caused her to seek higher and higher amounts of the drug as a way to assuage her shame. Finally, when she could no longer obtain the drug in secret, she revealed her "true self" to him. Soon after, she sought help from our facility.

Several areas of this case are particularly relevant to merging phenomena: first, her experience with me at the tail end of her detoxification, an experience that she frequently referred to throughout our years of treatment together; second, her sporadic use of outpatient treatment, necessary as infusions to bolster her damaged self; and third, her relationship with the drug itself as it relates to parental introjects and to her ongoing insistence on remaining an unsoothable, unreachable sufferer.

The Immersive Touch

At the height of her detoxification, Susan was extremely vulnerable and frightened. She was unsure of the hospital's ability to care for or to nurture her. Given her mother's narcissistic parenting, she transferentially assumed the hospital staff, and I in particular, would respond in a similar manner. Given this transference, she did not ask us for help in reducing her pain, and she refused to follow any of the remedies we offered, because she assumed nothing could help her. Instead, she sat in her bedroom "waiting it out." Her silent suffering indicated her infantile adjustment to a world that never provided for her what she needed most—attention and soothing. Susan recalled a picture of herself from age 3 in which, rather than smiling, she was frowning into the camera. "My family says I never smiled as a kid, that I was a colicky baby and never could be soothed. I think it was just my nature to be unhappy. My mother always told me that I was the only one out of the four of us who was never happy. She always told me I was difficult—sulky-like, you know."

Of note, Susan interpreted from this childhood description that nothing, and no one, could make her happy. Her fate was to remain an unsoothable person.

Susan assumed that her suffering was inevitable, an assumption that I challenged. I told her that I hoped to be a different kind of person than she had been used to and that she might begin to experience the inpatient unit, as a whole, in a different way than she had experienced others in the past. I challenged her ingrained belief that her suffering was infinite and impenetrable. At the start of one of our sessions, for example, I noticed she was shivering uncontrollably, a symptom of detoxification. I went out of her room and brought back a woolen comforter and hot tea. As she stopped shaking, she began to cry because she had never expected to be helped, or even noticed, by an other. She spoke of her surprise that not only did I act in a caring way but also that my ministrations had been effective. Susan had been so unused to help that she had stopped believing in the power of others. Later in this session, I spoke to Susan about ways to encourage others to care for her. Just as I wanted to help her, she needed to let the nursing staff know when she was in pain, when she needed a warm bath to soothe her aching joints or a back rub to relieve her muscle spasms. I showed Susan that this process involved both of us as well as the entire nursing staff.

In making this intervention, I likened the process to the movie E.T., in which the alien being needed the devoted relationship of the little boy who had found him to recontact the home ship. In the movie, both the boy and E.T. become empathically joined together so that one experienced the same affective state as the other. Susan immediately connected with this image, as she had often felt like an alien being surrounded by untouchable others. I pointed my index finger toward hers, to demonstrate that I wanted to touch her suffering, her pain, and her alienated being. She stretched her finger outward and met mine. It was a dramatic moment neither of us ever forgot, a moment when touching symbolized the maternal merging she had never received. Throughout the rest of her stay, Susan was able to seek moments of empathic, emotional touch. When she left the hospital two months later, it was with a newfound hope that relationships could be empowering and soothing.

Lack of Immersive Contact: Relapse

After Susan left the hospital and began outpatient treatment in a clinic near her home, she was unable to make a similar connection to her new therapist and soon dropped out of treatment. She did not contact me at that time because she worried I would be disappointed in her, a feeling based on her relationship with her mother. She called me two years later when, back on the methadone, she again felt stuck in the fated position of sufferer. Susan spoke of the alienated pain she felt in the outside world, pain that had led her to seek again the embrace of methadone.

My husband needed me to be strong for him. He is really like a baby who needs me to nurture him. So I couldn't very well look to him to bolster my own self, could I? And the meetings didn't feel real enough to me—I couldn't feel connected there somehow. The first time I took the methadone again, I felt whole, relaxed, soothed. And once that happened, there was no turning back.

The Power of Methadone and the Power of Fate

For over two years, Susan remained in sporadic treatment with me. She continued to take methadone, in part because of her fear of the detoxification process itself and in part because the substance still held enormous transformative powers. The drug established an ongoing connection both to her mother, with whom she was estranged, and her dead father. In part, the methadone served to unite her with her parents—an opiate like the one her father so enjoyed and a drug administered by a staff of nurses like her mother. The use of the synthetic opiate joined her to her father, whereas the clinic administration of the methadone tied her to her mother.

Susan remained a "fated" individual because she could not shake her identity as a sufferer. Yet, she allowed herself to have at least a few moments of positive mergings with me and found our contact uplifting and energizing, indicating the importance of these therapeutic immersions. Also indicative of the value of her treatment, even though it was sporadic, is that she stopped abusing the methadone and took only the prescribed dose. But she could not tolerate an ongoing therapeutic ingestion because she remained too attached to her parental introjects. Keeping herself at an emotional distance from me, utilizing me only for crisis immersions, enabled her to remain her mother's child. Further, attachment to the drug caused her to remain an unsoothable individual.

The issue here is not whether she should have become totally drug-free; certainly there is controversy in the field of addiction as to whether individuals should be encouraged to maintain a prescribed methadone dose for years or whether the goal should always be complete sobriety. Methadone is referred to as "the golden handcuffs" for this reason, because detoxifying from this drug is so difficult, and it is a legal drug. Even counselors and physicians who work for the methadone program may advise long-term maintenance. I am not debating whether this patient should have sought a goal of total abstinence; rather, my concern is understanding the psychodynamics behind her use. That she could become controlled in her use was certainly an accomplishment. I think that in this case, should she have wanted to attempt total abstention, she would have had to utilize psychopharmacologic assistance. This again supports Treece and Khantzian's (1986) position that drug addicts are often medicating underlying psychiatric conditions, and that opiate abusers are more often medicating underlying, severe depressions.

Susan surrounded herself with the protective covering of the methadone and was aware that this substance made her feel empowered in the world. Although she struggled with feelings of shame for utilizing the methadone in this way, she also believed that "methadone is really a medication like heart medication or medication for diabetics. There is a lot of research to support that this substance is okay to use for life, as long as it is not abused. I feel that, with your help, I no longer need to abuse the methadone. But at times it still nags at me that I can't do without it at all."

By continuing to feel shame over her use of methadone, she kept herself from fully enjoying other aspects of life, such as her ability to complete medical school and to pursue other successful areas of her career. In this regard, Susan kept herself very much in a relationship with her mother—she remained the "sulky" child who was never happy. She knew she continued struggling to enjoy life, as evidenced by a note on a Christmas card I once received from her:

I continue to be surprised at how good my life is and I thank you for showing me that I deserve good things in life. I'm glad that we still have sessions when I need them, because I often lose sight of this, and I need refreshers from you. Thanks. I love you and will call to see you soon!!"

Susan understood the dilemma she placed herself in, but was unable to utilize the treatment relationship in a different manner. She was typical of many chemically dependent patients I have treated because she utilized me as if I were a drug. When needing a powerful infusion, she would seek contact, and when filled up again, she would disconnect so as to continue the illusion that her power was generated solely by herself.

JOHN

In this case, the lack of physical contact between the patient and his mother flavored both his choice of drug and his difficulties in recovery.

John was 40 years old and a highly successful real estate broker when we met. He had been married for twenty years and had four children. From a blue-collar background, he catapulted himself to the wealthiest percentile, all before the age of 35. Although outwardly successful, the patient felt a piercing inner void and a tugging at his core that continually battled with these financial accomplishments. He had been in recovery for cocaine addiction for six years, although previously he had had many alcohol binges. In these six years, he had never had more than three months of continuous sobriety. He had attempted various structured outpatient programs, but resisted the rigidity and time constraints these programs placed upon him.

History

John was the third of six boys raised in a strict Irish-Catholic home in an exclusively Irish-Catholic neighborhood. His parents were demanding and rigid, keeping a "close eye" on John because he was seen as the troublemaker. He was frequently involved in fights at school with neighboring boys and in physical altercations with his older brothers. The patient feared his father because of his heavy-handed approach to discipline. Any infraction of the rules brought stiff punishment with the belt. The scenario was always the same—as judge, jury, and executioner, his father would decide the number of blows each offense merited and then administer the punishment in complete silence. John would never cry, always resolved to keep his inner self privately tucked into his own being.

John's mother was unaffectionate and witholding. He has no recollection, after the age of 5, of her telling him that she loved him. For most of his childhood John felt isolated, alone, and unlovable. His only physical contact came from the beatings by his father; he was only touched when he was "bad." In treatment, John remembered a recurring dream from his childhood that epitomized his relationship with his parents. In it, John was being followed by an angry force that kept coming closer and closer to him. He wanted to cry out for help, but his vocal cords would not work. He tried again and again, but his voice would not speak. John believed this dream signified the extreme prohibition he felt in asking for help, in looking for a protective other in any relationship. He always felt alone in what seemed to be a difficult and unloving world and always felt that his gestures for attunement, his longings for soothing, would go unnoticed.

Just as he learned early not to cry when his father beat him, he learned never to share his internal wishes with anyone.

Not surprisingly, this untouchability remained at the core of his personality. Unions occurred with a punishing other rather than with a protective, nurturant soother. Nurturance and love were craved but feared by him because they were always connected with control and dominance. The external other was feared because he experienced it as all powerful and, concurrently, all punishing.

Immersions with the Resistant Patient

One of the essential difficulties in treating a patient with this kind of punitive fusion experience is that he will anticipate, and look for, the same kind of moments with the therapist. John presented me with this dilemma quite early in the treatment. He began therapy following a three-day binge and agreed with me that, should he relapse again, he would consider an inpatient hospitalization. After three months of outpatient, weekly sessions, John relapsed again. He followed his usual modus operandi, simply disappearing from his family, friends, and job without warning. He spent three nights in various hotel rooms in Manhattan, inhaling large amounts of cocaine. Finally when he had had his fill, he called his wife and told her he was coming home.

John and his wife came to an emergency session immediately upon his returning to his suburban home, and we discussed his relapse and the options now available to him. I reminded him of his prior agreement to try inpatient hospitalization. John looked frightened and said that he knew he had agreed, but he could not pursue this kind of treatment. He was worried about the kind of punishing other this institutionalized setting would provide for him. He pleaded with me to think of an alternative plan—anything but hospitalization. I was struck by the intensity of his pleas and by his view of me, in that moment, as an all-powerful, yet punishing, other. My years of experience as a therapist specializing in drug counseling told me that I should confront him, insist on hospitalization, and threaten to terminate treatment unless he comply. I reminded myself of this possible strategy while I analyzed the meaning behind John's resistance to hospitalization and his appeal for some other approach. Essentially, he was asking for more contact with me. In his "untouchable" state, he was looking to me for contact and involvement. If I hospitalized him, I would remain a punishing other – abandoning him in his badness. If instead I provided more contact, if I insisted on more sessions rather than isolating him in the hospital, he might begin to experience the healing power of interpersonal immersions.

I offered John the option of twice-weekly individual sessions and a marital session as well, rather than hospitalization. I put into words my dilemma regarding the standard drug counseling approach and my alternative suggestion that we intensify our work together. I hoped my intervention would lead to the establishment of a different kind of transferential relationship. John immediately relaxed and became tearful. When he spoke again, he talked about how important it was to him that I had not abandoned him in his badness, that rather than rejecting him or punishing him, I was offering more of myself instead.

Fusion and Self-Cohesion

During this period of intensified treatment, I frequently commented to John how unintegrated the drug addict in him was from the rest of his personality. He could easily find ways to forget about this badness, to simply blot out the existence of this piece of himself. Although he went to AA meetings, for example, he rarely referred to himself as a drug addict, preferring to call himself an alcoholic. He had never discussed his urges with his wife, nor had he ever asked her to attend Alanon or Naranon meetings. He was more comfortable leaving her on the periphery of this piece of himself. No friends or even family knew of his six-year struggle with cocaine. Thus, John had attempted to isolate this badness and leave it totally unintegrated from his character.

One of the important functions that merging provides is the integration of the child's budding core self. Personhood depends in part on the mother's ability to provide a protective covering that weaves together the child's diffuse pieces of self. She essentially lends her ego to develop his. There are multiple facets of his self that she brings together: she contains his aggression, soothes his anxiety, praises his developmental milestones, offers cognitive stimulation, and gives cuddles and hugs. In another case, for example, a patient at age 5 had developed an internal, imaginary friend who seemed so real that he even gave "him" a name. This piece of self was a split-off parental introject that helped the child whenever he felt anxiety or fear. Because his parents would lock their bedroom door at night, signifying their unavailability, his "friend" would provide the protection and comfort he needed to cope with his nightmares and fear of being alone. During the day, he might call upon him to answer questions on a school test because he was overcome by anxiety. This imaginary figure remained unintegrated in the patient's self until treatment when, through the internalization process of the therapist, this friend was replaced by the therapist-introject and later by the individual's own ego.

Therefore, a mother like John's, who hated his badness, would certainly not provide ego protection over this part of his character. Having no one to help him integrate this aspect of his self into his character, this piece was cut off from the rest of his core. Unloved by his mother and beaten by his father, this piece of him, rather than becoming integrated, became completely isolated from the rest of his self.

It was crucial, therefore, to begin this process of self-integration. I suggested that John write down all the ups and downs of his latest binge and place this description in his wallet to look at, should he ever be tempted to use again. He did in fact write himself a letter and referred to it several times during the next few months. As well, John began a journal, but would not reread earlier entries, another sign of his disintegrated core self.

Whenever he would refer to himself as an alcoholic, I would add "and drug addict." This was important because he would otherwise deny the extent of his substance abuse problem. I also wanted him to understand why he chose this drug and no others, why he sought the powerful rush of this substance rather than the more calming and depressive effect of alcohol. In time, John discovered that, after the initial high, cocaine mimicked his relationship to a punitive, powerful other. He initially felt an extreme high, a rush of energy and excitement that brought him a sense of powerfulness he rarely experienced in his most intimate relationships. After the high, he felt an intense loneliness and abandonment coupled, understandably, with some marked moments of paranoia. In these moments, he was again the split-off, bad self that was totally unlovable and undesirable. The cocaine experience, then, fit perfectly with his history. He sought the fusion with cocaine when he felt particularly unempowered, when he felt alone and frightened. Unable to ask an other to hold him, to protect him in some way, he sought the drug instead. After the initial high, his split-off self became punishing and abusive. In this way the drug relationship became just like the one with his punitive, witholding parents. The paranoia of the drug simply exacerbated his own sense of alienation and unlovableness.

The intensification of treatment provided a frame to develop other merging moments. For example, I often spoke with John about ways to hold onto me outside session, of ways to develop immersion aids. The patient was able to make some attempts in this direction, but he became quite frightened by budding feelings of dependence on me. After several months of intense contact, he took a summer vacation with his family. When he returned, he requested a move to once-a-week sessions. Although I acquiesced, I questioned his fear of the immersive process and the sense he had that he was so dependent on me. How could a forty-five-minute contact with me mean I was controlling his life? How was it possible that he was still not the initiator of his own actions? In analyzing this feeling of dominance, we were touching on his subjective feeling of powerlessness. In his family, contact was based on badness and signified weakness. John had grown up in an alienated world in which he had learned to harden his defenses against immersive opportunities. Even in his marriage, he had resisted psychological intimacy. For example, he was either high or hung over during each of his children's births. He could not tolerate the powerlessness he felt in watching his wife's labor; he had to fortify himself as well as place himself outside a shared experience with her.

Over the years, his marriage had evolved into a re-creation of his childhood home because he and his wife had become so distanced that they had no physical contact whatsoever. Indeed, his parents' marriage was an example of the hostile, punitive unions he was so accustomed to. His father and mother had for years slept in separate bedrooms and were on opposite shifts in their work schedules. Their only communication revolved around schedules and family arrangements. John usually had separate conversations with each parent, often repeating the same story to each because he knew they never discussed things together. Thus, for John, relationships were never intertwined, but always separate and distanced.

John and I were discussing his resistance to immersive contact when a life event significantly affected the treatment. He had been fired from his job after his last binge and had spent the last six months in an earnest search for a new job. Finally he secured an even better, more lucrative position in another city and was now contemplating moving. I asked him about the effect such a change would have on his newly found recovery, a comment that enraged him. He felt I was belittling the progress he had been making and that I was doubting his ability to maintain his sobriety "on his own." He was angered by his own developing attachment to the therapy and wanted me to join him in denying the importance of the immersive process. He was used to relying only on himself: from infancy on, no one had offered him comfort, no one had been a subjective object for him. Relationships were bound by separation and separateness. John found the positive, therapeutic merging exhilarating but alarming, because it indicated that he was "hooked in" to the treatment relationship.

In questioning the value of detaching from his AA meetings and from therapy at this time, John felt that I was challenging his ability to be self-reliant. In fact, I was questioning his fear of interdependency. John was unable to put into words the depth of his narcissistic injury and ensuing rage. Instead, he began a three-day binge during the hour of our next scheduled appointment. When he returned home, John called me for session, saying that he had had a "major breakthrough" during his relapse.

Transformation: Immersion with a Powerful Other

Just before bingeing at the peak of his use, with $1,000 of cocaine in his possession, John experienced a moment that quite literally transformed him. He found himself stopping his hand from taking more cocaine, feeling as though a "force" had intervened and had prevented him from going forward with his self-destructive binge. He went for a ride in a cab and saw a pattern of the crucifix in the lights of the street. He followed this pattern of lights and found himself in front of an unfamiliar hospital that offered emergency drug counseling. He spent an hour with a drug counselor, found himself calmed down, and then spent the night sleeping with the cocaine lying untouched next to him. The next day John came home, exhausted but feeling transformed by this miraculous experience.

John discussed the significance of this event with me. Although denying that it all could have been simply a hallucinogenic experience due to the amount of cocaine he had sniffed, he preferred to view the episode as a forceful encounter with his God. For the first time, God had responded to him in his badness and had not shunned him during his plight. John felt a sensation of "being held, as though a force had actually held my hand and led me to the drug counselor rather than to a cocaine dealer. I've never had an experience like this before in my life. I've always wished for, but never found, a benevolent God surrounding me with love and affection. And now I'm beginning to believe it."

This was indeed a moment of transformation. In it, John had found himself surrounded by a soothing, protective other. And, rather than dismiss this feeling, this relationship, he had allowed himself to be held and to be protected.

In part, John was able to envision this comforting presence, this protective covering, because of the therapeutic relationship. We had been building a bridge joining us, to keep my presence with him even between sessions. The practice he had gained by evoking my image, an image of soothing protection, had been drawn upon during a period of therapeutic misattunement. After learning to open himself to external soothing, he had been able, when he could no longer have me because of his rage, to feel external soothing from another source.

His anger at me can be understood as a rupturing of the illusion of control he felt he had had with me. My misattunement caused him to feel that I was usurping his burgeoning sense of power, power he was finally feeling within a relationship. My comment, designed to help him examine his resistance to the process of therapeutic immersion by moving out of state, instead caused him to feel wronged and criticized. He could not verbalize his feeling to me, nor could he continue to hold onto me in any internalized way. He responded as always when confronted with a feeling of infantile powerlessness—he turned to an infusion from the drug. That this time, however, he experienced help from a soothing, protective God representation indicated some carryover from the therapeutic process. Rather than an infusion from me, he had found comfort and solace from his God.

Once he resumed his recovery, John continued to embrace and embellish on the tranquility he had found from his experience with God. He made a substantive switch from using me to using God as a subjective object, which seemed safer to him because it seemed more reliable. He did move to another city for his new job and, after several transitional sessions with me, stopped the therapy. Indeed, the narcissistic injury had been too deep; continued treatment was experienced as an ongoing sign of his powerlessness.

DAN

In this case, the patient craved merging moments, but struggled with feeling weak and powerless when immersed too long in this experience. One fascinating aspect of this case was the ontogenetic root to his struggles with merging—his mother's smothering yet ineffective love as contrasted to his father's physical and emotional violence. Dan experienced the world as an unyielding and overpowering place, which elicited feelings of rage and self-hatred. Therapy became his respite from the world and, whenever he allowed contact, provided moments of immersion.

Dan, a 45-year-old recovering heroin addict, lived with his wife and three children in a three-bedroom apartment. He had been sober for the last five years, but had struggled with recovery for the last ten. Dan originally attended twice-weekly sessions in addition to marital sessions, but over the years tapered to weekly and then to intermittent therapy sessions. The frequency of these sporadic sessions might be as many as four or five weekly sessions followed by a lapse of several months. It was important to him that he control the frequency of these appointments so that he could determine the amount of contact we had. After a year of intermittent contact, he (or his wife) would call periodically to touch base. Invariably, the timing of their calls was simultaneous to my own thoughts about them.

History

Dan grew up in a rural community outside Cincinnati, Ohio, with his parents and two sisters. His father was an abusive alcoholic who continually focused his attention on his only son. Dan remembered multiple incidents in which he was beaten with a belt for not completing his homework or was slapped across the face for being impolite. Although a bright child, he was unmotivated because the strict Catholic school he attended mirrored his abusive home so accurately. Dan remembers one instance in which, although he actually had completed his homework and gotten an "A" on a pop quiz, the nuns were convinced he had cheated and called his parents to a disciplinary meeting. This incident furthered his resolve to become an academic failure.

At home, Dan was both emotionally and physically abused. He was called "lazy," "stupid," and "wimp" quite frequently by his inebriated father. His mother was unable to assert herself with her husband and was herself a victim of his physical abuse. Several times over the years she had tried to file for divorce, but was always too frightened to proceed. Her husband would frequently leave after damaging household items and then return several days later when sober, apologizing with gifts for the family. Dan was secretly delighted each time his father left and disappointed at his inevitable return. The physical abuse was of course painful, but Dan found the emotional humiliation more excruciating. His father would often sit him in front of his sisters and make him recite his homework. If he did not do so correctly, he was beaten in front of them. It became important to Dan never to show his pain, and he would try to grin while being hit rather than allow his father the pleasure of seeing him suffer.

At age 10, Dan began to struggle with what would become lifelong fantasies of suicide. He would sit in his room and wonder why he had been born, what purpose his life would serve, and why he had to tolerate the abuse he always received. He would imagine ways to die, such as jumping in front of a car or train. He also fantasized multiple ways to kill his father. At age 12, he started to carry out a plan to kill his father, but did not have the courage to actually enact his fantasy. He never forgave himself for avoiding the opportunity to kill this abusive, rageful man.

Dan and his father fought viciously throughout his adolescence, including episodes of car chases and bar brawls. By the time he was 16 he worked in the bar his father frequented and often had to carry him home after a night of heavy drinking. When Dan was 18 he wanted to go to college, but his father insisted he enlist in the Air Force instead. Dan never forgave him for sending him to his possible death. Soon after he was sent to Vietnam, however, his father killed himself. Dan was totally surprised by this act, but felt more anger than compassion: his father had denied Dan the final revenge of patricide.

By the time Dan returned home from the war, his mother and sisters had moved to another state, and he decided to live with some of his Vietnam army buddies. He had switched from alcohol to heroin while overseas and found this substance a "miracle cure" for his depression and rage. Indeed, until recovery, heroin remained his drug of choice.

Achieving recovery was important to him because he felt shamed at succumbing to the same affliction as his father. He felt that being a heroin addict was one step lower than an alcoholic, a continuous reminder that he was indeed the loser his father had predicted. Furthermore, as time went on, Dan began financing his heroin habit by selling other drugs. He purposely did not sell heroin, so as to prevent himself from using his own selling supply. He decided to seek recovery in part because he realized that drug enforcement officials were investigating his drug-dealing friends. Sensing an imminent drug sting, he abruptly quit and entered his first rehabilitation program. He did so just in time, as some of his buddies who had remained in the business were soon arrested and incarcerated.

The Immersive Effect of Heroin

Dan fully understood the significance of his drug of choice. He felt that heroin gave him a sense of well-being and a feeling of warmth and nurturance. He described it as taking a "warm bath, so soothing and calming" and believed the heroin provided him with the love he had not found in his relationships. He did not get loving devotion from his wife, mother-in-law, or other family members, but he did have an illusion of this feeling with his drug. It was as though he felt a continuous infusion of love. Winnicott writes that the breast is both an internal and external object because the milk is ingested, but the breast is not. Heroin is similar in that the drug is injected, but the needle is not. The choice of this substance, then, demonstrates the intensity of immersion that he so desired. In some ways a repetition of his early relationship with his mother, the drug provided him with an overwhelming feeling of well-being. His mother's attentiveness had been overingratiating and intrusive, causing him to feel weak and powerless. As a child he had learned to push her away; he preferred the solitude of his room to the solicitude of his mother's devotion.

For a long time, Dan could generally regulate the intensity of the high and determine the duration of the experience. Indeed, he would often forego using the drug if he was feeling extremely depressed or suicidal. He preferred being dope-sick to possible overdosing in an impulsive act of self-hatred. Heroin also calmed him down when he was raging and soothed him when he was depressed. He did not feel like an emotional "wimp" when using the drug to obtain this calming, soothing effect. To the contrary, he felt proud that he was using the "hard stuff," not the "soft" drugs like marijuana. Further, he was proud of the fact that he had taken care of himself without involving others.

Life Without Heroin – A Slow Road to Therapeutic Immersions

Dan came to treatment expecting criticism and ridicule, as though I were like his father, and alternately worried that I would be smotheringly sweet like his mother. He was suspicious of my exploratory questions and non-hostile responses. He seemed to weigh his words so as to avoid telling me too much of his thoughts and feelings. He did, however, discuss the loneliness he was now experiencing in his marriage. His wife was a somewhat passive-aggressive individual who was frightened by intimacy and had chosen him in part because of his schizoid character. Now that Dan was maintaining sobriety, he was able to focus on how little emotional contact he actually got from her. He realized that, with the infusion of heroin inside himself, he had been oblivious to her inaccessibility. Her lack of attentiveness was once a welcome change from his smothering mother, and he had enjoyed the emotional freedom it brought him in the marriage. Once in sobriety, however, he began to feel stirrings of the kind of love he wanted and was saddened and frustrated by the inadequacies of their marriage.

Furthermore, his sobriety inevitably led to his awareness of her own alcoholism, which had blossomed when he began recovery. As he queried her about late-night drop-ins to the local bar, she became more oppositional and stayed out even later. Desirous of more emotional contact, Dan was frequently enraged and humiliated by this hostile, distancing behavior. Her scornful rejection frequently caused him to move into a depressive spin, which always led to suicidal fantasies. Typically, in re-creation of his childhood, he would withdraw from all contact with her and stay in his room while contemplating ways to die. After several days of this withdrawal, Dan would regroup and return to his daily activities. It often took him over a week to begin speaking again with his wife, an action he always regretted because he felt it gave her permission to be unloving the rest of the time. Intermittently, she would shower him with enough tenderness and love to sustain him for a while. In general, their relationship was a mixture of alienated rejection and brief intimate contact. The unpredictability of their immersion was quite difficult for Dan, who had begun to long for a relationship with more consistent affection.

Without heroin, Dan found that he wanted more intimacy than he was receiving in his AA meetings, from his family of origin, or from his wife. Feeling again alienated and unhappy, for the first three years of treatment Dan attempted to find the excitement and attention he needed by experimenting with gambling. In part out of an identification with his father, who had also gambled, Dan was attempting to find another object he could omnipotently control. Although he was beginning to form a therapeutic attachment, he was afraid at this time to utilize this relationship fully. Feeling alone and alienated, with no omnipotent other by his side, he turned to gambling so that he could still have a relationship with a powerful object, an object with some of the same characteristics as his father. For some time, he was fairly successful in the betting strategies he planned and the risks he took, although when depressed he would gamble away the monies he had accrued. Dan's judgment was highly influenced by his mental state: a depressed period would cost him dearly. In fact, he finally gave up gambling after a period of tremendous financial loss. This loss helped him see that, again, he had been trying to control an uncontrollable object. He put down the gambling as he had put down the heroin—it was over, and he refused to return to what he now understood to be a destructive relationship with an unpredictable, unforgiving other.

Immersions in Treatment: Using the Therapist as Heroin

That left only one other constant relationship in his life—his therapeutic relationship with me. Dan was always quite eloquent in sessions and marvelously adept at describing his inner feeling states. He evoked in me a sense of urgency to listen to his every word, to be involved with him on every level. He would immerse himself in the therapeutic process and call upon me to be just as involved as he. Dan would speak about his discomfort in disclosing his inner world, and yet, simultaneously, he would share his rageful and suicidal fantasies with me. He would speak about his sense of alienation and loneliness and yet add that, with me, he felt safe and nurtured.

We did not start at this level of comfort; rather, it evolved out of my continual challenging of his transferential expectations of me and his view of himself as unlovable and impenetrable. In part it occurred simply by my listening to his feelings and thoughts. He had never had an other attending to his self-experience without misunderstanding him. He frequently measured how much of himself he wanted to reveal. When he would want to change topics, I would question what he was holding onto that he did not feel he should share. He would describe his reluctance to continue because of his fear of humiliation or shame. He did not want me to "take pity" on him or to criticize his inner experience. I would trace this reluctance to the historical figures of his father and mother and point out that, rather than feeling anger or pity, I was simply allowing myself to sit, side by side with him, in the experience he was describing. I encouraged Dan to describe his self-experience in detail and praised his talent for self-expression. In my responses, I wanted to show him that we were a team, that I wanted to join him in his world. We were building an immersive realm in which he and I could reside together.

Dan frequently brought his rage to sessions, but had difficulty allowing himself to explode fully during the session hour. He would grit his teeth rather than scream about his experience of the world as unforgiving and hostile. In his childhood Dan was sent to his room to deal with his rage alone, an example of the damage caused by parental non-intervention during a child's temper tantrums. His silent fury was endemic to his character and pervasive in his marriage. His wife and mother-in-law, for example, knew to avoid him when he was angry and at times would stay at a relative's home rather than be around him. His anger surrounded him like "Pigpen's" ball of dirt—it encircled the rest of his character. Because of this, it was crucial to the immersive process that I become witness to and welcoming of his anger. Indeed, my insistence on being present during rageful moments helped him feel that I wanted to know and understand all aspects of his character. Just as important, he found that, by sharing his rage with me, the intensity of this feeling was diffused. The presence of a soothing, protective other reduced his fury to a more manageable affect.

In a similar manner, Dan frequently discussed his suicidal fantasies, at first rather gingerly and, later, after he knew that I would not overreact, in great detail. Dan initially worried that his disclosure of these thoughts would alarm me and cause me to insist on hospitalization. In fact, I did think about this modality at times during the therapy, but did not discuss it with him, because Dan had had several inpatient stays in the past, with little success. If I had moved to hospitalize him, I would have become the intrusive, smothering mother who was infantilizing and ineffective. I once suggested antidepressant medication, but he stated he had also tried this approach with no success. He refused this option now, stating that he wanted to "deal with himself" unaided by medication. Each suicidal crisis was a further opportunity to understand his core self and a further chance to enhance his connection to me. I saw his suicidal wishes as a reaction to his wife's coldness and a further way to connect with his father. I encouraged Dan to discuss his rageful feeling towards his wife and also to examine why he wanted to attach more deeply to his father than to me. By inserting myself into the suicidal fantasies, by insisting that his death would be painful for me, I encouraged him to look at his need to retreat rather than to cope with the disappointing moments of his relationships. I often told him that I would be furious if he were to end his life, and our relationship, in this manner. I told him that to kill himself would also be to kill us as well and that I did not want to be abandoned by him. Dan was shocked by my assertion because no one else had ever reacted to his suicidal raging with anger, nor had anyone ever fought with him to stay alive. His wife, for example, would ignore him and retreat to the bar. He had never had an other who wanted to be inside his angry world with him. For the first time in his life, an other was encouraging the discussion of his anger, disappointment, and self-hatred, rather than pushing him away.

In most sessions, Dan treated me as though I were heroin. He came to me for an infusion of his worthiness and his purposefulness in this life. He came to me for an infusion of merging, for contact with an other who was warm, nurturant, but not suffocating. He needed me to be a subjective object, to answer his gesturing. Like heroin, he needed to feel that he could regulate our contact. But he insisted on merging moments, moments of intense emotional impact, whenever he came to session.

Love and Fusion

In one poignant session in our fifth year, Dan spoke of his frustration that he was still in his marriage, saying, "I guess I just don't know what love is or how to love." I asked him to discuss this more fully. He spoke of the frustration he felt by the coldness of their relationship. He wondered if he was unable to have a loving relationship at all. "What about here?" I asked He responded rather guardedly, "Yes, love is involved here." I encouraged him to continue, because I knew that helping him verbalize this feeling was of paramount importance. He went on to say that he did love me, which was "one of the most confusing things about the treatment process—you aren't supposed to love your therapist." He had been struggling with this emotion for some time, he told me, never knowing how to bring it up and even feeling shamed that he was feeling this way. I replied

> Why should you not love me and hope to be loved in return? We
> have developed quite an intimate relationship here, one that you

have never had in your life. Here, you can share your thoughts and feelings and are able to feel understood. Of course that could stimulate loving feelings. Where else in your life do you even get five minutes of attention, let alone forty-five minutes? Where else do you feel safe enough to share most of your thoughts and feelings?

Dan sighed in relief that this secret was finally out. He had tormented himself by thinking he had done something wrong by feeling love toward me. I went on to discuss with him that

not many patients will allow themselves to express their loving feelings toward their therapist. It is a sign of your ability to love, and your capacity to tolerate the intensity of this emotion, to be able to verbalize and discuss this feeling. [Pause] I get the feeling that you want to know if I love you also. [He nodded yes.] Yes I do, because you continue to share yourself with me and allow me to be with you, no matter what kind of emotional pain you are feeling. You allow me to be with you throughout your life. You most certainly know how to love, and you are having here a most important experience of being loved as well.

Dan's eyes welled with tears as I spoke, and he answered, "I'm glad you feel that way. It's true, I guess, that I hadn't ever realized that I do know how to love. I want even more of this—I want this in all of my relationships."

To this I answered, "Then let us figure out why you so stubbornly insist on staying in a hostile, alcoholic relationship rather than having a loving relationship instead!"

Love is affectively connected to the merging process. In immersing herself within her child's self, the mother is deepening her capacity to love as well as her ability to empathize with her child. The child builds an internalization of his mother not just because he is cognitively prepared to do so, but because emotionally, out of his love for his mother, he wants to stay connected to her at all times. Similarly, a patient does not build an internal representation of the therapist simply because of the intellectual intensity of the process, but because the relationship with the therapist is so powerful that he wants to continue cathecting to the therapist's image even outside the office.

For Dan, this session was indeed transformative. His affect greatly improved, and he embarked on a more extended period of time without suicidal fantasies. He also became motivated to actively seek a job promotion because "I don't have to take this shit any more." He was empowered by the feeling that he was lovable, a self-concept he had never experienced. Sessions became more relaxed as he basked in the feeling of love.

Suicidal Ideation as Rebirth

Winnicott suggests that in infancy the baby feels helpless if separated from mother for too long or at too early an age. He experiences his separateness, his smallness, with great fear and anxiety. Alternately, we can assume that if the baby is emotionally smothered by his mother's presence and has been given too little chance to discover his own self, he can feel just as fearful and anxious *in the presence of* the more powerful other; by comparison, his size is tiny!

Dan grappled with feeling small, weak, and ineffective. He became self-hating when he felt overpowered by the world around him. Sometimes these feelings would stimulate a suicidal rage and precipitate a reclusive episode. In these periods, he would always seek to stop therapy. Like his decision to avoid heroin when markedly depressed, he would want to avoid therapy because I might say "the one thing" that could push him into suicidal action. He withdrew into himself out of a fear that he could be damaged by an other, even a loving other, who was nevertheless experienced by him as being more powerful than himself. He was aware that again he was trying to control the uncontrollable, omnipotent other. He knew that he could not trust his suicidal self even to me. Because he always returned to therapy after the crisis abated, I once suggested that he instead "take a vacation" rather than insist on stopping treatment altogether. Dan liked this idea because it lessened his sense of enfeeblement when he returned again to sessions. My intervention was designed to emphasize that our immersive area could not easily be destroyed.

Dan fit perfectly into Guntrip's conception of the schizoid. He was compelled to move quickly into a "regression into himself" that could lead either to suicide or rebirth. In each separation Dan teetered between life and death, but always chose life. He would return to his activities with a new vigor and a deepened commitment to living. For example, during one hiatus he quit smoking, and during another, he joined a nutritional program and lost twenty pounds. These "vacations" enabled Dan to "rebirth" himself and to feel that he was in charge of his own self. When overwhelmed by too many affects, when surrounded by too much disappointment, Dan moved into hibernation. His mother had been so smothering that he had had to retreat from her, whereas his father was so punitive that he had had to run from him. There was no one to rely on but himself. Guntrip talks about the regression to a womblike state, and indeed, Dan's retreat to his bedroom, where he would stay under his covers, can be seen as a replication of the womb. It was as though he placed himself under the protective covering of the amniotic sac and then waited to be reborn a new man, with greater power and strength.

Even though he hibernated from our relationship during these episodes, he kept his internal image of me close at hand. He would think of me often, imagine what I would say to assuage his sadness, and talk with me about his rage: "I tell you all my anger and shame and you always tell me to hang in there. I know you think I should call you when I feel so miserable, but to me that would make me feel too weak. I prefer just to sit in my room by myself, and pretend you are telling me what I want to hear to calm myself down."

Indeed, just like with heroin, Dan was empowered by infusing the therapeutic substance in a manner in which he could regulate both its intensity and duration. In this way he could remain a separate individual and yet, simultaneously, experience the intensity of the immersive relationship through internal fantasy.

This case demonstrates the importance of helping the patient develop the immersion process. Treatment afforded him the opportunity to experience the quality and duration of mergings he had been deprived of in his childhood and addictive adulthood. When I correctly attuned to him, when I encouraged him to involve me in his world and to bring my presence into his daily life, I helped him experience fusion. When I put myself into his suicidal fantasies, when I matched my anger with his, I merged into his world.

One of the crucial aspects of treatment was my encouragement of these fusion experiences so that Dan could find comfort in an interpersonal area. By fusing with me, he could disengage from the powerful substance of the heroin and reattach to the therapeutic relationship. By fusing with me, he could build an internal, loving representation that could fight his critical, unloving self-experience and the hating introjects of his father. By fusing with me, he could feel powerful within the context of a relationship and leave the drugs, food, and cigarettes behind.

He or his wife continues to check in periodically. Recently they bought a home, which was a monumental goal for both and which solidified their commitment to stay together in their marriage. Simultaneously, a life circumstance has gravely affected their lives and their relationship. Their daughter has been stricken with childhood leukemia. He and his wife have joined together in their efforts to take care of and nurture this sick child. His wife has been able to express her gratitude for his help. He continues in his sobriety and, although he still has moments of suicidal fantasy, has learned to ignore these urges and has stopped giving in to the temptation to die. Indeed, he has a different purpose in life now—to provide care and devotion to his daughter.

Literary works abound with alcoholic references and scenes. One reason to look to poetry and drama is the powerful way in which literature can evoke what theory cannot. One play that is centered on addiction is Eugene O'Neill's *Long Day's Journey Into Night*. Written in 1941, some fifteen years after he achieved his own sobriety (with the exception of mini-binges), the play is primarily an autobiographical account of his parents and older brother. His father, a famous actor, was an alcoholic throughout his life, and his mother became addicted to morphine after it was used to assuage her pain during and after the birth of Eugene himself. His older brother, ten years his senior, died after years of chronic alcoholism, a year after his mother's death. Of particular interest to me is the recovery of Eugene's mother from her morphine addiction. She was addicted to this drug for twenty-six years, finally achieving a long-awaited sobriety, which lasted throughout the last eight years of her life, during a stay at a convent. She had always been extremely religious and in fact, in the years before she met her soon-to-be husband, had wanted to be a nun. O'Neill, too, moved into recovery in what seems to have been a conversion experience, albeit of another kind. He began reading books by Freud in 1925 and, after six weeks of intensive psychoanalysis, ended the bulk of his years of alcohol abuse. The two members of the family who maintained sobriety, then, had had conversion experiences that significantly altered their compulsive addictions.

In the play, in fact, it is Edmund Tyrone (O'Neill's representation of himself) and his mother, Mary, who speak the most candidly about their need for transcendency. Neither his father nor older brother Jamie has much use for this kind of discourse, preferring instead to dwell on their self-hatred and mutual animosity. James Tyrone, the father, is blamed by everyone else in the family for his wife's morphine addiction. He had taken her to a second-rate doctor and, as well, had never given her the kind of home she had wanted. As an actor, he was constantly on the road and would often insist that she be with him rather than with the children. Mary says to Edmund that her husband was always jealous of her relationship with her children. In fact, she blames the death of her second son on her husband's insistence that she leave the boys with her family while she traveled with him during his acting season. It is this second son, in the play named Eugene, who died at age 2 after being exposed to the measles already contracted by Jamie. Mary's mother had been left in charge of the children, and she allowed Jamie, while he was still contagious, to go into his little brother's room. The toddler thereby contracted the measles that caused his tragic death.

In the Tyrone marriage, there was an intensity of the parents' neediness for one another. James Tyrone, away on tour, often wrote to his wife, complaining of his loneliness, which caused her to leave her young children and attend to her husband's needs. Separation between the couple was so unbearable that the children were often left with others so that husband and wife could be reunited.[1] In this way, the marital couple resemble Mark's parents discussed in Chapter 5, who were a unified force at the expense of the children. It is certainly possible, in fact, that James Tyrone's early childhood separations caused him to fight any extended absences from his wife. In fact, we learn that his own father deserted his mother and five sisters when James was only 10 years old, forcing him to leave school and go to work instead.

Accusations and blame cause each family member to have an excuse for his addiction. Jamie, of course, has lived with a lifetime of guilt for the death of Eugene. And Edmund feels guilt for causing his mother so much pain during his birth that she was given the morphine to which she remained addicted throughout his entire childhood, adolescence, and

---

1. According to Carpenter (1979), O'Neill's most painful childhood memories were of his many years spent in boarding school. He rarely lived with his parents during the school year because they were traveling on the road with his father's acting troupe. He remembered even having to spend Christmas vacation at the school. He felt deeply what in his own words he termed "betrayal" (p. 26) by his parents for their abandonment of him during the holiday season. Carpenter comments, "The first and deepest unhappiness of his life was that of homelessness—both psychological and physical" (p. 26).

mid-twenties. Mary blames herself for choosing marriage rather than religious service, and James blames Mary's addiction on his own continued alcoholism. Despite this animosity and hatred, the family rallies around the just-discovered relapse of Mary. Each of the men struggles with his sense of hopelessness in stemming her relapse. In several episodes (primarily when drunk), each character has an opportunity to disclose an aspect of his inner feelings to at least one other family member, kindling in each instance a sense of closeness and connectedness. It is in these scenes, not surprisingly, that we understand the powerful loneliness of Mary and Edmund. They reveal to us the important connection between alienation, addiction, and the wish for transcendence.

Mary herself is a fated individual. She views life as a series of events that, like a movie, are "done to" (p. 61) her. These events, she explains, cause other choices to be made, "until . . . everything comes between you and what you'd like to be, and you've lost your true self forever" (p. 61). She feels that she has been alienated from all that she loves. The fog that surrounds her house is, in metaphor, the detached wall that isolates her inner core. The fog allows her to hibernate from the world, to remain sheltered from the rest of humanity. She feels safe in her fog-encased home, where she lives undiscovered, untouched, and invulnerable. As another metaphor of her detached, alienated core, she never has had a permanent home, because her husband's career has so often taken them on the road that they own only a summer home, a home that only her husband loves. Edmund compares her drug use to the fog, because it is a "blank wall" (p. 139) that she uses to separate herself from her family, to get away from any involvement with them. He feels that, beneath her overt love for her husband and children, she harbors an underlying, invisible hatred that is manifested in the drug use itself.

Indeed, it does seem that Mary does, at least in part, hate them all. Each has pulled her farther and farther away from her primary attachment to God, and each has disappointed her again and again. She used to feel rooted in her religion, but has become frightened of the Virgin Mary, and is no longer able to find comfort in her faith. She has long held the idea that the death of her son Eugene was punishment from God and the Virgin Mary, because she chose to marry rather than to become a nun. This alienation from her faith has left her alone, alienated, despondent. Although she sees her opiate addiction as another affliction from God, it can also be seen as a replacement—as the only replacement powerful enough to imprison her—for her spiritual death. She hopes that one day she will "find [her soul] again, . . . [when she doesn't] have to feel guilty any more" (p. 94).

The play ends with Mary in a morphine stupor, reliving, in her own fantasy world, the moment when she lost her faith. She is searching for her wedding gown and remembers how fulfilled she was in her faith before her marriage. "When I had it," she says, "I was never lonely nor afraid" (p. 173) Until she married, she continually felt the Virgin Mary's presence. She evokes the memory of those spiritual moments when she felt connected, loved, and strengthened by her faith. She says, "I knew . . . she [the Virgin Mary] . . . would always love me and see no harm ever came to me so long as I never lost my faith in her" (p. 176).

That is one of the last lines of the play, a fitting end, given the importance of transcendence, faith, and spirituality as alternatives to addiction. Edmund too describes his own sense of transcendence, but his concern is nature and the ocean. Interestingly, his soliloquy conjures up the oceanic feeling once more. He has always felt unwanted and unloved, and indeed he was not conceived with Mary's wishes. Her husband had thought it best that she have another child to take away some of the grief she was experiencing from the death of her 2-year-old child a few years earlier. She felt otherwise; her guilt over the loss of this child pervaded her entire being. She remembers being nervous throughout the whole pregnancy, worried that something would harm this baby also. Because she felt that God was continuing to punish her for her abandonment of Eugene, she felt certain that He would continue to inflict retribution, for her loss of faith, upon this new baby as well. She viewed Edmund as an unhappy, unhealthy boy, of frail constitution and neurotic temperament. Indeed, we can imagine how impaired the early bonding was with this child because of her newfound addiction (which probably was covering her grief and depression).

Edmund echoes his mother's perceptions in a later passage, ostensibly unaware of her earlier words. "It was a great mistake, my being born a man, I would have been much more successful as a sea gull or a fish. . . . I will always be a stranger who never feels at home, who does not really want and is not really wanted, who can never belong, who must always be a little in love with death!" (pp. 153–154). How similar are his words to those of Thomas Wolfe, how similar the sentiments of these two lonely, alienated souls. Edmund describes the only moments when he has expe-

rienced a feeling of oneness; not surprisingly, these have occurred outside
the realm of human contact, in association with the world of nature and
the sea.

> I lay on the bowsprit, facing astern, with the water foaming into
> spume under me, the masts with every sail white in the moonlight,
> towering high above me. I became drunk with the beauty and
> singing rhythm of it, and for a moment I lost myself—actually lost
> my life. I was set free! I dissolved in the sea, . . . became beauty and
> rhythm, became moonlight and the ship and the high dim-starred
> sky! I belonged, without past or future, within peace and unity and
> a wild joy, *within something greater than my own life*, or the life of Man,
> to Life itself! To God, if you want to put it that way. . . . And several
> other times, . . . I have had the same experience. Became the sun,
> the hot sand, green seaweed anchored to a rock, swaying in the
> tide. . . . For a second you see—and seeing the secret, are the secret.
> For a second there is meaning! Then . . . you are alone, lost in the
> fog again, and you stumble on toward nowhere, for no good reason!
> (emphasis added) [p. 153]

Sometimes, in describing psychological realities, literature says it
best. And here again we have evidence of the oceanic feeling, the
spirituality of moments of oneness, which are powerful enough to evoke a
sense of transcendency in yet another most detached, alienated soul.

10

GASLIGHTING

One's outer life passes in a solitude haunted by the masks of others; one's inner life passes in a solitude hounded by the masks of oneself.

Eugene O'Neill, *Memoranda on Masks*

THE TRANSFORMATIONAL aspects of drugs and alcohol, then, help the user to feel connected and indeed immersed in his life and his relationships. He often feels helpless and detached, freakish in some cases, when separated from the drug that has so often soothed and protected him. In his relationships with others, he rarely feels the immersive connection that has been described and discussed earlier. Rather, he feels separated. Often, in marriage, these individuals become disappointed with their spouses because the original transformational quality of the other has waned and the spouse is no longer deemed able to provide soothing mergers. Very often, the relationship becomes repetitive of childhood experiences—the addict is deemed infantile and helpless, whereas the spouse has become the overly responsible, resentful parent. A study of the relationship reveals a consistent pattern in which both members sacrifice the expression of their inner selves for the good of the marriage. Conflict is avoided, falseness encouraged, and separation, like an infectious disease, spreads.

For example, Mack, a 60-year-old recovering alcoholic, has been married for thirty-five years. He has been sober for almost twenty years, but his wife still views him with suspicion. Barbara, age 58, long ago gave up any hope of finding a soulmate in her husband. She shifted her attachment focus from her husband to her five children and is still devoted to these now-adult children who continue to flood her with their many problems: drug addictions, marital conflicts, and financial troubles. Mack long ago relinquished his own self to try and create a happy merger. He bought the house she wanted and sold the house he loved. He worked two jobs to support the children and essentially gave her sole custody of their emotional life. He learned to stifle any critical thought regarding the way she was raising their children and shifted his focus to work and work alone. Over the years, Mack became quieter and quieter. He came home only between shifts at his jobs and spent most of his evenings socializing with customers who frequented the saloon where he bartended. And of course, he drank. He drank during all those lonely years while feeling so separated, so disillusioned by the woman he had thought would save him from isolation.

His mother had been an alcoholic, and he had spent much of his childhood rescuing her from bars, working to help pay their bills, and waiting up nights in terror that she may have met with an untimely death. He was an only child. His mother had told him in a drunken rage that he had been illegitimate and unexpected. His father deserted the family when Mack was 5, never to return.

He had thought that he had found, in his wife, a loving and devoted soulmate. They were in love at first, and then the children became his wife's focus and monetary provisions became his. His wife too had hoped for a lifetime of love in her husband. She was the fourth of eight children, with a depressed mother who frequently ruminated about suicide. Barbara was an excellent caregiver who had taken over many household responsibilities at a young age. She was a good student, the only one of her siblings to show much promise. And yet, when she showed her mother her accomplishments, she was answered only with a request to do more. She never felt she did anything well enough or that she deserved anything for herself. This relationship she repeated with her children, always putting their needs before her own, never allowing herself any luxury.

As for her husband, Barbara felt he viewed her as never good enough, never pleasing him well enough. She became more and more removed from him, ever wishing for the marriage she had never had. His drinking angered and worried her, and she became frightened of him. When drunk, he sometimes shifted out of the quiet falseness she had grown accustomed to and became an angry, at times violent, man. He never hit her or their children, but he might throw a lamp or punch a wall. Over the years, she resigned herself to a lifetime of separateness. Divorce? Not likely, because she believed this was her "lot in life," her "cross to bear." Again, another fated individual. She did not drink, but turned instead to sweets as companions. Despite high blood pressure and other medical complications, she craved the soothing, rewarding taste of chocolate and ice cream. When her husband stopped drinking, she had a renewed sense of hope for their relationship. Her feeling was short lived, however, because he became an angrier man and more withdrawn, silent, and tense. Her fear of him was concretized. She became quieter and quieter. She poured her heart and soul into her church, her job, and her children.

By the time the two came in to see me for a consultation, Mack had already discussed divorce with Barbara. They had such separation in their marriage that they slept in different beds, were never sexually intimate, and never exchanged more than daily pleasantries with each other. To avoid any conflict, Mack had relinquished other responsibilities, thus placing himself in the position of child to his wife's mothering role. Although the bills were all in joint accounts, Mack had no idea what monies were where—he did not even have his own ATM card, or access to their checks, or a mailbox key. He left all of these responsibilities to Barbara. Yet, in fact, he was a competent businessman and actually excelled in small-time investments; still he felt it best to shed himself of this talent in relation to his wife.

This is not an uncommon phenomenon in marriages, where the two are so angry and so fearful of their anger that they resort to compromise and sacrifice at the expense of the expression of their inner selves. To attempt some semblance of what they believe is connectedness, they shed their souls. Merger has been blamed for this process, in which the couple is viewed as symbiotically attached, as enmeshed beyond any separateness. The couple is seen as infantile in their need for oneness and their search for infantile fusion. Although I agree with Peck (1978) that separateness must balance merger, he also sees most marriages as having erred on the side of merger.

> I have come to realize that it is the separateness of the partners that enriches the union. Great marriages cannot be constricted by individuals who are terrified by their basic aloneness, as so commonly is the case, and seek a merging in marriage . . . . The ultimate goal of life remains the spiritual growth of the individual, the solitary journey to peaks that can be climbed only alone . . . . Marriage and society exist for the basic purpose of nurturing such individual journeys. [p. 168]

In actuality, a couple such as Mack and Barbara have no connectedness. They are as separated, as isolated as is humanly possible. Their

attempt at merger has mistakenly rested on the idea that anger is dangerous, that expression of the inner self is poison. When I work with couples
like this one, I tell them that our job is to create a middle, to create an area
of immersion, in which the two can find some connectedness. I tell them
to remember the beginning of their relationship. I say to them:

> Originally you were two separate beings, who then joined together.
> And in the process of joining together, you tried to become one. But
> oneness is an impossibility, it is a longing you have in part because of
> the years of separateness you felt in your own families. You wanted
> so very much to become one that anger felt like a dangerous intruder
> serving to separate you both. And so you each have kept your anger
> inside yourselves and over time have learned to keep everything else
> about yourselves secret. In marriage, the best we can do to create a
> feeling of oneness is to *communicate* our inner thoughts and feelings,
> to make a middle where there has been no middle before, to build a
> bridge between our separate selves. And that can only be done if you
> are willing to share a piece of the internal you, the part that long ago
> shut down and hid away.

Over time, we began discovering how the two had distorted the
relationship between each other, how the multiple projections of childhoods past were infecting the marriage of the present. Mack then began to
assert himself in the area of their finances and to insist on being kept
involved in all its aspects, and Barbara disclosed to him her sense that he
was always critical and ungiving. We discussed in detail his chain smoking
and how it makes her feel disregarded, belittled, and ignored. We discussed her sweet tooth and the reasons behind her need to self-soothe. In
every case, the two had to fight against their instinctive reaction to hide
their thoughts and feelings. In every instance, the room became less tense
and constricted when they were able to share their inner feelings.

The outcome of whether they stayed married or decided to divorce
was, to me, not the point at issue here. If, for example, in the process of
shedding some of their hidden thoughts, the two had discovered they
really disliked, or even hated, one another, a divorce might have ensued.
The important aspect, however, was that the two learned to gain access to
their inner selves and to share that communication, as much as possible,
with the other. So very often, in these kinds of marriages, each spouse

sacrifices his or her individual being for the sake of the other. The spouse is seen as powerful and dangerous; the self is viewed as weak and little.

I call this process *gaslighting*, and suggest to patients that they view the brilliant 1944 film entitled *Gaslight*, starring Ingrid Bergman and Charles Boyer. In the movie, Bergman plays a young woman, Paula, who is slowly and systematically stripped of her self. She is a willing target: lonely, depressed, and long suffering from abandonments. She never knew her parents, her mother having died during her birth. She was raised by her aunt, a famous opera singer, who is murdered just as the movie begins. As a teenager, Paula is essentially alone in the world, with no family alive and few friends. For ten years she remains an isolated soul, studying opera in the tradition of her aunt, until she falls in love with her soon-to-be husband, Gregory. She feels so powerful in his presence that she could conquer the world. All her fears, she tells him, have melted away. They marry quickly, she, no doubt, in disbelief that she could be loved so dearly and utterly. This is an important aspect of her love: originally he was her object of transformation and salvation.

In order to devote herself to her husband, she ignores and abandons her own musical talent that would have maintained her own self and self-confidence, as well as her connections with other human beings, such as her teacher, and so on. Throughout the rest of the movie, her acceptance of her husband's maltreatment and even cruelty must be viewed against the backdrop of her idealization of him. She continues to "chase the high" of their early romance. The husband soon puts into effect his plan to make her go crazy so that he can gain possession of her inherited great wealth and find her aunt's missing jewels. He is obsessed with the jewels, and he must have them at any cost (not unlike a drug addict in pursuit of his drugs). And, like a drug addict, he must render her helpless and powerless and destroy any credibility she may have with others. He proves to her, by his manipulations, that she is forgetful, that she is always losing jewelry or pictures, and he wears down any self-confidence she has had. For example, she knows that the gaslight that dims every night when he goes out must somehow be related to his leaving, and yet she cannot believe it. She has been so assaulted that she believes she is dreaming or hallucinating. The gas dimming and the sounds that rumble above her head, she decides, are her own fantasies.

Paula knows the reality of what she is seeing and she knows her husband is responsible and yet, in the face of this most powerful other, she abandons her self. I have seen this phenomenon of shedding the self in numerous patients. For example, one patient described incident after incident of her husband's uncontrollable drinking. He would drink and drive, for example, or spend weekends in their summer home totally drunk, or come in from the commuter train obviously inebriated. And yet she continued to ignore her own reality. In alcoholism counseling terms, her denial was tremendous and her enabling behavior extreme. I prefer to describe her behavior differently, because the fact is, she knows what she sees, but consciously chooses to deny the inevitable confrontation that would ensue. Does she enable his alcoholic progression? Yes. Of equal importance, what is this phenomenon in terms of her *own* self? She is detaching from her own feelings and thoughts, from her own reality. When she accepts his lies of "I only had one beer" and when she co-opts to his belief system, she has left herself behind. She has shed her self to serve the other; she has placed herself in the infantile role of child to the controlling, demanding nature of the powerful other. I prefer to use the term *self-sacrificer* rather than enabler, because the spouse loses her own self in an attempt fully to merge with the other. Some years later, this patient called me, just to check in, after she had filed for divorce. She wanted to know if it was terribly "mean" of her to have closed out the few hundred dollars they had in their joint checking account, worried that several checks would then bounce. Meanwhile, her husband had just withdrawn the many thousands of dollars they had had together in a joint savings account. She had so lost her own self that she could not justify her own self-preservation. In another example, a patient would not believe the proof in front of him that his wife was having an affair. He would ask, and she would deny. He would find her out late, she would offer an excuse. He would sense her distance, she would cajole him. It was only after the divorce was final that a friend revealed to him the truth of his wife's adultery. Again, to crave the embrace of the powerful other, the self is lost.

What enables these individuals to petrify their inner selves? Is it simply the result of a persuasive lover, a charismatic seducer? I think not. In the individuals whom I have treated, underneath an exterior of self-sufficiency is a powerful craving to give in to, and to let go of, their own selves. In most cases the dynamics can be traced to childhood experiences with domineering and controlling parents. The child's world was consistently viewed as related to the mother: her needs came first. One patient described having to spend every Saturday waiting at the beauty parlor for her mother while her hair was washed, dyed, and styled. This child was given no activities of her own to pursue while her mother indulged in her beauty regime, but was expected to wait patiently, hour after hour, until the ordeal was over. Another described a mother who never agreed with her daughter's choices and always overrode decisions on such matters as dresses to wear, hairstyles to try, and foods to eat. Today, although she is a successful corporate executive, she is pained by the fact that she is over 40 and has never married. In each of the several times she has been engaged, she became so chameleon-like that she was frightened by her self-disintegration. To prove her love, for example, she once relocated to a foreign country so as to be nearer her lover, leaving behind friends, family, and a well-established career. When the relationship ended, she returned to her hometown and re-established herself all over again. In her next relationship, she quickly allowed her new boyfriend to move in all of his belongings and simultaneously redecorated her home to suit his tastes.

Jordan (1983) terms this phenomenon an inability to self-empathize, which is prominent in childhoods filled with domineering, narcissistic mothering. I agree with her thoughts, although I would add that these patients, like the alcoholic, have attempted to immerse themselves in a powerful other who undermines their own selves. They are returned to their infantile state of helplessness, powerlessness, and dependency; they have become shells of their former selves. Another patient comes to mind. Married for ten years, Linda thought she had found the man of her dreams. They never fought, which indicated to the patient that their marriage was harmonious, loving, and peaceful. She did whatever he asked her to do, consciously deciding that nothing was worth fighting over. So, when he suggested that she pay all the household expenses from her own salary (she was the bigger wage earner, by far), she readily agreed. His money was to be banked, saved for their future plans. When he wanted to buy expensive "toys" like sports cars, speed boats, or a winter ski house, Linda reminded herself that "this is no big deal." Having a marriage without conflict was desperately important to her because she had been raised in a house filled with arguing and violent fights. Had her parents not had children, she was convinced, they would never have stayed together. She believed she was the cause of their misery because they had married after her unplanned conception. Similar to Paula in *Gaslight*, whose mother had died in giving her life, Linda's guilt revolved around the years of suffering that her parents had endured so that she was given a "stable" home.

She was well prepared, then, for a life of caring for her husband. For example, although she had been a Phi Beta Kappa scholar in college, her husband insisted that she downplay her academic prowess with his friends because he thought her intelligence would make them "uncomfortable." She therefore kept careful watch over showing her intellect, refraining from making comments that might be over their heads or talking about subjects she knew he and his friend would not be interested in discussing. Linda was "gaslighting" herself, slowly diminishing her worth for the sake of the other. She stopped socializing with long-time friends, stopped pursuing hobbies and sports that she previously had enjoyed.

She had thought that the less she did for herself, the happier he would be. Instead, the more demanding he became. Over time, she became more and more unhappy. He never came home before ten o'clock from his job, began traveling frequently, and always asked her for money. When she finally sought treatment, she had almost convinced herself that she had driven him away. What we discovered was that he had been involved in an extramarital affair for over a year and had taken all the money earmarked for savings and had spent it wining and dining his new lover. In a way, Linda had been right: she had driven him away. The sacrificing of her self, all done in the fantasy of love, had robbed her of her intelligence, her charm, her person. Originally he, too, had sought in her a powerful transformation. In giving away her self, Linda had given away her power and, therefore, any possibility of remaining his transformational object. We discussed this dissolution of her self, and she was able to see the depth of her self-destruction. She began, piece by piece, to reclaim her own being. She started socializing with friends and returned to her hobbies. She was surprised at "how good" she was beginning to feel.

> I haven't felt like this for many years. There's a powerful surge of energy in me, a feeling of self-confidence I haven't had in years. It's as though I've been sleeping for a long time, and am just finally waking up. I realize some of the thoughts that used to keep me from doing what I wanted to do, thoughts like "Well, I really should wait for him," or "Well, it's okay to sacrifice this for him." There are so many movies I've wanted to see, for example, and I've always just waited for him, hoping we'd go together. And then it would never happen, we'd never go. And you know something? Now, I'm going to the movies, even if I go by myself. I'm doing what I want to do, and it feels heavenly.

The fantasy, then, that merger means "no conflict," that it means "one being," had caused Linda to deny her own existence. Now, she was reclaiming her self and learning that moments of oneness can truly exist only between the separations of two distinct beings. She, like so many others, had mistakenly believed that to feel herself into an other meant to *give* herself to an other. She had mistaken a feeling for an action; she had hoped to sustain what can only be momentary immersive experiences into a lifetime by attempting to *become* the other.

In the following example, the patient explains her compulsion to take on the emotional state of her lover. Spotnitz (1976) has underscored the frequency of "induced" feelings, and I have found it useful to discuss with patients the difficulties inherent in this phenomenon, especially with patients who attune so readily to others. The patient, Jacquelyn, was involved with a man who often suffered from self-doubts, depression, and a sense of hopelessness. She found herself becoming depressed, viewing the world from his sad-colored glasses and lessening her involvement in the vibrant life she had been living. I pointed out to her that she was viewing his depression as if it were an infectious disease that she could catch. To this she agreed, adding, "Well, isn't it?" We discussed this idea, that she could "catch" his depression and become depressed too. I said, "I suppose so, if you feel that you must feel the same things he feels and live the same way he lives." Jacquelyn was puzzled by this, saying, "But I do think that. It would be a *betrayal*, don't you see, if I didn't feel what he feels, if I wasn't so in tune with him. How can I go out and have fun, for example, if I know he is home feeling discouraged and unhappy? How can I pursue my own accomplishments if he can't achieve anything?"

I pointed out to her that she was attempting to *be* him, which was an impossibility. "How does it help him, I wonder, for you to join his depressed world? What has caused you to think that this is expected of you?" Jacquelyn knew exactly where this expectation had come from: her mother had insisted on total attunement from her when she was a child.

> I remember going to school and worrying about my mother. If I was having too good of a time with my friends, I would feel guilty, thinking that it was a betrayal — a betrayal of how I was supposed to be. I was supposed to think only of her, wasn't I? I've always thought it was a sign of good mothering, to be so "hooked in" with your kid. Not that she was, with me. Actually she never comforted me when I was sick, or if I had fallen down. But I thought that's what mothers do.

I suggested that this is what she wished mothers would do; this is what she had done for her younger sisters and for her mother, and for the many people in her life whom she had since "mothered." I asked her, "Do you really think this is so? The child has fallen, his mother comforts him, and puts a bandage on the 'boo-boo.' Now, does she still go and make dinner for the family, or do the two of them stay in this fallen moment?" Jacquelyn laughed, realizing that of course the latter scenario was not realistic. As we spoke further, I suggested to her that she was not just having a moment of empathic understanding of her lover, but she was infecting herself with his emotion. She was not keeping herself separate while remaining connected. I said to her,

> I would rather that you feel deeply his emotional pain, when you are talking with him or are visiting with him, but that then, when you have completed the phone call, when you have left his home, you remind yourself of all that you are; you return to all that you can accomplish. And then, the next time you speak with him, you can again resonate with his emotional pain, feel yourself into his world view, and immerse yourself into his being. But when you leave, it is time again to return to YOU.

Jacquelyn had to have me say this a few times to her for her to really understand the idea. She felt "freer" from our discussion, freer to be able both to join his world and yet not to have to give up her own. In the next case, presented below, Diane exemplifies a more extreme false self who was so surrounded by malevolent, powerful others that she had no ability to attend to herself.

DIANE

Diane, a strikingly attractive yet heavy-set woman of 34, spoke in a soft, melancholy voice that served to dramatize the depth of emotional pain she had experienced. Frequently, she became tearful and would sit silently to compose herself. After six months of treatment, she had not yet told me all the details of the emotional abuse and physical beatings she had experienced at the hands of her parents. But I did not need the specifics to feel the depth of her damaged core.

Diane was the oldest of five children and, because of this, received most of her parents' rage. She told me that her father was an active alcoholic who frequently raged when drunk, calling her "stupid," "fat," or "ugly." She was regularly beaten by him and for years had fantasized about calling child protective services to report his abuse. He had repeatedly threatened her with death—if she misbehaved, if she had too many friends, or if she ever dated. Her parents had actually forbidden her to date at all, even during her college years. She began to hate her attractiveness, dreading the attention men would give her, attention other women would have craved. She found herself developing strategies to look unappealing, such as wearing out-of-date clothes and gaining weight. Her avoidant behavior included making no eye contact, saying nothing in class, and hurrying out of buildings to limit any socializing with her peers. She was terrified that her father would follow her movements and would indeed carry out his threat to kill her even if what he had seen was simply an innocent interaction with a fellow student.

When Diane was 28, she finally became determined to move out of her parents' home, despite her fears of being on her own. She was successful in her move, but began to think that they were watching her. In fact, she tried to protect herself by getting an unlisted phone number and leaving no forwarding address. To her dismay, her parents began writing her cruel, critical letters. She never knew how they found her, but believed they had hired a private detective. After this episode, she again moved, hoping to get loose from their grip. Six months later, however, she received an invitation to attend a family reunion. They had again found a way to harass and torment her, to keep her frightened focus on them.

Treatment

Diane viewed me with a mixture of fear and interest. From a previous outpatient treatment experience several years before, she knew that her assumptions about me might very well be transferentially based. For example, she was involved with an older, recovering alcoholic she had met at her AA meetings. She frequently asked me if I thought she should terminate the relationship, if I thought the relationship was "no good" for her. I told her that her need to make me decide was a replication of her parents' relationship with her. Diane knew that this was the position she had attempted to place me in, and after I had pointed this out, she refocused on her own feelings instead.

Diane often took a minute in the beginning of each session to "find her own center." In this fascinating ritual, she would sit quietly while clearing her throat. This sound seemed to re-evoke an infantile gesturing and caused her to shift from focusing on me to attuning to herself. In a similar manner, she would sometimes stop our discussion midway to throw out a seemingly unrelated thought, saying "I just had to say that. I feel better now." These thoughts usually were related to an internal feeling-state, such as "I am feeling stronger right now" or "I know what I have to do." Actually, these comments were similar to the clearing of her throat—they were ways for her to tune in to her own self and to tune out her focus on me. Diane had been so criticized as a child that she never learned to trust any of her wishes, thoughts, or initiative. She had been taught early on to attune only to the emotional state of others; the relationship with her parents was so parent-centered that she learned only to follow, not to lead; to imitate, not to create. She became preoccupied by the emotional state of the powerful others around her, an adaptation that had originally been necessary for her survival.

The therapy helped her to clarify and hold onto her own thoughts and feelings. She began to experience, within the relationship, her own powerfulness and began to feel a sense of confidence she had not experienced throughout her childhood. Diane became more empowered. When we first met, she was an accountant who was being overworked and underpaid. She had little confidence in herself, and despite realizing that she was indeed being taken for granted, she felt she had no recourse but to accept this mistreatment. Over time, Diane began to gain the courage to request overtime pay, and she practiced with me the words she would say in her meeting with her boss. To her amazement, he granted her request and even gave her a promotion. The therapeutic value of her immersion with a protective, nurturant other was the key to her improved level of confidence. Through the experience of sharing her internal self with me, she was able to gain a sense of importance and faith in herself. Having a powerful other listen and attend to her developing self made the difference in her ability to ask for, and receive, something that she had wanted.

Building a Protective Container

To help Diane understand the frequency of her other-focus, I drew an analogy to the "bubble babies," those children who are so germ-sensitive that they must spend every waking moment encased in a protective bubble, separated from the outside world. Diane had no protective bubble surrounding her, so that she absorbed every interaction, every comment, every glance that came her way. Being so outwardly attuned left her no opportunity to explore her own thoughts and wishes. Explaining this, I suggested she begin developing that external bubble, that protective coating between herself and the external world that would give her space to experience herself. Diane immediately embraced this idea. She started a diary and began going to the library and to church for some peaceful inner attunement. She told me that she often thought of me during her quiet time and would imagine me there with her, so that the silence was not abandoning or painful. She also began lessening the intensity of her relationship with the older man because she decided she had used him to "fill herself up" with an other.

This bubble baby metaphor also helped Diane tune into one of the major factors that contributed to her overeating. She began to focus on how food felt comforting and protective, a respite from the cruel and threatening world. Diane usually ate at night when she was alone. She used food to build an inner sanctum, but inevitably became ashamed by her indulgence and "weakness." Through the metaphor of the bubble, she began to find other soothing techniques that revolved around immersion into the therapeutic relationship rather than submersion in the food.

Diane typifies many individuals who have been thwarted in their emotional development by immersions with malevolent others. In most cases the individual has become solely focused on the needs and wishes of others, causing him to be well suited to alcoholic relationships. Helping the individual notice his other-focus and by providing accurate mergings to encourage his stunted omnipotence, can enable the individual to begin to awaken his own powerfulness instead.

One patient gave me some of his writings, to offer me his thoughts on the ideal relationship he had always hoped for but inevitably never found. A recovering alcoholic, he had also sought fusion and comfort from blissful moments with alcohol. Married twice, he always started the relationships with great promise and hope. Again in the throes of divorce, he wrote of his dream for salvation from an other. He wrote of his willingness to give away his own self in the process of getting an other.

Since I was a child, I have always believed that there was always some one person whom I could quite simply give my heart and soul to, and she would in turn do the same. Nothing would matter but the love and caring we would hold for one another. We would deal with each other in nothing less than endearing terms. Even when we would be upset, even with one another, that would quickly fade away, giving way to the bond that remained, that could not be broken . . . .

Where are you? I look for you everywhere. I search for you in so many faces that pass me by each day. Could she be you? Could she have been you, I wonder? I look for the light, the light in the eyes, that tells me she might be you. I know you are out there, somewhere, looking for me, asking: "When will he find me? Will he know me when he sees me? I am waiting". . . . There are times when I thought I had found you, times when the world was briefly transformed into my own domain, where laughing and loving overshadowed all else . . . .

I have always been convinced that only love for another human being could ever make us a whole and happy person . . . . Yet lately, in the AA Program, I have come to realize that happiness is the realization of oneness with one's Higher Power. We must let go of our will, to will everything, let go and let God take our lives into His hands. We must trust His will for us. In that vein, then, when I "cry out" in my heart for that one person I search and yearn for, I try to hold in my mind the phrase: "only if it is meant to be."

I want to be at peace with Him and with myself, but it is so sad when I have no one to share these feelings with. I don't want to devour someone; I want to hold us both in a light that will warm and satisfy our fears and anxieties, so that we can experience inner peace together.

"Where are you? . . ."

In some ways, these individuals crave an other just as the addict craves his drug. In fact, rather than being consumed by the drug, these patients have become compulsively attached to the other. Indeed, the program of Alanon, developed by Bill Wilson's wife, uses the same Twelve Steps as AA. The emphasis is on helping the spouse develop his or her own self rather than continually focusing on the alcoholic. The more recent co-dependency groups have the same focus: to help the individual shift away from his powerless position in his relationships. There are many similarities between the addict and the co-dependent, although one distinction certainly is that, in a human relationship, there can always be new demands, different requests, and ever–changing needs from the powerful other. And while the drug insists on ever-larger consumption, there is a certain consistency in the entire pursuit. In every case of "gaslighting," the individual has allowed himself to become totally dependent on the other—careers have been put off, friends have been left, and family have been ignored. The individual has become totally alone, his alienation that much greater, and his desperation for the other more intense.

In one case, a patient had been quite active in performing music before his marriage. He had many friends and was always asked to perform his songs in front of guests at parties and get-togethers. He owned a successful business and was thriving in all areas of his life. And yet, within the first year of marriage, he had refused all social invitations and had stopped creating his music. As he later told me, "I thought I was supposed to give it all up for the good of the marriage. I thought that is what being 'one' was all about." Indeed, in his childhood he was frequently reprimanded for being non-cooperative and oppositional to his parents' wishes. This had been so painful for him that, in marriage, he had chosen to ignore his multifaceted abilities. The moment of truth came for him when, after months of sadness and rejection in his marriage, months of shutting off his anger before it could emerge, he punched a wall during the first and only argument with his wife. "And in that moment, I felt all the emotions I had been blocking come through. It's as if my walled-off self came alive, and I was flooded with the sense of connectedness to me that I realized had been pushed down so far I had forgotten it had even existed." The marriage did not survive, but the patient has become more solidified in his own being and has resolved never to lose himself in the effort to merge again.

In another marital case, the husband reminded me of a snapping turtle. He only took his head out of an inner shell when he was desperate, when he had no recourse but finally to offer a moment of his internal self. Like so many other couples, he had reverted to passive–aggressive communication as the only way to keep a tiny piece of himself alive. He would forget important dates that his wife would remind him of, would come home an hour later than he had promised, or would forget to buy her favorite ice cream when shopping for food. These were all indirect attacks, but nevertheless quite powerful. His wife knew to expect little from him, to keep her distance, and to stifle any possible communication that might break through the barrier. She was a recovering alcoholic who, like so many others, attributed part of her need to drink to the intensity of the loneliness she felt *within* the relationship. For his part, her drinking represented the enormity of his failings as husband, lover, and friend. The two were separated by a vast emotional distance. The momentary peepings-out of his head from this shell were the only attempts he could offer in his own defense. In the marital work of therapy, the two struggled to reconcile their years of anger and disappointment in each other. Simultaneously, they attempted to become closer by planning a few household projects together. But they were unable to handle the frustrations involved with intimacy. They retreated back into their detached marriage, resigned to live together in separateness.

I wish to stress the distinctions between immersive moments that allow for and respond to the inherent separateness of all individuals and the enslaving illusion of merger that entraps and freezes two detached individuals. In the first, both partners are able to develop and grow while feeling held in the indissoluble bond of the other; in the latter, both are inhibited by the strangling power of a merger that is, in actuality, only a fantasy. In the kinds of relationships described in this chapter, neither member is fully embraced by the other. One spouse sheds her spontaneity in the hopes of becoming more connected to her husband, while her husband seeks a new partner to be the powerful other he so needs; in another relationship, one spouse quiets her sadness and distances her love, while her husband drinks in attempts to find oneness. In all of these relationships, what is missing is the spontaneous core of the two partners. Without moments of true self contact, there is no true oneness.

In these cases, I agree with Freud that idealization can be defensive in nature, that it serves to exalt an other beyond his realistic stature. In this regard, the idealized other is the salvation, the transformative object, who is *unrealistically* imbued with overesteemed value. In this regard, the self is then devalued, and the process that I have described above begins. Yes, this does hearken back to early infantile feelings, when mother was larger than life and as important as the air the baby breathed. But the reason for its importance is not because the baby is merged, but because the baby is separate, tiny, helpless. Attachment is inherent to the human condition. The baby looks to his mother to save and protect him, and originally, in this infantile state, that is a *realistic* evaluation of her greatness. Over time, if he has not been valued and has not therefore learned to value himself, to imbue his own being with pride or with love, then he continues seeking powerful others to care for him. As an adult, this individual finds himself ever searching for the powerful one who will rescue him from the abyss of powerlessness and alienation. He idealizes each potential other he encounters in the desperate hope that he will, this time, find the value in himself that has never been given. He idealizes to find salvation; he devalues to ensure permanent access to this transformational relationship. It is not the salvation, however, nor even the idealization, that is pathological. When experienced, the conversion can be so powerful that the individual is pushed into a transformation that raises his true self to a greater degree of spontaneity and freedom. What is pathological, however, is when this transformational power is seen as only part of the other and has not been incorporated into part of the self.

Moments of oneness provide transcendence from the isolation of separateness. These moments join true self-experiences and in that way are powerful, evocative, and spiritual. These moments bring love to the self and purpose to the being. These moments tell us that we are all, indeed, connected to each other and comfort us in confirming that we "cannot fall out of this world."

LVII

somewhere i have never travelled,gladly beyond
any experience,your eyes have their silence:
in your most frail gesture are things which enclose me,
or which i cannot touch because they are too near

your slightest look easily will unclose me
though i have closed myself as fingers,
you open always petal by petal myself as Spring opens
(touching skillfully,mysteriously)her first rose

or if your wish be to close me,i and
my life will shut very beautifully,suddenly,

as when the heart of this flower imagines
the snow carefully everywhere descending;

nothing which we are to perceive in this world equals
the power of your intense fragility:whose texture
compels me with the colour of its countries,
rendering death and forever with each breathing

(i do not know what it is about you that closes
and opens;only something in me understands
the voice of your eyes is deeper than all roses)
nobody,not even the rain,has such small hands

                                                              e.e. cummings

REFERENCES

Alcoholics Anonymous. (1939). New York: Alcoholics Anonymous World Services.

Angier, N. (1994). Mother's milk found to be potent cocktail of hormones. *Science Times, The New York Times,* May 24, p. C1.

Balint, M. (1968). *The Basic Fault: Therapeutic Aspects of Regression.* New York: Brunner/Mazel, 1979.

Bollas, C. (1987). *The Shadow of the Object: Psychoanalysis of the Unthought Known.* New York: Columbia University Press.

_____ (1989). *Forces of Destiny: Psychoanalysis and Human Idiom.* London: Free Association Books.

Bowlby, J. (1969). *Attachment.* New York: Basic Books, 1982.

_____ (1973). *Separation: Anxiety and Anger.* New York: Basic Books.

_____ (1979). *The Making and Breaking of Affectional Bonds.* New York: Routledge.

_____ (1980). *Loss: Sadness and Depression.* New York: Basic Books.

Buie, D. H. (1981). Empathy: its nature and limitations. *Journal of the American Psychoanalytic Association* 29: 281–307.

Buxton, M., Smith, D., and Seymour, R. (1987). Spirituality and other points of resistance to the 12-step recovery process. *Journal of Psychoactive Drugs* 19: 275–285.

Carpenter, F. (1979). *Eugene O'Neill,* rev. ed. Boston: G. K. Hall.

Clinebell, H. (1962). Philosophical-religious factors in the etiology and treatment of alcoholism. *Journal of Substance Abuse Treatment* 9:473–488.

Druck, A. (1989). *Four Therapeutic Approaches to the Borderline Patient.* Northvale, NJ: Jason Aronson.

Eigen, M. (1981). The area of faith in Winnicott, Lacan and Bion. *International Journal of Psycho-Analysis* 62: 413–433.

Fairbairn, W. R. D. (1941). A revised psychopathology of the psychoses and psychoneuroses. In *Psychoanalytic Studies of the Personality,* pp. 28–58. New York: Routledge and Kegan Paul, 1986.

_____ (1943). The war neuroses—their nature and significance. In *Psycho-*

analytic Studies of the Personality, pp. 256–288. New York: Routledge and Kegan Paul, 1986.

———— (1946). Object-relationships and dynamic structure. In *Psychoanalytic Studies of the Personality*, p. 137–151. New York: Routledge and Kegan Paul.

Freud, E. L., compiler and ed. (1964). *Letters of Sigmund Freud*. Trans. T. Stern and J. Stern. New York: McGraw-Hill.

Freud, S. (1909). Analysis of a phobia in a five-year-old boy. In *The Sexual Enlightenment of Children: Sigmund Freud*, ed. P. Rieff. New York: Collier Books/Macmillan, 1963.

———— (1914). On narcissism: an introduction. *Standard Edition* 14:67–102.

———— (1926). Inhibitions, symptoms and anxiety. *Standard Edition* 20:75–175.

———— (1927). The future of an illusion. *Standard Edition* 9:126.

———— (1930). *Civilization and Its Discontents*. Trans. J. Strachey. New York: W. W. Norton, 1961.

Gaslight. (1944). Metro-Goldwyn-Mayer film directed by George Cukor, based on the play by Patrick Hamilton.

Gawain, S. (1978). *Creative Visualization*. New York: Bantam Books, 1982.

Gay, P. (1987). *A Godless Jew: Freud, Atheism, and the Making of Psychoanalysis*. New Haven: Yale University Press.

———— (1988). *Freud: A Life For Our Time*. New York: W. W. Norton.

Glenn, J. (1980). Freud's advice to Hans' father: the first supervisory sessions. In *Freud and His Patients*, ed. M. Kanzer and J. Glenn, pp. 122–127. Northvale, NJ: Jason Aronson.

Greenacre, P. (1957). The childhood of the artist: libidinal phase development and giftedness. *Psychoanalytic Study of the Child* 12:27–72. New York: International Universities Press.

Greenberg, J. R., and Mitchell, S. A. (1983). *Object Relations in Psychoanalytic Theory*. Cambridge, MA: Harvard University Press.

Guntrip, H. (1961). *Personality Structure and Human Interaction*. New York: International Universities Press, 1977.

———— (1969). *Schizoid Phenomena, Object Relations, and the Self*. New York: International Universities Press, 1985.

Howard, M. P. (1994). A halfway house for me. *The New York Times Magazine (HERS)*, August 7, p. 18.

James, W. (1901). *The Varieties of Religious Experience: A Study in Human Nature*. New York: Penguin Books, 1958.

Jones, E. (1959). *Free Associations: Memories of a Psychoanalyst*. London: Hogarth.

Jordan, J. V. (1983). Empathy and the mother–daughter relationship. In *Work in Progress: Women and Empathy—Implications for Psychological Development and Psychotherapy* (no. 82–02), ed. J. H. Hall, pp. 2–5. Wellesley, MA: Stone Center, Wellesley College.

Kaplan, A. G. (1983). Empathic communication in the psychotherapy relationship. In *Work in Progress: Women and Empathy—Implications for Psychological Development and Psychotherapy* (no. 82–02), ed. J. H. Hall, pp. 12–16. Wellesley, MA: Stone Center, Wellesley College.

Karen, R. (1994). *Becoming Attached: Unfolding the Mystery of the Infant-Mother Bond and Its Impact on Later Life*. New York: Warner Books.

Kernberg, O. (1975). *Borderline Conditions and Pathological Narcissism*. New York: Jason Aronson.

_____ (1980). *Internal World and External Reality. Object Relations Theory Applied*. New York: Jason Aronson.

_____ (1984). *Severe Personality Disorders: Psychotherapeutic Strategies*. New Haven: Yale University Press, 1986.

Kierkegaard, S. (1846). *Purity of Heart*. New York: Harper and Row, 1938.

Kohut, H. (1971). *The Analysis of the Self*. New York: International Universities Press, 1989.

_____ (1973). The psychoanalyst in the community of scholars. In *The Search for the Self: Selected Writings of Heinz Kohut: 1950–1978*, vol. 2, ed. P. H. Ornstein, pp. 685–724. Madison, CT: International Universities Press, 1978.

_____ (1977). *The Restoration of the Self*. New York: International Universities Press, 1988.

_____ (1980). Summarizing reflections. In *Advances in Self Psychology*, ed. A. Goldberg. New York: International Universities Press.

Kuhn, T. (1962). *The Structure of Scientific Revolutions*, 2nd ed. Chicago: University of Chicago Press.

Küng, H. (1979). *Freud and the Problem of God*. Trans. E. Quinn, additions, C. Murphy. New Haven: Yale University Press, 1990.

Kurtz, E. (1979). *Not-God: A History of Alcoholics Anonymous*. Center City, MN: Hazelden Educational Materials.

Lemkow, A. F. (1990). *The Wholeness Principle: Dynamics of Unity within Science, Religion and Society*. Wheaton, IL: Theosophical Publishing House.

Liedloff, J. (1975). *The Continuum Concept: Allowing Human Nature to Work Successfully.* New York: Addison-Wesley, 1987.

Mahler, M., Pine, F., and Bergman, A. (1975). *The Psychological Birth of the Human Infant: Symbiosis and Individuation.* London: Maresfield Library, 1985.

Masson, J. M. (1980). *The Oceanic Feeling.* Dordrecht, Holland: D. Reidel.

McElderry, B. R. (1964). *Thomas Wolfe.* New Haven: College and University Press.

Meissner, W. W. (1987). *Life and Faith: Psychological Perspectives on Religious Experience.* Washington, DC: Georgetown University Press.

Miller, A. (1981). *The Drama of the Gifted Child: The Search for the True Self.* Trans. R. Ward. New York: Basic Books.

————— (1990). *Banished Knowledge: Facing Childhood Injuries.* Trans. L. Vennewitz. New York: Anchor Books/ Doubleday.

Mitchell, S. A. (1988). *Relational Concepts in Psychoanalysis: An Integration.* Cambridge, MA: Harvard University Press.

Moore, B., and Fine, B., eds. (1990). *Psychoanalytic Terms and Concepts.* New Haven: The American Psychoanalytic Association and Yale University Press.

Niederland, W. G. (1974). *The Schreber Case: Psychoanalytic Profile of a Paranoid Personality.* New York: Quadrangle/The New York Times Book Co.

Nowell, E. (1960). *Thomas Wolfe.* Garden City, NY: Doubleday.

Ogden, T. H. (1986). *The Matrix of the Mind.* Northvale, NJ: Jason Aronson.

O'Neill, E. (1941). *Long Day's Journey Into Night.* New Haven: Yale University Press, 1989.

Parsons, W. B. (1993). *Psychoanalysis and Mysticism: The Freud–Rolland Correspondence,* 2 vols. Chicago: University of Chicago, Joseph Regenstein Library.

Peck, M. S. (1978). *The Road Less Traveled: A New Psychology of Love, Traditional Values and Spiritual Growth.* New York: Simon and Schuster, 1985.

Peele, S. (1989). *Diseasing of America: Addiction Treatment Out of Control.* Lexington, MA: D. C. Heath.

Rank, O. (1929). *The Trauma of Birth.* New York: Harper & Row, 1973.

Rieff, P. (1959). *Freud: The Mind of the Moralist.* New York: Viking Press.

Rinsley, D. B. (1988). The dipsas revisited: Comments on addiction and personality. *Journal of Substance Abuse Treatment* 5:1–7.

Ritter, A. (1936). Schreber: Das Bildungssystem eines Arztes. Erlangen: Inaugural dissertation.

Rizzuto, A.-M. (1979). *The Birth of the Living God: A Psychoanalytic Study.* Chicago: University of Chicago Press.

Searles, H. (1961). Phases of patient–therapist interaction in the psychotherapy of chronic schizophrenia. In *Collected Papers on Schizophrenia and Related Subjects,* pp. 521–559. New York: International Universities Press.

Seinfeld, J. (1991). *The Empty Core: An Object Relations Approach to Psychotherapy of the Schizoid Personality.* Northvale, NJ: Jason Aronson.

Slap, J. (1961). Little Hans' tonsillectomy. *Psychoanalytic Quarterly* 30:259–261.

Spotnitz, H. (1976). *Psychotherapy of Preoedipal Conditions: Schizophrenia and Severe Character Disorders.* New York: Jason Aronson.

Stepansky, P. E., compiler and ed. (1988). *The Memoirs of Margaret S. Mahler.* New York: Macmillan.

Stern, D. N. (1985). *The Interpersonal World of the Infant: A View from Psychoanalysis and Development Psychology.* New York: Basic Books.

Stolorow, R. D., and Lachmann, F. M. (1980). *Psychoanalysis of Developmental Arrests.* New York: International Universities Press, 1986.

Surrey, J. L. (1983). The relational self in women: clinical implications. In *Work in Progress: Women and Empathy—Implications for Psychological Development and Psychotherapy* (no. 82–02), ed. J. H. Hall. pp. 6–11. Wellesley, MA: Stone Center, Wellesley College.

Thomsen, R. (1975). *Bill W.* New York: Harper and Row, 1985.

Tiebout, H. M. (1949). The act of surrender in the therapeutic process with special reference to alcoholism. *Quarterly Journal of Studies on Alcohol* 10: 48–58.

———— (1954). The ego factors in surrender in alcoholism. *Quarterly Journal of Studies on Alcohol* 15: 611–621.

Treece, C., and Khantzian, E. J. (1986). Psychodynamic factors in the development of drug dependence. *Psychiatric Clinics of North America* 9: 399–412.

Webster's New Universal Unabridged Dictionary, (1983) ed. J. L. McKechnie et al. 2nd ed. New York: Simon and Schuster.

Weinstein, R. S. (1988). Should analysts love their patients? The resolution of transference resistance through countertransferential explorations. In *Love: Psychoanalytic Perspectives*, ed. J. Lasky and H. Silverman, pp. 192–199. New York: New York University Press.

Wilson, W. (1950). Alcoholics Anonymous. *New York State Journal of Medicine* 50: 1708–1716.

―――― (1952). *Twelve Steps and Twelve Traditions*. New York: Alcoholics Anonymous World Services, 1981.

―――― (1957). *Alcoholics Anonymous Comes of Age*. New York: Harper and Brothers.

Wilson, W., and Jung, C. (1968). The Bill Wilson and Carl Jung letters. *AA Grapevine*, January, pp. 26–31.

Winnicott, D. W. (1935). The manic defence. In *Through Paediatrics to Psycho-Analysis*, pp. 129–144. New York: Basic Books, 1975.

―――― (1945). Primitive emotional development. In *Through Paediatrics to Psycho-Analysis*, pp. 145–156. New York: Basic Books, 1975.

―――― (1974). Hate in the countertransference. In *Through Paediatrics to Psycho-Analysis*, pp. 194–203. London: Hogarth, 1978.

―――― (1951). Transitional objects and transitional phenomena. In *Through Paediatrics to Psycho-Analysis*, pp. 229–242. London: Hogarth, 1978.

―――― (1952a). Anxiety associated with insecurity. In *Through Paediatrics to Psycho-Analysis*, pp. 97–100. Basic Books, 1975.

―――― (1952b). Psychoses and child care. In *Through Paediatrics to Psycho-Analysis*, pp. 219–228. New York: Basic Books, 1975.

―――― (1958). The capacity to be alone. In *The Maturational Processes and the Facilitating Environment*, pp. 29–36. New York: International Unversities Press, 1965.

―――― (1960a). Counter-transference. In *The Maturational Processes and the Facilitating Environment*, pp. 158–165. New York: International Universities Press, 1965.

―――― (1960b). Ego distortion in terms of true and false self. In *The Maturational Processes and the Facilitating Environment*, pp. 140–152. New York: International Universities Press, 1965.

―――― (1960). The theory of the parent–infant relationship. In *The Maturational Processes and The Facilitating Environment*, pp. 37–55. New York: International Universities Press, 1965.

―――― (1963a). Communicating and not communicating leading to a study of certain opposites. In *The Maturational Processes and the*

Facilitating Environment, pp. 179–192. New York: International Universities Press, 1965.

———— (1963b). From dependence towards independence in the development of the individual. In *The Maturational Processes and the Facilitating Environment*, pp. 83–92. New York: International Universities Press, 1965.

———— (1963c). Morals and education. In *The Maturational Processes and The Facilitating Environment*, pp. 93–105. New York: International Universities Press, 1965.

———— (1971). *Playing and Reality*. London: Routledge, 1986.

Wolf, E. S. (1988). *Treating the Self: Elements of Clinical Self Psychology*. New York: Guilford.

Wolfe, T. (1929). *Look Homeward, Angel: A Story of a Buried Life*. New York: Charles Scribner's Sons, 1957.

Wright, K. (1991). *Vision and Separation: Between Mother and Baby*. Northvale, NJ: Jason Aronson.

Zuckerberg, J. O. (1988). The struggle to love: reflections and permutations. In *Love: Psychoanalytic Perspectives*, ed. J. Lasky and H. Silverman, pp. 147–158. New York: New York University Press.

INDEX

Absolute dependence, stage of, 87
Addiction. *See* Alcoholics/addicts
Aesthetic moments, 104–105, 112, 115
Affirmations, 179
Ainsworth's Strange Situation experiment, 68
Alanon, 288–289
Alcoholics/addicts, 9, 75. *See also* Immersive transference; Immersive treatment
 conversion experience and, 167–168, 170–171
 language and, 95–96
 near-death experiences, 172–173
 psychotherapy and, 126
 spirituality and, 123–137
Alcoholics Anonymous (AA)
 critique of, 156–158
 dependency and, 180–182
 disease model approach and, 170, 182–185
 historical background, 166–174
 powerlessness and, 181–182
 Twelve Step program of, 174–180
Alienation, 2, 9, 60
Angier, N., 54f
Attachment. *See also* Separation-individuation paradigm
 insecure, styles of, 68–69

 mothering and, 67
 needs, of child, 8–9
 objects of, 223–224
 resistance to, in therapy, 235–237
 separation threats and, 66–67
 theory, 52, 64–69
Autonomy, 1

Balint, M., 2, 116, 124
 on merging, 56–58
Basic fault, 2, 10, 56–57
Biddle, W. E., 118
Birth, 3–4
Birth trauma, 3
Blos, P., 44
Bollas, C., 77, 112, 115, 124, 147, 155, 177
 on aesthetic moments, 104–105
 on fated individual, 159–160
Bowlby, J., 8, 9, 18, 39–40, 224
 on analysts and separation/attachment, 54–55
 developmental schema of, 64–69
 on separating children from parents, 55–56
 on substitute objects, 99–100
 on walking, by toddlers, 52
British object relations school, 55–69
Brown, J. S., 79

Bueti, G., 56
Buie, D. H., 53, 82
Buxton, M., 134, 170

Carpenter, F., 271n
Castration anxiety, 38
  in Little Hans, 39
Clinebell, H., 127, 134
Co-dependency, 289
Connectedness, 2
Consolidation of
    individuality/beginnings of
    emotional constancy phase,
    47
Core self, 93, 255
Countertransference, to
    immersive transference,
    230–238
Creative visualization, 179

Demand feeding, 92
Detachment, 2
  normative abuse and, 10, 66
  relational, 101
  temper tantrums and, 84–85
Developmental schema
  of Fairbairn, 58–60
  of Freud, 38
  of Kohut, 78–79, 80, 81, 82
  of Mahler, 44–53
  of Stern, 82–97
  of Winnicott, 73–78, 87–98
Disease-model approach,
    alcoholism and, 170, 182–185
Druck, A., 232
Drugs. See alcoholics/addicts

Eigen, M., 113
Empathy, 82–84

in psychoanalysis, 104n
Empty core, 2, 10, 60

Fain, M., 54
Fairbairn, W. R. D.
  developmental schema of, 58–60
False self, 2, 10, 66, 76. See also
    True self
  alcoholics and, 134
  development of, 243–246
Fated individual, 160, 251, 276
Fine, B., 104n, 118–119
Freud, S., 3, 109, 112
  addiction and, 124–125
  analysis of Little Hans, 40–44
  attachment of analysts to, 55
  developmental schema of, 38
  on oceanic feeling, 116–118, 246
Fusion. See Immersive
    transference; Merger

Gaslighting, 275–291. See also
    Merger
Gawain, S., 179
Gay, P., 118, 125
Glenn, J., 40
God. See Spirituality
Graf, M., 38
Grandiosity, child's sense of, 43
Greenacre, P., 6
Greenberg, J. R., 45–46, 55
Guntrip, H., 61–63, 120, 124

Hatching phase, 46
Howard, M. P., 44–45

Idealization, 81–82, 112–114
  pathological, 290–291
  of therapist by patient, 113–114

in immersive treatment,
    187–221
Kernberg on, 231–233
Illusion, moment of, 87–89, 92, 97
Immersive moments, 103–137,
    119, 122–123
    defined, 104
    idealization and, 112–114
    love and, 107
    in psychotherapy, 109–111
    spirituality and, 116–137
    alcoholism/addiction,
        123–137
Immersive object, 99
Immersive transference
    case illustrations, 187–221,
        248 259
    countertransference to, 230–238
    merger issues, 260–270
Immersive treatment
    analytic neutrality and, 229–231
    case illustration, 139–163
    crisis issues in, 227–228
    Kernberg's strategies contrasted
        with, 204, 228 234
    objects of attachment and,
        223–224
    relapse prevention and, 224–226
    transference in. See Immersive
        transference
Individuality, 1
Individuation. See
    Separation-individuation
Intersubjective relatedness, 94

James, W., 127, 170
Jones, E., 38f
Jordan, J. V., 82–83, 281
Jung, C., 166

Kaplan, A., 83
Karen, R., 68, 69
Kernberg, O., 53
    on idealization, 231–232
    treatment strategies, immersive
        approaches contrasted
        with, 204, 228–234
Khantzian, E. J., 125, 252
Kierkegaard, S., 51
Kohut, H., 53, 65
    developmental schema of,
        78–82, 84
Kuhn, T., 37, 53
Küng, H., 117, 119
Kurtz, E., 169, 170, 180

Lachmann, F. M.
Language acquisition, 94–96
    alcoholics/addicts and, 95–96
Lemkow, A. F., 106
Liedloff, J., 4, 126
Little Hans, Freud's analysis of,
        39–44
Long Day's Journey Into Night
    (O'Neill), immersive
    experience of alcohol and,
        270–274
Love, 107
    in psychotherapy, 109–111

Mahler, M., 6, 37
    developmental schema of, 44–53
Masson, J. M., 116n
Mature dependence, 59, 65, 120
McElderry, B. R., 128
Meissner, W. W., 120–121
Merger, 2, 37. See also Immersive
    moment; Immersive
    transference

Merger (*continued*)
  British object relations school
    Balint, 56–58
    Fairbairn, 58–60
    Guntrip, 61–63
    Seinfeld, J., 60–61
    Winnicott, 73–78, 87–98
  as danger, 1
  denial/devaluation of, 1–2
  empathy and, 82–84
  experiences, lack of, 14
  as infantile phenomenon, 111
  pathological, 275–292
Methadone, 251–252
Miller, A., 8, 117
Mitchell, S. A., 9, 45–46, 55, 230,
    232
Moore, B., 104n, 118–119
Moro response, 65

Narcissism
  pathological, 79
  primary, 38, 45, 46, 50
Narcissistic rage, 84–86
Near-death experiences, alcoholics
    and, 172–173
Neutrality, analytic, 229–231
Niederland, W. G., 69, 70–71
Non-nutritive sucking, 99–101
Normal autistic phase, 45
Normative abuse, 8–14, 71. *See
    also* Little Hans, Freud's
    analysis of
  alcoholism and, 14–36
  detachment and, 10
  examples, 10–30
  name-calling and, 13–14
  Schreber case and, 69–71
  separation and, 66–67

  separation/individuation and,
    8–9, 54
  societal sanction for, 8–9, 18–19
Nowell, E., 129

Oceanic feeling, 2, 36, 52,
    116–119, 274
Ogden, T. H., 54, 88
Omnipotence, infantile, 38, 79
  addiction and, 129–130
  critique of concept, 8, 79–81,
    84, 154
  development of, 88
Oneness/separateness paradox,
    73–101
  Kohut and, 78–82, 84
  Stern and, 92–97
  Winnicott and, 73–78, 87–98
Oxford Group, Alcoholics
    Anonymous and, 166–167,
    169, 170

Parsons, W. B., 119, 246
Pathological narcissism, 79
Peck, M. S., 109, 110, 111, 119
Peele, S., 166, 182–185
Potential space, 88, 91, 93–94,
    104
Powerlessness, 2. *See also*
    Alcoholics Anonymous (AA)
  addiction and, 124, 134–135
  alcoholism and, 171–172
  child's experience of, 4–6, 9,
    38–39, 79–80
Practicing phase, 46
Primary identification, 59
Primary objects, 57
Psychosis, separation-
    individuation and, 50–51

Psychotherapists
   separation-individuation
      paradigm and, 54–55
   as transformational objects, 114
Psychotherapy. *See also* Immersive
      transference; Immersive
      treatment
   immersive framework for,
      139–163
   love in, 109–111
   spirituality in, 119, 122–123

Rank, O., 3
Rapprochement phase, 46
Regressed ego, 62
Regression, schizoid states and,
      61–63
Relative dependence, 65
Religion. *See* Spirituality
Religious patient, 201
Resistant patient, immersions
      with, 254–255
Rieff, P., 40
Rinsley, D. B., 120, 134
Ritter, A., 70
Rizzuto, A. M., 121–122

Schizoid state, 60, 123, 124
   regression in, 61–63
Schreber case, 69–70
Searles, H., 44, 53, 206
Seinfeld, J., 17, 53, 60–61, 111,
      180, 213, 227–228, 232
Selfobjects, 65, 79
Self-reliance, 1
Separateness, 1, 2. *See also*
      Attachment; Oneness/
      separateness paradox
   baby's experience of, 4–5

Separation anxiety, 69
   Little Hans and, 40–41
   threat of separation and, 66–67
Separation-individuation
      paradigm, 37
   analysts and, 54–55
   critique of research on, 47–53
   phases of, 44–47
   psychosis and, 50–51
   shift away from, 53, 106
   societal sanction for, 37, 53
   symbiosis phase, 45–46
Sexual phobia, alcoholics and, 135
Seymour, R., 134
Slap, J., 40
Smith, D., 134
Spirituality, 115–137
   alcoholism/addiction and,
      123–137
   Freud and, 116–118
   psychotherapy and, 119,
      122–123
Spotnitz, H., 111, 235, 283
Stern, D. N., 4, 45, 50, 77, 88
   on oneness/separateness
      paradox, 82–97
Stolorow, R. D., 232
Subjective object, 80–81
   patient's wish for, 232–233
Substitute object, 99–100
Sucking
   non-nutritive, 100–101
   thumb, 59
Suicidal patients, 63
Surrey, J. L., 101
Sutherland, J. D., 53
Symbiosis. *See also* Attachment;
      Merger; Separation-
      individuation paradigm

Symbiosis (*continued*)
  as developmental phase, 45–46
  importance of, 53
Symbiotic state, 1

Temper tantrums, 84–85
Thomsen, R., 168
Thumb-sucking, 59
Tiebout, H. M., 170–171
Transcendence, addiction and,
  272. *See also* Alcoholics
  Anonymous; Spirituality
Transference. *See* Immersive
  transference
Transformational objects, 77. *See
  also* Attachment
  drugs/alcohol as, 173, 275
  spirituality and, 115–116
  therapists as, 114, 155, 197–198,
  223
Transitional objects/process,
  97–101

Treece, C., 125, 252
True self, 73–74, 76. *See also* False
  self
Twelve Step program, of AA, 156,
  165, 174–179

Walking by toddlers, significance
  of, 51–52
Weinstein, R. S., 109, 110–111,
  238
Wilson, W., 166–170, 175
Winnicott, D. W., 2, 64, 116, 142
  oneness/separateness paradox,
  73–74
  religious patient, 201
Wolf, E. S., 82, 84
Wolfe, T., 127–129
Wright, K., 122, 140

Zuckerberg, J. O., 111